At War with
Civil Rights and
Civil Liberties

At War with Civil Rights and Civil Liberties

Edited by
Thomas E. Baker and
John F. Stack, Jr.

ROWMAN & LITTLEFIELD PUBLISHERS, INC.
Lanham • Boulder • New York • Toronto • Oxford

Contents

Acknowledgments

We are pleased to acknowledge the assistance of several colleagues who made this volume possible. Dr. Thomas A. Breslin, former vice president for research at Florida International University (FIU) conceived of a series of books on contemporary public policy and provided financial support leading to the publication of seven books with the final volume nearing production.

Thanks are due for the support of Dr. Mark B. Rosenberg, FIU's provost and executive vice president of academic affairs and Dr. Ralph S. Clem, director of the Center for Transnational and Comparative Studies. At the Florida International University College of Law we want to thank Dean Leonard P. Strickman and Associate Dean Scott F. Norberg for their official support and encouragement. We are personally grateful as well to Danielle Strickman for her gracious hospitality. Thanks also to Vania E. Orozco and the special students of the inaugural class of the College of Law, the Class of 2005.

Of course, we are more-than-we-can-say grateful to a number of scholars who gave rise to this project and to the actual contributors to this book: Philip Chase Bobbit, Lee Epstein, Louis Fisher, Mark Graber, Michael Greenberger, Peter Irons, Jules Lobel, and Mark V. Tushnet.

Ms. Jennifer Knerr, vice president and executive editor for political science and international relations at Rowman & Littlefield, deserves special thanks for her support of this volume and several others published by Rowman & Littlefield.

This work would not have been possible without the support of the Jack D. Gordon Institute for Public Policy and Citizenship Studies at Florida International University and the tireless assistance of Ms. Elaine Dillashaw who has worked so hard in bringing this volume and six others to life.

Finally, we acknowledge permission to reprint the following: Stephen G. Breyer, associate justice of the United States Supreme Court, *Liberty and Security: A Speech before the Association of the Bar of the City of New York,* April 14, 2003; Attorney General John Ashcroft, *Preserving Life and Liberty: A Speech before Law Enforcement Officers in Boise, Idaho*, August 25, 2003; Jules Lobel, *The War on Terrorism and Civil Liberties,* 63 U. Pitt L. Rev. 767 (2002); Peter Irons, *Politics and Principle: An Assessment of the Roosevelt Record on Civil Rights and Liberties,* 59 Wash. L. Rev. 693 (1988).

1

At War with Civil Rights and Civil Liberties: An Introduction

John F. Stack, Jr., and Thomas E. Baker

On July 28, 2004, the Supreme Court of the United States decided three cases at the center of the constitutional balance between civil rights and civil liberties and the powers of the government to wage war. In the minds of many Americans, the September 11, 2001, attacks fundamentally changed the nature of constitutional protections and dramatically expanded the power of the executive branch at the expense of the judiciary. The Bush administration launched the War on Terrorism, followed by the war in Afghanistan, followed by war in Iraq. These wars were not declared in the only way the Constitution provides that wars should be declared,[1] but nonetheless these military adventures are wars in every other sense of the word. American lives are being lost; our country's standing in the world is at stake and its treasures are being spent. Battlefield prisoners are being captured and pursued.

The outcomes and reasoning of these three decisions were somewhat mixed. These decisions reinforced the nation's commitment to the rule of law and constitutionalism, but the justices took a decidedly pragmatic view of the executive power over foreign affairs and waging war. In *Rasul v. Bush*,[2] the administration contended that it had the inherent power flowing from the War on Terrorism to hold foreign terrorist suspects indefinitely outside of the contiguous United States without access to legal counsel. Thus, more than six hundred non-Afghan nationals (Australians and Kuwaitis) were confined at the isolated American naval base at Guantanamo Bay, Cuba. In *Hamdi v. Rumsfeld*,[3] the administration went further to maintain that it could designate an American citizen captured in Afghanistan, who allegedly was fighting against American troops in support of al Qaeda and the Taliban regime, as an enemy combatant and deny him legal counsel in order to protect the national security interests of the United States. In the third case, *Rumsfeld v. Padilla*,[4] an American citizen was arrested on a flight from Pakistan to Chicago and held incommunicado in military custody—without ever being charged—because the government suspected him of planning acts of terror such as exploding a so-called dirty bomb, a device that would explode and contaminate a wide area with nuclear radiation. For many Americans, the Bush administration's policies constituted a dramatic and threatening transformation of traditional constitutional civil rights and civil liberties, even recognizing that the country was waging a de facto if not a de jure war. The Court's opinions in *Rasul v. Bush* and *Hamdi v. Rumsfeld* constitute landmark cases and appear in chapter 9 of this book. These opinions document how members of the Supreme Court have responded thus far to the current crisis in the name of the Constitution. The justices were obliged to explore the same constitutional leitmotifs that shape the warp and woof of this book. The stakes could not be higher for our country and for our way of life. Constitutional self-government and individual liberty lie in the balance in a number of vital areas:

- the constitutional implications of the War on Terrorism
- the delicate balance between civil rights and civil liberties of citizens and noncitizens during times of war
- the significance of the great writ, habeas corpus, as a shield against arbitrary detention
- the scope of the executive's powers in wartime
- Congress's responsibilities during times of war and national emergency
- the proper role of the Supreme Court and the lower federal courts
- the importance of the rule of law for our polity

This is American constitutionalism writ large for our generation. In the words of the Preamble, this is how "We the People . . . provide for the common defense, promote the general Welfare, and secure the Blessings of Liberty to ourselves and our Posterity."[5]

The book unfolds in three parts designed to provide a way to understand these political and legal issues. Part I provides an overview and some perspective. The manner in which constitutional issues are framed necessarily reflects the political, social, cultural, and legal contexts of the times. Chapter 2, "Perspectives on Liberty, Security, and the Courts" places the aftermath of September 11, 2001, between two different institutional perspectives as perceived by Associate Supreme Court Justice Stephen G. Breyer and then–Attorney General John Ashcroft.

Justice Breyer's "Liberty and Security" was a speech delivered before the Association of the Bar of the City of New York on April 14, 2003, based on remarks he had delivered in November 2002 in France before a meeting of members of the Paris bar. He addresses the institutional context in which Americans will confront and resolve multiple concerns about national security and human rights. The context directly implicates the role of courts but also calls for the involvement of the American citizenry.

The rule of the Constitution as an expression of the supreme law of the law is central to Justice Breyer's perspective in three areas: first, the rule of law as stated in the Constitution will apply to situations of dire emergency; second, the Constitution seeks a balance in defining basic rights, even in times of emergency; and third, the courts must balance individual rights against government powers within the context of an American history that learns from past mistakes. For Justice Breyer, this constitutional learning curve is a powerful means of transcending past mistakes ranging from the censorship of the Alien and Sedition Acts during the eighteenth century to the suspension of the writ of habeas corpus during the Civil War to the internment of more than 110,000 individuals of Japanese ancestry after the attack on Pearl Harbor in 1942.

Justice Breyer ultimately calls for judges and lawyers to ask questions that challenge too-easy restrictions on civil rights and civil liberties, based on an understanding of the first principles of constitutional government. "Asking these questions—looking for alternatives—will not guarantee perfect constitutional results. But when lawyers, judges, security officials, and others, try to find alternatives, they help to avoid the kinds of constitutional mistakes previously described." According to Justice Breyer, the search for alternatives itself helps avoid past mistakes:

> More importantly, the search for alternatives helps avoid two extreme positions. The first says that, insofar as war is concerned, the Constitution does not really matter. That is wrong. The Constitution always matters, perhaps particularly so in times of emergency. The second says that, insofar as the Constitution is concerned, war or security emergencies do not really matter. That is wrong too. Security needs may well matter, playing a major role in determining just where the proper constitutional balance lies.

Chapter 2 also gives the perspective of one of the most significant actors during this crisis, now-former Attorney General John Ashcroft, in a speech entitled "Preserving Life and Liberty," delivered in 2003 before an audience of first-line law enforcement officers. Attorney General Ashcroft begins with the stated assumption that the first obligation of government is "to preserve the lives and liberty of the people." Indeed, apropos of its immediate audience, the speech is a call to arms for the nation's law enforcement officers:

> In this struggle, we must never forget what we face: Our enemies have placed themselves on the side of oppression and domination. They have launched a campaign against innocent men, women, and children. Where they have gained power, they have extinguished political and religious liberty. Where they have ruled, they have enslaved women, strangled education, and sought to kill Americans whenever and wherever they can.

The speech also sought to justify the USA PATRIOT Act, the controversial legislation passed by Congress in the immediate aftermath of the September 11, 2001, attacks. Ashcroft argues that the Patriot Act eliminates restrictions on the government's ability to investigate terrorism, updates federal laws to meet the new challenges posed by terrorists using new technology, and permits the United States government to build an inclusive enforcement network that shares information to detect and defeat terrorism domestically and abroad. But the USA PATRIOT Act is more than a sharing of information among discrete federal law enforcement and national security agencies. It is a vehicle that unites federal and state governments in a common cause to protect the citizens of the United States from the threats posed by transnational terrorists operating beyond the traditional nation-state.

In chapter 3, "The War on Terrorism and Civil Liberties," Professor Jules Lobel considers the threats to civil rights and civil liberties that have been posed throughout American history and politics from the protection of national security. Central to his concerns is an imbalance he perceives that has cumulatively favored the power of the executive branch—the president of the United States—as commander in chief. For Professor Lobel, the protection of national security also has steadily resulted in a serious erosion of Congress's law-making authority during times of crises and national emergencies.

Most threatening have been national emergencies in the twentieth century—namely World War II and the Cold War. Deferring to military commanders during World War II, most notably over the internment of the Japanese in 1942, set a dangerous precedent that maximally expanded the executive branch's authority. This trend was intensified by the constant crisis atmosphere of the Cold War. Here a near-permanent (1947–1990) national security crisis became a justification for the abridgment of civil rights and liberties for immigrants, foreigners, and political dissenters. Indeed, the USA PATRIOT Act can be situated as an extension of this abdication of judicial and congressional authority in the face of perceived threats to national security. Lobel worries about this kind of brinkmanship in international and domestic affairs.

Chapter 4, "Politics and Principle: An Assessment of the Roosevelt Record on Civil Rights and Civil Liberties," by Professor Peter Irons, is a critical assessment of the administration of Franklin D. Roosevelt. In spite of the oft-celebrated liberal values of President Roosevelt, an effective and consistent agenda supportive of workers' rights and African American civil rights was never realized. Irons suggests that, properly understood, the protection of civil rights depends on a national agenda. The attorney general plays a central role in how that agenda is formulated and implemented—a story worth retelling today because it underscores the power of the Department of Justice during periods of national crises and emergencies.

Professor Irons underscores the critically important role played by the attorney general in setting a national agenda for the protection or attenuation of civil rights and civil liberties in the United States during that era. Irons suggests that the Department of Justice is a key federal agency forming the nexus between the federal government and state governments. The federal/state distinction is fundamentally important because the Constitution explicitly enumerates rights and obligations of the United States in the context of the powers of the states.

Part II of the book turns to an assessment of civil rights and civil liberties and the constitutional and political issues raised following the attacks of September 11, 2001, the War on Terrorism, and the wars in Afghanistan and Iraq. Three dimensions are critical to an understanding of constitutional law during these phases of the crisis currently facing the nation. The first is the articulation of a national agenda that privileges and gives priority to national security and military objections as being of paramount significance to the survival of the United States. The second examines the acquiescence of the Congress of the United States in implementing the USA PATRIOT Act and ratifying and supporting the War on Terrorism. The third dimension traces the activities of the Department of Justice to implement the domestic and international security objectives of the Bush administration.

Chapter 5, "Indefinite Material Witness Detention without Probable Cause: Thinking outside the Fourth Amendment," by Michael Greenberger, assesses the power of the Department of Justice under Attorney General John Ashcroft. This chapter provides a detailed assessment of the detention of material witnesses by the Department of Justice after the September 11, 2001, attacks and the wars in Afghanistan and Iraq. Greenberger places a human face on the detention of thousands by focusing on the detention of Osama Awadallah and Abdallah Higazy. His narrative of the role of lower federal courts is instructive because of the power and reach of the federal court system and the deference federal judges were willing to afford to the Department of Justice. Vindicated by the Supreme Court's July 28, 2004, decisions, Michael Greenberger's assessment is as chilling a reminder of the federal government's reach in our time as was Peter Irons's assessment of the Department of Justice's abuses during earlier national emergencies.

Chapter 6, "Constitutional Safeguards after 9/11" by Louis Fisher, traces the exploitive techniques of law enforcement, the establishment of military tribunals, the concealment of the names of hundreds of detainees, the use of the material witness statute, the designation of enemy combatants without charging them with a crime, and other techniques. Fisher details the dramatic expansion of executive power with a noted absence of checks from Congress and the lower federal courts. His is a sobering assessment of the aggrandizement of power by the Bush administration in the aftermath of September 11.

How constitutional safeguards are best understood comprises the theme of part III, including a discussion of the specifics of the incarceration of foreign terrorist suspects and the detention of Hamdi, Padilla, and others—issues characterized by the failure of Congress and lower federal courts to check the administration's policies. Two constitutional scholars offer perspectives on the nature of civil rights during times of emergency as a way of contextualizing the shifts in constitutional guarantees during times of war and national emergency. In chapter 7, "Voting Rights and Other 'Anomalies': Protecting and Expanding Civil Liberties in Wartime," Mark A. Graber argues, contrary to the conventional wisdom, that the right to vote has progressively expanded during wartime. He challenges the widespread belief that the tension between national security and civil rights during wartime is invariably resolved in favor of the state resulting in the contraction of civil rights and civil liberties. His assessment should be carefully considered.

Mark Tushnet's carefully crafted essay, "Emergencies and the Idea of Constitutionalism," constitutes chapter 8. He traces three basic positions that incorporate war into American constitutionalism in fundamentally different ways. The first position is that the Constitution's general standards should be applied in wartime although the fact of war may make the determination of such constitutional standards difficult and problematic. The second position suggests that constitutional rules applicable during times of war simply are categorically different during peacetime. The third position treats war as a possibility of justifying widespread suspensions of illegality. Tushnet argues that the third approach should be taken seriously as a way of avoiding pragmatic and moral justifications for actions during wartime that ultimately undermine a spectrum of values expressed in the rule of law tradition. He explores these positions from the perspective of a constitutionalist and a theorist.

Chapter 9, "The Terrorism Detention Cases of 2004," edited by Thomas E. Baker, consists of shortened and abbreviated versions of the Supreme Court opinions. They represent the culmination, at least up to the moment, of the historical, contemporary, and philosophical perspectives that run throughout this book. These accessible versions of the opinions allow the reader to appreciate the debate within the Supreme Court on its own terms. The decisions themselves are also significant for revealing how the Supreme Court addresses complex and difficult issues going to the heart of American constitutional law, politics, and society. As Baker writes in his introduction to the cases:

> Thus, here is how the Justices on our High Court have responded in the name of the Constitution — in their own words. These opinions oblige every American to contemplate the nature of the War on Terrorism, civil rights and civil liberties of citizens and non-citizens, the great writ of habeas corpus, the warmaking power of the executive, the power and responsibility of Congress, and the proper role of the Supreme Court. The stakes could not be higher for our country and for its citizens: our way of life and our system of constitutional self-government lie in the balance.

At War with Civil Rights and Civil Liberties suggests that American constitutional law is an evolving process of self-government. Two hundred and eleven years ago, Congress proposed and the states ratified the Bill of Rights. For two centuries, the interpretation, application, and extension of those constitutional guarantees preoccupied both the legislative and judicial branches. The transformation of American politics and society during historic periods of internal and external upheaval, however, have dramatically affected how the federal government respected the protections afforded its citizens. The Alien and Sedition Acts, the Civil War, the "Red Scares" during World War I and II, the Cold War and its permanent crisis atmosphere, the Vietnam era, and now the War on Terrorism are points along a line of contested history and conflict. Each of these crises generated stresses and strains for our constitutional guarantees of civil rights and civil liberties.

For some, the Roman maxim *Inter arma silent leges* (that during times of war the laws are silent) best describes the pragmatic necessity that government power should trump individual rights in a crisis. For others, civil rights and civil liberties are absolutes that allow for no adjustments of personal freedoms whatsoever. The Constitution is prejudiced against absolutist claims, however — both claims of absolute government power as well as claims of absolute individual rights. The Supreme Court functions as our balance wheel. History and prudence teach the lesson that government power and individual liberty are arrayed in a zero-sum relationship that is in constant flux. National security and individual rights do fluctuate from normal times to times of crises. A time of crisis often is the occasion for reassessing civil rights and civil liberties. When people fear their security is threatened, they often are willing to acquiesce in incursions of civil liberties as a perceived trade-off to gain a sense of greater personal safety. Conversely, when people feel secure, they are inclined to bridle at even minor constraints on their personal liberties. How such tensions are resolved is part of an ongoing struggle to situate individual rights within the context of national security, a struggle itself defined in part by interbranch checks and balances, partisanship politics, divided government, and changing perceptions of national interest, both domestically and abroad.

The changing ambit of constitutional safeguards, therefore, is dependent on more than the outcomes of high profile litigation and even landmark Supreme Court cases. It goes to the heart and soul of American politics. Writing for the court in the flag salute cases[6] decided at the height of World War II, Justice Robert Jackson paraphrased Lincoln to ask the rhetorical question: "Must a government of necessity be too *strong* for the liberties of its people, or too *weak* to maintain its own existence?" The Constitution does not allow us to choose either of these two extremes, nor should we want to choose one or the other. The twenty-first century promises to challenge this generation of Americans to maintain this balance in the face of grave threats to our national security and equally grave threats to our civil rights and civil liberties. As we have learned from previous generations, so too will future generations learn from us.

NOTES

1. U.S. Const., art. I, § 8, cl. 11. See Authorization for the Use of Military Force, Pub. L. 107-40, §§ 1-2, 115 Stat. 224.

2. 542 U.S. ___, 124 S. Ct. 2686, 159 L. Ed. 2d 548 (2004).

3. 542 U.S. ___, 124 S. Ct. 2633, 159 L. Ed. 2d 578 (2004).

4. 542 U.S. ___, 124 S. Ct. 2711, 159 L. Ed. 2d 513 (2004).

5. U.S. Const., preamble.

6. West Virginia State Board of Education v. Barnett, 319 U.S. 624 (1943).

I

CONTEXT

2

Perspectives on Liberty, Security, and the Courts

Liberty and Security
A speech before the Association of the Bar of the City of New York
April 14, 2003

STEPHEN G. BREYER
Associate Justice of the United States Supreme Court

Your President, Judge Leo Milonas, has asked me to repeat remarks I gave last November at a meeting of members of the Paris bar. My object was to help foreign lawyers understand the institutional context in which Americans will resolve their concerns about security and basic human rights. I described the kinds of issues that might soon arise, explained the courts' role, set forth a general framework that would help guide judicial decisions, and made clear that, not only judges, but many other Americans as well, would determine the ultimate outcome. I shall repeat the essence of that talk.

I

First, the current situation: Post September 11 civil liberties issues fall into three categories. The first includes the rights of detainees. These detainees include (1) approximately 600 individuals from 42 different countries who fought against allied forces in Afghanistan and are presently detained at Guantanamo Bay; (2) two American citizens, accused of crimes related to terrorism, who have been detained in military prisons; and (3) 200 of the thousand or so individuals arrested by the government after September 11 who are still being detained. This group includes aliens illegally present in the United States, material witnesses, and a few individuals accused of terrorism-related crimes.

The second category involves statutes increasing the government's information-gathering powers, for example, laws making it easier for the government to obtain a magistrate's approval for a search or wiretap, to proceed without approval in certain emergency situations, to listen to certain terrorist-related lawyer/client conversations (though these conversations cannot be introduced into evidence).

The third category includes those matters that might happen, but so far have not, for example, trials before military tribunals. Consequently, from a judicial perspective, the civil liberties cases involving detainees now seem more urgent.

II

Second: the legal questions presented. The detainee cases may ask the courts to decide, among other things: What law applies to the detainees in Cuba? What rights or guarantees does the applicable law grant them? Have those rights been respected? Are the restrictions imposed upon the two American citizens detained in military prisons consistent with basic constitutional guarantees? What rights, if any, does the Constitution offer foreigners illegally present in the United States? What are the rights of material witnesses? In particular, to what extent and in what circumstances do ordinary courts lack jurisdictional competence to decide these questions?

I cannot tell you how the courts will answer these questions. But as you understand, answers will be forthcoming. Our judicial system is open. An individual detainee, or a "next friend" if that detainee lacks immediate access to a court, can file a court complaint. The complaint can ask the judge for relief, say freedom from detention, access to counsel, or an amelioration of detention conditions. The court will respond, yes or no, grant or deny. And the losing party can appeal—eventually to our Court. Indeed, a party concerned with delay can move for a speedy response and can seek review of an adverse ruling. And, if the government claims that the court lacks jurisdiction to decide a particular matter, the court, not the government, will decide if that is so, with the result in a lower court being subject to appeal.

Moreover, in our system, habeas corpus represents the norm, lack-of-jurisdiction the exception. The theory of the ancient habeas corpus writ is that anyone in detention can challenge the lawfulness of that detention by getting word to a judge, who can order the sheriff or other jailer to "bring me the body." If exceptions exist, courts will determine their scope and whether particular circumstances fall within them.

I emphasized these matters abroad because I wanted the European lawyers to understand that American courts remain open and will eventually answer the legal questions raised. Courts will decide how the law applies, what guarantees it provides, and whether the government has respected those guarantees. The recent decisions in the *Hamdi* and *Padilla* cases show that the process is well under way.

III

Third, a decision-making framework: We do not yet have authoritative judicial answers to many of the legal questions raised, but past experience during periods of emergency suggests several general principles that can help guide judicial decision-making.

1) *The Constitution applies even in times of dire emergency.* Who would think the contrary? Cicero did. He said *inter armes leges silent*—"once the guns begin to sound, the laws fall silent." And Justice Jackson worried that the Court majority in *Korematsu* might have implicitly adopted Cicero's dictum. In dissent, Jackson warned the Court that wartime decisions could create disastrous precedents that would remain, like loaded guns, ready to be fired in the future.

But our Court, along with other modern courts, has explicitly denied Cicero's view. During the Civil War, the Supreme Court, in *Ex parte Milligan*, wrote that the Constitution does apply "in time of war as in time of peace." Indeed, in 1941, in the midst of hostilities, an English law lord, Lord Atkins, wrote that "the laws are not silent. Their substance may change, but they speak the same language." He added that England was engaged in a struggle for the right to maintain a government that would protect the liberties of its citizens. That objective demands that independent judges place themselves between government and citizen—making certain that the government restricts liberty no more than the law permits.

These views embody the more ancient principle, summarized 350 years ago by Lord Coke, when he told England's king that his authority was limited, not "because the king" is "subject to human beings," but because "he is subject to God and to the law." We call this principle "the supremacy of law." No one in this country denies that principle. Its widespread acceptance keeps the courthouse doors open—even in times of national emergency.

2) *The Constitution, emergency or no emergency, typically defines basic liberties in terms of equilibrium.* Law itself seeks to reconcile each individual's

desire to act without restraint with the community's need to impose restraint in order to achieve common objectives. It is not surprising that Constitutional guarantees often demand a similar balance. They seek an equilibrium permitting the government to respond to threats without abandoning democracy's commitment to individual liberty.

An equilibrium that is right in principle will yield flexibility in practice. The Fourth Amendment uses the word "reasonable,"—a word that permits different results in different circumstances. That Amendment, which ordinarily insists that a magistrate issue a warrant before a search, can relax that prior authorization requirement when a dangerous killer is loose in the neighborhood. In doing so, it does not abandon its commitment to personal privacy; it applies those protections in changed circumstances. The value does not change; the circumstances change, thereby shifting the point at which a proper balance is struck. That is what happens in wartime when more severe restrictions may be required. Justice Goldberg, paraphrasing Justice Jackson, pointed out that "the Constitution is not a suicide pact."

3) *A proper equilibrium requires courts to learn from past mistakes.* What mistakes? They include the speech-censoring Alien and Sedition Acts enacted during the Republic's early years. They include President Lincoln's suspension of the writ of Habeas Corpus during the Civil War. As a result, the Union generals imprisoned between 13,000 and 18,000 people—all without benefit of judicial process. They include Congress's efforts during World War I to punish efforts to incite disobedience to the Draft and the executive's efforts to use that law to prosecute political dissidents, for example, the publisher of a political cartoon showing a giant, called "conscription," crushing a worker and a farmer.

They include treatment of Japanese Americans during World War II when, soon after Pearl Harbor, the Government removed 110,000 individuals of Japanese origin, 2/3 of whom were American citizens, from their homes in California, sending them to camps located in Mountain and Mid-Western States. The Government feared sabotage—though the FBI and J. Edgar Hoover himself *then* said they had no evidence of any act of sabotage or any sabotage threat. Politicians of the day, including our great civil liberties champion Earl Warren, supported the removal (much to their later regret). And the Supreme Court in *Korematsu*, a decision we now recognize as shameful, held that the Constitution permitted it.

Three justices, Jackson, Murphy, and Roberts, dissented. Justice Murphy pointed out that the evidence was not sufficient to accuse or convict any person of Japanese ancestry of espionage or sabotage directly after Pearl Harbor when these individuals were still free. Justice Jackson observed that the Court's holding posed a greater threat to liberty interests than the military order itself, which, "however unconstitutional, is not apt to last longer than the military emergency."

Most court historians now believe that these decisions were wrong. They benefit from hindsight. But, even so, the Court's overemphasis upon security demands seemed apparent to many at the time. And today, most believe the Court abdicated its review responsibilities, failing to find the kind of equilibrium that the Constitution demands. It seems fair to say that *Korematsu* now represents the kind of constitutional decision that courts should seek to avoid.

4) *To avoid those mistakes bench and bar must ask at least two questions: Why? and Why Not?* The question "why," when asked in respect to an unusual governmental restriction means "why is this restriction necessary?" Courts, as well as lawyers, ask this question of government officials. Those officials can explain the special need, backing up the explanations with relevant supporting material. Courts can examine that material, in camera if necessary, even *ex parte*, say, with counsels' permission. Courts can give weight, leeway, or deference to the Government's explanation insofar as it reflects underlying expertise. But deference is not abdication. And ultimately the courts must determine not only the absolute importance of the security interest, but also, and more importantly, its relative importance, i.e., its importance when examined through the Constitution's own legal lens—a lens that emphasizes the values that a democratic society places upon individual human liberty.

The second question, "why not," means why not achieve your security objective in less restrictive ways? Might the government, at little security cost, impose a restriction of shorter duration? Are sunset provisions possible? Might impartial administrative decision makers play a role in the restriction's application? What about periodic reports about the implementation of the restriction, as well as its continued need?

Other nations have explored alternatives: Does the government fear a lawyer might become a conduit for a suspected terrorist's coded messages? I listened to a British lawyer describe how Britain limits the suspect's choice to a list of "secure" counsel—a limitation that is restrictive compared to a suspect's ordinary totally free choice, but which is less restrictive than no counsel at all. Are the reasons for holding such a suspect powerfully compelling? I have heard Israeli lawyers describe how, in such circumstances, courts demand continued updates on the ongoing nature of that need.

Asking these questions—looking for alternatives—will not guarantee perfect constitutional results. But when lawyers, judges, security officials, and others, try to find alternatives, they help to avoid the kinds of constitutional mistakes previously described.

More importantly, the search for alternatives helps avoid two extreme positions. The first says that, insofar as war is concerned, the Constitution does not really matter. That is wrong. The Constitution always matters, perhaps particularly so in times of emergency. The second says that, insofar as the Constitution is concerned, war or security emergencies do not really matter. That is wrong too. Security needs may well matter, playing a major role in determining just where the proper constitutional balance lies.

IV

Fourth, the role of others: Judges alone do not determine the content of the law that eventually will emerge. To the contrary, the American law-making process is one, not of law being dictated by judges or, for that matter, legislators. It is one of law "bubbling up" out of the interaction of groups of interested, affected individuals, experts, organizations such as private firms, unions, bar associations, and many others as well. Interactions take place through discussion and debate in the press, in journals, at public meetings, at colloquia, at legislative hearings, and in dozens of other formal and informal ways. These interactions take the form of a national conversation, with proposals being made, criticized, revised. And out of this conversation will emerge a legal product—a product that often differs significantly from the original proposal.

That is why the many disagreements among us, reported in the press—about government restrictions, security threats, civil liberties—do not mean that disaster is upon us, but that the democratic process is at work. I believe that this is how the democratic process should work. My Court plays a role in the process, but it typically becomes involved fairly late in the day, to determine, say, whether that legal result, as applied, is consistent with basic constitutional norms.

That the Court's intervention comes late is often desirable, for we are relatively isolated from the facts and are aided by knowledge of how a particular provision has worked in practice. But that means that the job of reconciling civil liberties and security needs cannot possibly belong to judges alone. All of us—including lawyers, administrators, legislators—participate, and properly so.

Nor would I limit the "all" who can participate to Americans. We live in a world where communication is instantaneous, where other democracies have faced problems of terrorism, where other lawyers and judges have tried to make certain that the law respects basic individual freedom despite serious security problems. Indeed, the Council of Europe has issued Guidelines based upon Human Rights Court decisions. And the English Court of Appeal, in a case involving British citizens being held at Guantanamo Bay, held that the legal questions at issue were for American Courts to decide, while observing that "the United States courts have the same respect for human rights as our own."

I see no reason why Americans should not read the European Guidelines or consult the lawyers, the courts, or the executive branch officials in countries with similar experiences, in our efforts properly to reconcile the relevant interests at home.

That in part, is why I am pleased to have had the opportunity to speak in France. I learned from what I heard there as I participated in a continuing conversation about the seriousness of the security problem and the importance of simultaneously maintaining our guarantees of basic freedom. Ultimately, that discussion reinforced my own conviction that the community of those concerned about security, those who remain dedicated to the protection of basic liberties, and those who place trust in the democratic process, is a world wide community. Its members learn from each other.

I conclude by pointing out that I have not told you what you really want to know—how the civil liberties cases will be decided. I would like to know that too. I can only now describe a process. It is a process in which we all participate. And I can, and do, simply underscore the importance of your continuing participation.

Preserving Life and Liberty
A speech before law enforcement officers in Boise, Idaho
August 25, 2003

ATTORNEY GENERAL JOHN ASHCROFT

Thomas Jefferson wrote eloquently that governments are instituted among men to secure the inalienable rights of the people . . . treasured rights to life, liberty, and the pursuit of happiness.

This is the first responsibility of government: to preserve the lives and liberty of the people. This is a responsibility you know well. This is the responsibility to which you have dedicated your lives.

You are the doers. You are the achievers. You are the soldiers . . . on the ground and in the trenches . . . who put your lives on the line to defend Americans' lives and liberties. Your spirit is the heroic spirit we saw on September 11, when New York's finest and New York's bravest ran up the stairs of the World Trade Center as others were running down.

It is the work of unknown heroes . . . heroes whose stories may never be known, but whose spirit is the measure of hope we take from that terrible day. The cause to which these men and women gave the last full measure of devotion . . . the protection of the lives and liberty of their fellow Americans . . . has become the cause of our time. It has transformed the mission of the Justice Department.

Where a culture of law enforcement inhibition prevented communication and coordination, we have built a new spirit of justice. We have constructed America's defense . . . the defense of life and liberty . . . upon a foundation of prevention, nurtured by cooperation, built on coordination and rooted in our constitutional liberties.

Never in our nation's history have we asked more from the men and women of law enforcement. We have asked you to add to your duties. We have asked you to root out the networks of terror and forge new alliances to defend freedom from a ruthless threat. We have asked you to prevent terrorism, communicate information and evidence, and cooperate to build a stronger justice community. You have heeded the call. Thanks to you, your colleagues, and your cooperation, America has responded to the terrorist threat with speed and resolve. Thanks to you, we are preserving lives, liberty, and the rule of law. Thanks to you, we are winning the war on terror.

Our terrorist enemies underestimated America. They did not think that we could or that we would respond so decisively and so resolutely. The terrorists believed this nation would retreat when lives were threatened and liberty was attacked.

But we have shown them. We have shown the world: Usama Bin Laden is wrong. Al Qaeda is wrong. All who support and fight for terrorism are wrong. Their murderous vision of an America in flames has united this nation. September 11 has led to a new seriousness, a new appreciation, a renewed love for the noble vision of liberty and the rule of law that guides this nation.

In this struggle, we must never forget what we face: Our enemies have placed themselves on the side of oppression and domination. They have launched a campaign against innocent men, women, and children. Where they have gained power, they have extinguished political and religious liberty. Where they have ruled, they have enslaved women, strangled education, and sought to kill Americans whenever and wherever they can.

They have vowed to spread the disease of hate, but we have vowed to stop them. Together . . . we *are* stopping them.

As President Bush has said, "Our war against terror is a contest of will in which perseverance is power. . . . Whatever the duration of this struggle, and whatever the difficulties, we will not permit the triumph of violence in the affairs of men . . . free people will set the course of history."

It is an honor to serve a President with the courage to face tough challenges and the vision to lead. Under his leadership, America is not sitting back while terrorists wage war against us. We are waging war on them.

In the days after September 11, we vowed to do everything within the law to prevent additional terrorist attacks. We talked to individuals like you: law enforcement officers, investigators and prosecutors. We asked you what tools you needed to preserve life and liberty.

We then appealed to Congress to give us better tools to protect America, and Congress responded to our call. Democrats and Republicans united and they passed the USA PATRIOT Act with wide, bipartisan support. And while our job is not finished, we have used the tools provided in the Patriot Act to fulfill our first responsibility to protect the American people.

We have used these tools to prevent terrorists from unleashing more death and destruction on our soil. We have used these tools to save innocent American lives. We have used these tools to provide the security that ensures liberty.

The Patriot Act does three things: First, it closes the gaping holes in our ability to investigate terrorists. Second, the Patriot Act updates our anti-terrorism laws to meet the challenges of new technology, and new threats. Third, the Patriot Act has allowed us to build an extensive team that shares information and fights terrorism together.

First, the Patriot Act provides critical investigative tools to law enforcement.

The Patriot Act gives investigators the ability to fight terror, using many of the court-approved tools that have been used successfully for many years in drug, fraud, and organized crime cases.

For instance, the Patriot Act allows agents to conduct investigations without tipping off terrorists. If criminals are tipped off too early to an investigation, they might flee, destroy evidence, intimidate or kill witnesses, cut off contact with associates, or take other action to evade arrest. Therefore, federal courts in narrow circumstances have long allowed law enforcement to delay for a limited time when the subject is told that a court approved search warrant has been executed. As many of you know because you have used them, these delayed notification search warrants have been used for decades in drug and organized crime cases, and have been upheld by courts as fully constitutional.

Most Americans expect that law enforcement tools used for decades to fight organized crime and drugs be available to protect lives and liberties from terrorists.

Of course, notice of searches is provided, but the reasonable delay gives law enforcement time to identify the suspect's associates, eliminate immediate threats to our communities, and coordinate the arrests of multiple individuals without tipping them off prematurely.

For example, if the government becomes aware of a terrorist plot to use a pre-positioned, remote controlled explosive device at a major public event in

Boise . . . before tipping off the terrorists, who might explode the device due to the tip-off . . . we need to find and disable the bomb. Perhaps we learned that one of the known terrorists was staying in a hotel and we have reason to believe that a search of his hotel room will yield the location of the bomb.

For decades, normal criminal law has allowed us to use a court-authorized search warrant and delay notification of the search in order to obtain the information we need to protect the lives of the innocent.

Those who challenge this long-standing, Constitutional capacity to defend America would force us to tip-off the terrorists that we are on to them, and potentially enable the explosion of the device before it is located and disabled, endangering American lives.

Another tool the Patriot Act provides is court-approved access to business records to protect against international terrorism or clandestine intelligence activities.

Every cop and prosecutor in this room understands the value business records can play in an investigation. Investigators may need to look at records from chemical plants or hardware stores to discover who bought materials that could be used to construct a bomb. Law enforcement may need bank records to follow the trail of money being sent to terrorist organizers abroad.

And for many years, prosecutors have long been able to obtain the business records in criminal cases by using grand-jury subpoenas. But before the Patriot Act, agents had limited tools to obtain them in national security terrorism investigations. The Patriot Act recognized that the same type of records should be available in national security investigations, while providing special protections for the First Amendment activities of Americans.

All of these critical investigative tools help close the gaping holes in our ability to investigate terrorists.

Second, the Patriot Act brings our laws up to date with modern technology.

In an age when terrorists have cellular, even satellite, phones, we must anticipate, out-think, and adapt to the new tactics and technology of our terrorist foes. Under the Patriot Act, prosecutors may now use a "roving wiretap" to track a terror suspect's communication even when the suspected terrorist switches, changes, or abandons phones to avoid detection.

Since 1986, we have effectively used roving wiretaps to track suspected drug dealers. Thanks to the Patriot Act, we can now use them to track the terrorist threat.

Americans expect that law enforcement tools used for decades to fight organized crime and drugs be available to protect lives and liberties from terror.

This is an example of the way the Patriot Act brought our laws up to date with new technologies and new threats.

Third, the Patriot Act has expanded our capacity to build strong teams—teams that many of you are a part of—teams dedicated to uncovering and stopping terrorists before they strike.

We have stronger teams today because law enforcement and federal prosecutors can now share information and cooperate better with each other. From police officers to FBI agents to prosecutors and intelligence agents, the Patriot Act allows our expanded teams to "connect the dots" and save lives.

We know that information-sharing coupled with decisive action leads to results.

In Portland, Oregon, we have indicted several individuals for allegedly conspiring to travel to Afghanistan after the September 11 attacks in an effort to fight against American forces. In an example of improved information sharing among local, state, and federal authorities, the investigation was aided when a local sheriff in another state shared information with the Portland Joint Terrorism Task Force. Recently, one of the defendants from this investigation, Maher Hawash, pled guilty to illegally providing support to the Taliban and agreed to cooperate with the government. He faces a sentence of seven to ten years in prison.

The information-sharing that the Patriot Act allows has enhanced the capabilities of our Joint Terrorism Task Force to protect local communities. And this has allowed federal, state and local law enforcement officers to create a seamless anti-terror team with international law enforcement and intelligence agencies.

We saw the results when law enforcement apprehended Hemant Lakhani, an alleged arms dealer in Great Britain. Lakhani is charged with attempting to sell shoulder-fired missiles to terrorists for use against American targets. I think all Americans understand the devastation such a missile is capable of inflicting on a commercial airliner. After a long undercover investigation in several countries, Lakhani allegedly traveled to Newark, New Jersey, and was arrested, along with two alleged financial facilitators, as he allegedly prepared to finalize the sale of the first missile.

The Lakhani investigation would not have been possible had American, Russian, and other foreign intelligence and law enforcement agencies not been able to coordinate and communicate the intelligence they had gained from various investigative tools.

The Patriot Act has truly allowed us to build an extensive team that shares information and fights terrorism together.

To address all of the issues surrounding the Patriot Act would require more time than we have here. It is critical, however, for everyone to understand what the Patriot Act means for our success in the war against terrorism. I would encourage Americans to read about the Patriot Act's common-sense reforms and how it is keeping our nation safe by logging on to our new website, www.lifeandliberty.gov.

The common-sense reforms of the Patriot Act are the reason why the law is supported by the public by a two-to-one majority, and it is why the bill passed 98 to 1 in the United States Senate and by a five to one margin (357 to 66) in the United States House of Representatives. Both Idaho senators voted in favor. Around this nation, we can point to quiet, steady progress because of the combined and cooperative efforts of law enforcement and intelligence:

We have dismantled four alleged terrorist cells in Buffalo, Detroit, Seattle, and Portland; We have brought criminal charges against 255 individuals; 132 individuals have been convicted or pled guilty, including shoe-bomber Richard Reid, "American Taliban" John Walker Lindh, six members of the Buffalo cell, and two members of the Detroit cell; We have deported more than 515 individuals with links to the September 11 investigation; Our human sources of intelligence have doubled; Our counter-terrorism investigations have doubled in one year; Over 18,000 subpoenas and search warrants have been issued; and We have built our long-term counter-terrorism capacity by adding: Over 1,000 new and redirected FBI agents to counter-terrorism and counter-intelligence; 250 new Assistant U.S. Attorneys; and 66 Joint Terrorism Task Forces.

All told, more than 3,000 suspected terrorists have been arrested in countries around the world. Many more have met a different fate.

Make no mistake: Our strategy and tactics are working. Our tools are effective. We are winning the war on terror.

Nearly two years have now passed since American ground was hallowed by the blood of innocents.

Two years separate us from the day when our nation's stock of consecrated ground grew tragically larger: Ground Zero in lower Manhattan. The Pentagon. A field in Shanksville, Pennsylvania.

For the dead, the hallowed spaces of freedom are memorials, testaments to their sacrifice. For the living, they are a warning. They are a reminder that the first responsibility of government is to preserve the lives and liberty of the people.

In 1863, Abraham Lincoln stood on the hallowed ground of freedom at Gettysburg and expressed the sense of resolution familiar to anyone who has looked into the void at Ground Zero, surveyed the wreckage of the Pentagon, or seen the gash in the earth left by Flight 93.

"We cannot dedicate, we cannot consecrate, we cannot hallow this ground," Lincoln said. "The brave men, living and dead, who struggled here, have consecrated it far above our poor power to add or detract."

The responsibility of those who remain, said Lincoln, is to honor the dead, not with their words, but with their actions; to be, quote, "dedicated to the unfinished work which they who fought here have thus far so nobly advanced."

It is now as it was then. Our final tribute to the dead of September 11 must be to fulfill our responsibility to defend the living . . . to finish the work. Our greatest memorial to those who have passed must be to protect the lives and liberties of those yet to come.

Today, let us be clear. Let us be resolved. We will finish the work begun on September 11. Thank you. God bless you and God bless America.

3

The War on Terrorism and Civil Liberties

Jules Lobel

Throughout American history, we have grappled with the problem of balancing liberty versus security in times of war or national emergency. During the Civil War, Lincoln questioned whether a republic must "of necessity[,] be too strong for the liberties of its own people, or too weak to maintain its own existence."[1] Often repeated is the Roman maxim first coined by Cicero "*Silent leges inter arma*," which has been broadly interpreted to mean "the power of law is suspended during war."[2] Chief Justice Rehnquist recently reformulated Cicero's phrase, noting that the law is not quite silent during war—but speaks with "a somewhat different voice."[3] He could have added that during wartime, law's voice has often been so muted as to be almost inaudible. Rehnquist quotes Roosevelt's wartime Attorney General Francis Biddle: "The Constitution has not greatly bothered any wartime President."[4] Or, as Oliver Cromwell pithily put it, "necessity hath no law."[5]

Our history is littered with sordid examples of the Constitution's silence during war or perceived national emergency. The first war with a European power after the Constitution's ratification—the undeclared war with France in the late 1790s—led Congress to enact the Alien and Sedition Acts of 1798 authorizing the President to deport enemy aliens as well as any alien the President judged to be "dangerous to the peace and safety of the United States."[6] In addition, the Sedition Act made it a criminal offense to print "any false, scandalous and malicious writing . . . against the government of the United States."[7] Lincoln's incursions on civil liberties during the Civil War were numerous, most notably his suspension of the writ of habeas corpus.[8] The Wilson administration prosecuted and convicted hundreds of Americans for their criticism of World War I and the draft, including the socialist leader and presidential candidate Eugene Debs.[9] Many of those prosecutions were undertaken pursuant to the Espionage Act of 1917, which "authorized the government to confiscate property, wiretap, search and seize private property, censure writings, open mail and restrict the right of assembly."[10] Near the end of the war, Attorney General Gregory utilized unpaid volunteers from the American Protective League—an organization that grew to include 250,000 members and acted without police powers—to root out disloyalty through arrests, searches and seizures, tapping phones, and conducting what were termed "slacker raids" to root out draft dodgers.[11] Even if no law existed to punish a person's "disloyal acts," the authorities often prosecuted for other infractions.[12] After the war ended, the detonation of an anarchist terrorist bomb near his house led Attorney General A. Mitchell Palmer to launch the "Palmer" raid, in which 6,000 aliens were arrested without probable cause. Although no one was ever convicted of any crime, 500 immigrants were eventually deported for their political beliefs.

World War II again led to deprivations of civil liberties, the most serious of which was the internment of approximately 110,000 Japanese American citizens. After that war ended, the government's fight against the new enemy— Soviet Communism—resulted in the imprisonment and harassment of thousands of Americans for being communist or communist sympathizers.

The Supreme Court has generally acquiesced in these violations of civil liberties during war or emergency—at least until after the war or perceived emergency was over. Federal judges convicted dozens of people for violating the Sedition Act, all of whom were pardoned by Jefferson after he assumed the presidency.[13] The Supreme Court unanimously affirmed the Debs conviction for criticizing the draft, and the convictions of other Espionage Act violators during World War I.[14] Justice Black, one of the most ardent defenders of the Bill of Rights ever to sit on the Supreme Court, wrote the Court's opinion affirming Korematsu's conviction for disobeying his internment order during World War II, a decision concurred in by such civil libertarians as William O. Douglas, Felix Frankfurter, and Harlan Stone.[15] The Court also affirmed the convictions of Communists and upheld other anti-communist measures during the Red Scare of the late 1940s and early 1950s; the Court adopted a more rights protective jurisprudence only after the Communist Party had been virtually destroyed in the late 1950s and early 1960s.

While most of these measures later came to be considered mistakes after the war or emergency had passed, that lesson seems not to have prevented their repetition. Nor have the courts proven to be a bulwark for defending civil liberties in troubled times.

We once more are at war and are again being asked to balance liberty and national security in wartime. President Bush has stated, "[w]e believe in democracy and rule of law and the Constitution. But we're under attack."[16] President Bush, Attorney General Ashcroft, and other governmental leaders have argued that in war, "the Constitution does not give foreign enemies rights,"[17] conveniently forgetting that the enemy in this war is amorphous and that our constitutional rights are important precisely to ensure that the executive branch is not the sole prosecutor, judge, and jury of who is and is not an enemy terrorist. Administration officials have urged Americans to rally around the President in this time of war, with Attorney General Ashcroft arguing that those who criticize the government give aid to our enemies and Press Secretary Ari Fleischer stating that Americans "should watch what we say and what we do."[18] Dissidents have been subjected to increased harassment by government officials, private institutions, and groups.[19]

Since September 11 there has been a dramatic, and in some respects unprecedented, expansion of executive power, unchecked by the judiciary or Congress, increasing government secrecy (the government is aggressively asserting its privacy interest at the same time undermining the privacy rights of its citizens), and attacks on the most vulnerable members of society — immigrants. The government has instituted a level of unfairness in the treatment of alleged offenders, which is seen only in wartime and justified only as being a wartime measure. The catastrophic nature of the World Trade Center and Pentagon attacks has led many liberal law commentators such as Harvard Law Professor Laurence Tribe to acquiesce in many of these departures from traditional American notions of fairness, reasoning that the enormity of the danger justifies restrictive, emergency measures.[20] Justice O'Connor was proven prescient when she noted after viewing Ground Zero, "[w]e're likely to experience more restrictions on our personal freedom than has ever been the case in our country." [21]

A CRITIQUE OF THE WARTIME PARADIGM: THE CONTRADICTION OF PERMANENT EMERGENCY

The war/emergency balancing metaphor is subject to several critiques. First, as Professor David Cole and Professor Ronald Dworkin have argued, by reserving the most draconian measures for aliens suspected of some connection to terrorism, we are not balancing fairly. We are not deciding upon how to weigh our liberties against our security, but instead are balancing others' liberties for our security.[22] Most Americans would never consent to a rule that permitted the police to incarcerate them for months because of mere suspicions of a terrorist connection, nor would they consent to be tried in secret trials. Nor would they trade their liberty for security if it meant that they could be detained for months without trial on some trivial charge such as not wearing a seat belt while the FBI investigates whether they are terrorists. Hundreds of resident aliens have indeed been subjected to such practices after September 11. Rather than balancing, what is at issue instead is the fundamental fairness that the Constitution guarantees to the people—a word held to include resident aliens—when the government imposes the criminal justice system upon them.

A second critique of the war/emergency balancing metaphor is that it obscures the crucial question of whether the goal is long term or short term security. The mythical balanced scale, (I prefer the seesaw image) assumes that all the weights marked security are on one side of the scale and the weights denoted liberty on the other. But some measures which may have some short term security value at the cost of some quantum of liberty actually reduce security over the long term. Indeed, it is arguable that many of the Bush administration's responses to terrorism have just that effect. For example, questioning 5,000 residents of Arab descent about possible terrorist plots may yield some information helpful to national security, although even that is dubious, but in the long term it alienates the very community from which the FBI or CIA can recruit informants to wage the long term fight against terrorism. Similarly, refusing to accord captured Taliban fighters Prisoner of War (POW) status may result in some short term security gain—again dubious—but at the cost of fraying the multinational coalition so critical to long term security.

This essay focuses on a third critique of the war/emergency paradigm: one that derives from the paradigm's own basic assumptions. The notion that necessity hath no law, or that the laws fall silent during wartimes, assumes that war or emergency is a distinct event, and when over, society will revert back to normalcy. The Constitution's framers assumed that peace would be the normal state of affairs for the new Republic: war or other emergency crisis would be aberrational.[23] And so it was with our early wars in the nineteenth century.

The twentieth century challenged the constitutional assumption of war and peace, emergency and non-emergency as discrete spheres in which peacetime/non-emergency would be the norm. The United States' first war of the twenty-first century threatens to obliterate those constitutional distinctions. The most dangerous aspect of the current war on terrorism is its potential permanence and continued expansion.

THE TWENTIETH CENTURY AND THE PERMANENT CRISIS

World War I brought with it the "concept of a continuing war with an internal enemy composed of civilians who could no longer be trusted, even in peacetime."[24] The end of that war led some officials such as the Director of Washington's Military Intelligence Division (MID) to conclude that groups such as MID should be disbanded. Nonetheless, the MID was continued, and both military surveillance and FBI surveillance on thousands of individuals under vague terms like "subversion" and the investigation of potential crimes continued and expanded during the 1920s and 1930s.[25]

The Cold War against Communism that commenced after World War II dramatically accelerated the evisceration of the constitutional assumption that war and emergency were short, temporary exceptional departures from the normal rule of law. Emergency rule became permanent. Executive power became virtually boundless. The specter of Communism undergirding the Cold War was posed as an ongoing, continual threat to our very survival.[26] As Professor Gerhard Casper argued, this sense of emergency "fosters . . . a mentality which suggests that we live in a garrison state . . . we are in a state of alertness at all times. There is no such thing as normal times anymore." [27]

Every challenge to United States hegemony anywhere in the world began to be perceived as a threat to national security. Those perceived threats to United States power generated a profound sense of permanent crisis, leading many individuals such as Senator William Fulbright to argue that "the price of democratic survival in a world of aggressive totalitarianism is to give up some of the democratic luxuries of the past."[28]

The National Emergency that President Truman declared on December 16, 1950, in response to the developing Korean conflict remained in effect for almost twenty-five years.[29] That emergency proclamation triggered extraordinary presidential power to seize property and commodities, organize and control the means of production, call to active duty 2.5 million reservists, assign military forces abroad, seize and control all means of transportation and communication, restrict travel, and institute martial law, and, in many other ways, manage every aspect of the lives of all American citizens.[30]

Faced with this deeply held sense of indefinite crisis, Congress enacted hundreds of statutes providing the executive branch with broad emergency power. By the 1970s, some 470 such statutes existed, delegating power to the executive over virtually every facet of American life.[31] Some of the legislation contained positively draconian provisions. For example, the Internal Security Act of 1950 authorized the President to detain all persons whom the government had a "reasonable ground" to believe "probably" would commit or conspire to commit acts of espionage or sabotage.[32] While the detained person was entitled to an administrative hearing and appeal, the Act did not provide for trial before an Article III court, nor for the confrontation and cross-examination of adverse witnesses. Moreover, in most of the emergency legislation, vague terms[33] triggered executive power for unspecified lengths of time.

The judiciary was extremely deferential. The *Curtiss-Wright* court's dicta about the President's "plenary and exclusive power" over matters connected with foreign affairs[34] lent legitimacy to the doctrine of inherent and unilateral executive power to conduct foreign affairs. Furthermore, the Court's wartime detention rulings adopted an extremely deferential "reasonableness" standard of review, concluding merely that the Court could not "reject as unfounded" the military's claim of necessity.[35] Many lower federal courts simply refused to review the validity of actions taken during a national security emergency.[36] To the extent that the courts reviewed the exercise of emergency powers, they read Congress's delegations broadly and upheld executive authority.[37]

Even the bright spot in judicial restriction of executive emergency power—*Youngstown Sheet and Tube Co. v. Sawyer*[38]—had the effect of muddying the line between emergency and non-emergency power. Although advocates of congressional authority look to Youngstown's invalidation of the President's seizure of the steel mills as the basis for imposing limits on executive authority,[39] the decision contains the seeds for an expansion of the President's emergency power. The legal realist perspective of the concurrences of Justice Jackson and Justice Frankfurter, rather than the formalism of Justice Black's majority opinion, now dominates the national security establishment's view of the Constitution.[40] By emphasizing fluid constitutional arrangements between Congress and the President instead of the fixed liberal dichotomies bounding executive power, the legal realist approach to the Constitution and foreign affairs has effectively supported the extension of executive emergency authority.[41] The Burger and Rehnquist courts have subsequently utilized *Youngstown* to uphold broad assertions of executive power.[42]

Not until the 1970s, after the disaster in Vietnam and the Watergate scandal, did Congress move to terminate the ongoing national emergency that had existed since 1950 and to control executive emergency powers. The Church Committee and a host of other congressional committees detailed the innumerable abuses that had been committed under the guise of emergency or war authority.[43] These committees criticized the ongoing, virtually permanent emergency, which like Old Man River in the musical *Showboat*, kept on rolling along.[44] Congress enacted a number of reform statutes—the War Powers Resolution in 1973,[45] the National Emergencies Act in 1976, which terminated all emergency authority based on the past presidential declarations of emergency,[46] and the International Emergency Economic Powers Act.[47] Post-Watergate presidents have unfortunately sought to evade the structures of these statutes limiting executive authority, and neither Congress nor the courts have vigorously enforced them.

The end of the Cold War did lead to some relaxation of the feeling of perpetual crisis that had pervaded post–World War II America. The 1990s witnessed the United States defending against various threats—Saddam Hussein, drugs, illegal immigrants, terrorists, rogue states, human rights abusing dictators—but without the overriding sense of fear and national crisis of the prior four decades. The awful, devastating attacks on September 11 wrought a new, legitimate sense of fear and danger. Terrorism replaced Communism as the overriding evil propelling America's relations with the world.

The post–September 11 war against terrorism has taken on frighteningly similar aspects to the Cold War against Communism. The Bush administration states that we will again be involved in a long-term, virtually permanent war.[48] The war against terrorism threatens to form a backdrop to an increasing garrison state authority evoking the shadowy war that forms the background to George Orwell's novel, *1984*.[49] This new, low level, but always prevalent "warm" war, has the potential to lead us back to the worst abuses of the Cold War.

There is, of course, no end in sight to the war against terrorism, and as the Bush administration has defined the war, it is difficult to even foresee an end. First, it is unclear who the terrorist enemy is. As former CIA Director R. James Woolsey pointed out immediately after the September 11 attacks, "It is clear now, as it was on December 7, 1941, that the United States is at war. The question is: with whom?"[50] That question remains unanswered. While we clearly are at war with the Taliban and Al Qaeda, that military action is only the opening salvo in a broader war against the new evil. Various government officials have pointed out that their objective is not merely to destroy the perpetrators, aiders, and abettors of the September 11 attacks, which is all Congress has authorized, but "more broadly to go after terrorism wherever we find it in the world."[51] Under the rubric of defeating terrorism, the administration has sent troops to the Philippines, and Indonesia, and is contemplating a commitment of forces and monies to Georgia and Colombia. New military outposts for the extrusion of American power will be established throughout the world, most prominently for the moment in Central Asia.[52] International terrorism, like domestic murder will probably never be totally eliminated: it thus can justify continued emergency restrictions. Moreover, the administration has now expanded the war on terrorism to include rogue states such as Iraq, Iran, North Korea, and unnamed others—denoted the "axis of evil."[53] Every insurgency around the globe can potentially be linked to international terrorism, as they formerly were associated with Soviet Communism and states such as Cuba, which have no connection to international terrorism, but are obstacles to U.S. policy, may also be so defined.

As with the Cold War, the new war on terror will probably not involve massive pitched battles, but a continuous "lukewarm" war involving an ongoing low level of hostilities and covert operations. The war against terrorism has been defined in the same terms as the war against Communism—between good and evil, freedom versus barbarism, and the "fight of the free world against the forces of darkness."[54] This war on terror threatens, under the guise of wartime, emergency regulations, to return our society to the garrison state mentality of the Cold War, with its tragic and long term consequences for civil liberties. Indeed, we have already traveled a significant distance down that road.

THE CURRENT ASSAULT ON CIVIL LIBERTIES

Since September 11, the Bush administration has utilized two broad mechanisms to curtail civil liberties and restore practices reminiscent of the Cold War. The first has been the invocation of executive authority, utilizing the President's powers as commander-in-chief or inherent executive emergency power. Second, the administration secured Congress's passage of the USA PATRIOT Act, which provides for detention of suspected terrorists, defines terrorism vaguely and broadly, and accords the executive branch expanded surveillance power to fight terrorism.

Executive Emergency Power

The government has detained over 1,200, mostly Muslim, aliens in connection with its ongoing investigation into the September 11 attacks. Most of these were held for at least several months in jail; many are still being held.[55] Only one of these detainees has thus far been charged with any offense related to the terrorist attacks of September 11.[56] A handful are being held as material witnesses.[57] The rest of the over 1,200 detainees were either not charged with any violation, charged with minor immigration offenses for which they normally would not have been jailed, or charged with violations of federal law unconnected to terrorism such as lying to the FBI.[58]

Many of these detainees have been held in solitary confinement in which they are kept in their cells 23 hours a day. They are held virtually incommunicado, being allowed one call a week. Some were shifted from prison to prison to prevent their lawyers, family, or friends from contacting them.[59] The government has refused to release the names of those detained, a policy the Attorney General justified by stating that "[w]hen the United States is at war I will not share valuable intelligence with our enemies."[60]

Many of the detainees obviously had nothing to do with the September 11 attacks or international terrorism and were detained on the flimsiest of evidence. A Yemeni man was arrested after accompanying his American wife to her military base in Kentucky because his wife was wearing a hejab (the head scarf that many Muslim women wear), they were noticed speaking a foreign language—French—and they had in their suitcase box cutters which they had both used in their work.[61] He was held almost two months without any evidence ever being presented against him. His wife, who had also been detained, accepted an honorable discharge from the Army.[62]

Other similarly harrowing stories of detention based on no evidence have emerged.[63] Indeed the Justice Department has continued to indefinitely detain at least 87 aliens picked up on visa violations who have been given departure orders and simply want to be deported.[64] However, the government is waiting, sometimes months, for the FBI to complete background checks to clear them.[65] Some of these detainees are being held pursuant to the government's "mosaic" theory, which argues that the investigation into international terrorism is "akin to the construction of a mosaic and the involvement of any one suspect cannot be ruled out until the entire picture is understood."[66]

While the recently enacted USA PATRIOT Act provides the Attorney General with authority to detain a non-citizen for as long as seven days without being charged with a crime upon certification that he has "reasonable grounds to believe" that a non-citizen is engaged in terrorist activities or other activities that threaten national security, the government is apparently not relying on that Act for its authority to detain over 1,000 non-citizens. Instead, it has relied on an extraordinary emergency interim regulation announced by the Attorney General on September 17, 2001.[67]

The interim emergency regulation permits the INS in times of "emergency or extraordinary circumstances" to detain an alien, whom it has reason to believe is indefinitely in violation of a law, "for a reasonable period of time" while it investigates the detainee.[68] While this regulation is in conflict with the later enacted PATRIOT Act, which only provides for detention for seven days without some charge being filed against the detainee, the Bush administration has not repealed it. Indeed, many detainees were held for many weeks prior to being charged with any violation whatsoever.[69]

The detention of more than a thousand non-citizens for months has been aided by another emergency regulation promulgated by the Attorney General. Ordinarily a person detained on immigration charges receives a hearing before an immigration judge in which the judge decides whether to release the alien on bond.[70] If the judge decides to grant bond then the person is released unless the INS can convince the Board of Immigration Appeals—the appellate review body within the INS—to stay the granting of bond.[71] Pursuant to an interim rule issued by the Department of Justice on October 26, 2001, the INS now obtains an automatic stay of bond pending appeal, which de facto keeps the alien detained for at least another year pending the disposition of the appeal.[72] Of course, for most INS judges, the Attorney General's submission of an affidavit stating that national security—based on the mosaic theory of investigation requiring that the alien be detained—suffices to deny the bond. But those few judges who nonetheless have decided to grant bond have seen their bond decisions automatically stayed by virtue of the new emergency regulation.

Moreover, pursuant to another emergency regulation, the INS trials of those detained in connection with the terrorism investigation are conducted in secret with only the alien and his or her lawyer allowed to attend.[73] Nor are their cases "listed on any public docket,"[74] and the Justice Department will not confirm or deny whether such cases are even scheduled for a hearing.[75]

In essence, what the government has undertaken is a policy of preventive detention, using either mere suspicion or minor violations to hold aliens. For example, a 21-year-old Egyptian man, Wael Abdel Rahman Kishk, was convicted in February 2002 of lying to the FBI about his plans to study aviation.[76] The government, which had already held him in a harsh form of solitary confinement, sought a long prison sentence for Kishk even though it agreed that there was no allegation or evidence that he was in any way connected to terrorism.[77] District Court Judge Sifton rejected the prosecution's request stating, "[i]t will not do to prosecute people for a minor crime, . . . and then ask us to punish them based on some suspicion that they may have committed some more serious offense."[78] Through a myriad of mechanisms, the government is detaining people under harsh conditions on the mere suspicion that they may commit a crime, rather than any evidence that they have done so or will do so.[79]

The Justice Department also imposed new emergency restrictions that did not go through the usual procedures providing for extensive public comment. These restrictions permit the Justice Department to monitor confidential attorney–client conversations in any case in which the Attorney General finds that there is a "reasonable suspicion" to believe that a federal prisoner "may use communications with attorneys or their agents to further or facilitate acts of violence or terrorism."[80] Current law already accords the Justice Department authority to record attorney-client conversations where it believes the attorney is facilitating a crime; however, the Department must first obtain a warrant from a judge based on a showing of probable cause.[81] Under the new regulation, the Justice Department can itself determine when to monitor these conversations, based on a virtually standardless "reasonable suspicion," without being subject to any judicial review.[82]

In another, little known emergency regulation promulgated at the same time as the new attorney-client monitoring provision, the Justice Department is now allowed to hold an inmate incommunicado in solitary confinement for a year, which may be extended indefinitely where the head of an intelligence agency certifies that "there is a danger that the inmate will disclose classified information . . . [that would] pose a threat to the national security."[83] A number of leftist prisoners, such as seventy-seven year old peace activist Philip Berrigan, were placed in solitary confinement after the September 11 attacks, leading some to believe that the Justice Department's regulation has nothing to do with fighting terrorism but rather with penalizing radical dissent.[84]

Moreover, the Bush administration has used the September 11 attacks as a national security justification for increasing government secrecy. Subsequent to those attacks, Attorney General Ashcroft issued a new policy that reversed the Clinton administration's position of disclosing information pursuant to Freedom of Information Act (FOIA) requests unless it was "reasonably foreseeable that disclosure would be harmful."[85] The Ashcroft policy instead instructs federal agencies to withhold information whenever an argument could be made that there is a "sound legal basis" for doing so.[86] Under this standard, the government has denied a request for the CIA's budget for 1947, even though the 1997 and 1998 CIA budgets have been declassified and are public.[87] Similarly, an executive order issued November 1, 2001, gives the President the right to assert executive privilege to veto requests to open presidential records, including those where a former president wants his records released. This executive order violates the Presidential Records Act passed by Congress in 1978.

This secrecy issue is merely one subset of a broader push by the Bush administration "to draw a line in a different spot than previously has been drawn in the separation of powers." [88] Bush opposed Congress granting statutory authority to Homeland Security Director Tom Ridge, thus allowing Ridge to refuse congressional requests to testify. He at first ordered that sensitive intelligence briefings be limited to only eight members of Congress, in violation of current law, before backing down under congressional pressure. Bush has invoked presidential authority to sidestep a law requiring the executive branch to provide Congress with written notice of U.S. intelligence activities.[89] In sum, the administration has not only elevated government privacy while it dilutes the privacy of its citizens, it has used the anti-terrorism security rationale to extend its power vis-à-vis Congress.[90] The current emergency and war against terrorism has been thus used to justify a permanent expansion of executive power and secrecy.

The Bush administration has also openly resorted to racial profiling. In a November 9, 2001, directive, the Attorney General ordered the FBI and other law enforcement to conduct interviews with at least 5,000 non-citizen men who had come from countries where terrorist activities are known or believed to occur. Questions inquired into these men's political beliefs and those of their families and friends. This policy is not merely constitutionally suspect but has been criticized as counterproductive by former high FBI officials, including William Webster, in that it is unlikely to succeed in ferreting out any valuable information. One former high official has termed this technique, "[t]he Perry Mason School of Law Enforcement, where you get them in there and they confess."[91] In addition to these racially based interrogations, the Justice Department has also decided to speed up deportations of 6,000 people who are in violation of their immigration status, based solely on national or ethnic origin—in essence resorting to selective prosecution. These Justice Department actions have encouraged other governmental and private racial or ethnic profiling of Arabs, Muslims, or South Asians.[92]

Perhaps the best example of purported emergency action which threatens to indefinitely transform civil liberties is President Bush's November 13, 2001, "Military Order" permitting indefinite detention of any non-citizen accused of terrorism, and trial of such defendants by a military tribunal with limited due process protections and no judicial review.[93] The order announced that any non-U.S. citizen that the President declared a suspected terrorist, or believed "knowingly harbored" a terrorist could be tried before a military commission rather that an ordinary criminal court.[94] The order contained no definition of international terrorism and was so broad as to be potentially applicable to Colombian drug lords, revolutionaries, PLO fighters, IRA members, or foreign members of anti-globalization groups.

This order immediately came under intense criticism from civil libertarians and many conservatives such as columnist William Safire and Representative Bob Barr of Georgia. The government backtracked and announced that the rules it actually promulgated would respond to the criticism and incorporate more protections than the order facially provides.

Nonetheless, the increased protection likely to be provided in the rules eventually set forth are unlikely to alter the fact that the November 13 Military Order encapsulates the core of the current war on terrorism: the executive branch is carrying out an indefinite war against an ill-defined and amorphous enemy in which it claims the unilateral prerogative to define "terrorists" or those who "harbor" terrorists, and treat them under wartime rules and not accord them the ordinary protections of the criminal justice system. Congress has not provided the President with such power. It has not declared war, and its authorization for the use of force against those who committed or aided and abetted the September 11 attacks pointedly refused to grant the President the additional authority to use force to go after "international terrorism," which the Bush administration had originally sought.[95]

The defense of the military tribunals is premised on terrorism as essentially a new form of war—an ongoing war, without a clear beginning or end, conducted by enemies who are not entitled to protection under either the laws of war or the laws of peace. Therefore, the government has unilaterally refused to accord either the Taliban or Al Qaeda detainees held at Guantanamo POW status, has refused international demands that these detainees' status ought to be determined by a competent international tribunal, and has asserted the right to hold them indefinitely.[96] What the war on terrorism fundamentally eviscerates—as demonstrated by the President's military order and the government's treatment of the Guantanamo detainees—is any dividing line between war and peace. The war against terrorism takes place in the interstices between a state of war and peace. But are we as a nation really prepared to permit, for the indefinite future, the president to define the suspected terrorists as individuals in any one of "dozens of countries—including the United States"[97] and prosecute them in a manner inconsistent with the values we hold as a nation?

USA PATRIOT Act

On October 25, 2001, Congress enacted the USA PATRIOT Act ("Act"). The process by which the Act became law reflects the crisis environment pervading the country after September 11. The Senate passed the Act with only one dissenting vote, while in the House, a compromise bill that had broad bipartisan support and which the Judiciary Committee had unanimously voted out of committee was scrapped literally overnight in favor of a new bill supported by the leadership. The House voted overwhelmingly the next day to adopt the massive new bill with some members complaining that they had not even gotten a complete copy of what they were voting on.

The Act threatens to resurrect many of the abuses reminiscent of the Cold War. For example, in 1991 Congress repealed the much criticized provision of the McCarran-Walter Act which permitted the government to deny entry to any immigrant because their speech or writings supported Communism.[98] Section 411 of the Act resurrects this provision but substitutes terrorism for Communism.[99] The government can bar entry to non-citizens whom the Secretary of State determines make "public endorsement of acts of terrorist activity" or who use their "position of prominence within any country to endorse or espouse terrorist activity" where such speech undermines United States anti-terrorism efforts. Similarly Section 411 of the Act vastly expands the class of immigrants that can be removed on terrorism grounds, just as communist immigrants were removed in the 1950s.[100] Section 411 defines terrorist activity to encompass any crime that involves the use of a weapon or dangerous device other than for mere personal monetary gain.[101] Similarly, the phrase engage in terrorist activity has also been expanded to include providing material support to a "terrorist organization" even when that organization has legitimate political and humanitarian ends and the non-citizen seeks only to support those lawful ends.[102] Thus, an alien who supports a day care center run by the IRA can be deported for terrorism. And as already mentioned, Section 412 of the Act gives the Attorney General the authority to effectively detain indefinitely an alien who has been charged with a criminal or immigration violation when he determines that the non-citizen is engaged in terrorist activities or other activities that threaten national security.[103]

The Act also revives another practice that characterized the Cold War which allows intelligence agencies to circumvent the Fourth Amendment and potentially resume domestic spying on domestic groups under the guise of collecting foreign intelligence. In 1975, a special Senate Committee, the "Church Committee," found that the FBI had conducted a broad campaign of surveillance on disruptive political groups that were not engaged in illegal conduct.[104] One of the important abuses that the Church Committee reported was that intelligence agencies had infringed upon privacy interests through the executive branch's use of electronic surveillance and other intelligence collection techniques for national security purposes.[105] The Church Committee recommended that all electronic surveillance for intelligence purposes within the United States be restricted to FBI monitoring, undertaken pursuant to a judicial warrant.[106] The eventual result was the enactment of a compromise statute, the Foreign Intelligence Surveillance Act (FISA) in 1978.[107] FISA creates an exception to the general rule that wiretapping is permitted only when there is probable cause to believe a crime has been committed and a judge signs a warrant. The FISA permitted wiretapping to be carried out to gather foreign intelligence without a showing of probable cause where a special secret court, the Foreign Intelligence Surveillance Court, approved such wiretapping.[108] Critics have accused that court of being no more than a rubber stamp for the intelligence agencies, and in its 22-year history it has authorized over 13,000 wiretaps without apparently ever denying a request.[109]

Nevertheless, the FISA did contain a critical restriction to ensure that foreign intelligence gathering was limited to situations where "the purpose of the surveillance is to obtain foreign intelligence information."[110] While that language suggests the sole purpose of the wiretapping must be for gathering foreign intelligence, some courts required only that the surveillance be conducted "primarily" for foreign intelligence reasons.[111]

Section 218 of the USA PATRIOT Act amends the statute to permit wiretaps under FISA's lax standards even if the primary purpose of the surveillance is criminal investigation, as long as the gathering of foreign intelligence is "a significant purpose" of the surveillance.[112] This allows law enforcement to circumvent the Fourth Amendment and could lead to the resumption of domestic spying on government enemies under the guise of combating terrorism. Indeed, even prior to the Act, there is evidence that police forces were using anti-terrorism to justify spying on purely lawful domestic legal and political groups.[113] What Section 218 and other provisions of the Act clearly do is encourage "a closer working relationship between criminal and intelligence investigators than has previously been the case."[114] In doing so, the Act muddles the line between foreign intelligence gathering and domestic law enforcement that led so pervasively to abuses during the Cold War. Not only does the Act permit warrantless wiretaps where foreign intelligence gathering is not the primary object of surveillance, it also allows for increased sharing between criminal and intelligence operations.[115] While all these measures have arguable justifications as counter-terrorism measures, they open the door to a resurgence of domestic spying on political groups by the FBI and CIA.

The executive branch's justification for what hitherto was perceived by courts to be unconstitutional is the wartime authority of the President. In a letter sent to key Senators while Congress was deliberating over the USA PATRIOT Act, Assistant Attorney General Daniel J. Bryant of DOJ's Office of Legislative Affairs argued:

> As Commander-in-Chief, the President must be able to use whatever means necessary to prevent attacks upon the United States; this power, by implication, includes the authority to collect information necessary to its effective exercise. . . . The government's interest has changed from merely conducting foreign intelligence surveillance to counter intelligence operations by other nations, to one of preventing terrorist attacks against American citizens and property within the continental United States itself. The courts have observed that even the use of deadly force is reasonable under the Fourth Amendment if used in self-defense or to protect others. . . . Here, for Fourth Amendment purposes, the right to self-defense is not that of an individual, but that of the nation and its citizens. . . . If the government's heightened interest in self-defense justifies the use of deadly force, then it certainly would also justify warrantless searches.[116]

Therefore, as long as the war on terrorism continues, the executive branch's argument would justify warrantless searches.

Congress also reacted to the emergency by granting the administration its long-standing wish list of enhanced surveillance tools, along with little or no judicial or congressional oversight.[117] Congress gave the executive branch authority to disregard the Fourth Amendment's "common law" knock and announce principle for searches, and instead engage in "sneak and peek searches," or covert searches of a person's home or office that are conducted without notifying the person until after the search has been completed.[118] The Act permits the government to spy on web surfing by innocent Americans by merely asserting to a judge that the spying could lead to information that is relevant to an ongoing criminal investigation. The person spied on does not have to be the target of the investigation. The court must grant the application which requires no subsequent report to either the court or the spied upon individual.[119]

Finally, the Act creates a number of new, often vaguely defined crimes. One of the most dangerous to domestic dissenters is the new crime of "domestic terrorism." Section 802 defines domestic terrorism as those "acts dangerous to human life that are a violation of the criminal laws," if they "appear to be intended . . . to influence the policy of a government by intimidation or coercion" and if they "occur primarily within the territorial jurisdiction of the United States."[120] Under this definition, the anti-globalization demonstrators against the World Trade Organization in Seattle, could be subject to prosecution as "domestic terrorists." Another provision of the Act makes it a crime for a person to fail to notify the FBI if he or she has "reasonable grounds to believe" that someone is about to commit a terrorist offense, a definition so vague as to render innocent Americans subject to prosecution if they have a connection to a person who turns out to be a terrorist.

The good news about the USA PATRIOT Act is that Congress wisely included a sunset clause providing that some, but not all of the Act's provisions will expire on December 31, 2005.[121] However, most of the Act, including the provisions involving immigrants, new crimes, and some of the new expanded surveillance powers such as the "sneak and peek" searches are not included in the sunset provision. Moreover, it is unclear how Congress will review how several of these key provisions have been implemented, since some of them are implemented by a secret court, there are no reporting requirements to Congress, and in many cases, no reporting requirements even to a judge. Most fundamentally, if by December 2005 we are still engaged in "warfare" against terrorism, as we are very likely to be, the pressure upon Congress will be immense to continue these provisions into the future. To use Justice Jackson's metaphor, the question will be whether the sunset will devolve into a hazy twilight zone, where executive emergency powers are believed needed to protect against the harkening forces of darkness.

CONCLUSION

The response to the September 11 attacks threatens to place our nation in a permanent war footing. The war on terrorism is now being extended to justify actions that have little, if anything, to do with responding to Al Qaeda or other terrorist organizations. The enunciation of a new doctrine permitting preemptive strikes against other countries has been justified by the new post–September 11 environment, which Bush administration officials claim no longer allows us the luxury of waiting until threats become imminent or eventuate. Similarly, the threat of war against Iraq has also been tied to the ongoing war against terrorism. The war against terrorism thus seems likely to justify continued, ongoing, American military intervention abroad, just as the struggle against Communism performed that function during the Cold War.

Domestically, the September 11 attacks create the possibility that the Government will revive the permanent state of emergency that existed for most of the cold war era. Only if we constantly remember the excesses and violations of civil rights and liberties that stemmed from the cold war invocation of national emergency, will we be able to avoid repeating those errors in responding to the threat posed by terrorism.

NOTES

1. 6 James D. Richardson, A Compilation of the Message and Papers of the Presidents 23 (1898) (President Lincoln's Message to Congress, July 4, 1861).

2. *See, e.g.,* Jeff Bleich, Kelly Klaus and Deborah Pearlstein, *When War Comes to the Court: The True Limits of Our Freedoms May Soon Be Revealed*, Or. St. B. Bull., Nov. 2001, at 21, 21.

3. William H. Rehnquist, All the Laws But One 225 (1998).

4. *Id.* at 191.

5. Max Radin, *Martial Law and the State of Siege*, 30 C. L. R. 634, 640 (1942) (quoting Oliver Cromwell).

6. Alien Act, 1 Stat. 570 (1798); The Alien Enemies Act, 1 Stat. 577 (1978); The Sedition Act, 1 Stat. 596 (1798).

7. The Sedition Act, 1 Stat. 596 (1798).

8. *See generally* Rehnquist, *supra* note 3.

9. Debs v. United States, 249 U.S. 211 (1919); *see also* Frohwerk v. United States, 249 U.S. 204 (1919) (upholding Frohwerk's conviction for conspiracy to publish an antiwar pamphlet); Schenck v. United States, 249 U.S. 47 (1919) (*affirming* Schenck's conviction for sending antiwar literature via U.S. mail and holding that the Espionage Act of 1917 did not violate the First Amendment).

10. William C. Banks and M. E. Bowman, *Executive Authority for National Security Surveillance,* 50 Am. U. L. Rev. 1, 22 (2000).

11. *Id.* at 23. In New York, over a three-day period, "tens of thousands of men, most of whom simply were not carrying their draft cards, were rounded up and temporarily incarcerated." *Id.* at n.159.

12. G.J.A. O'Toole, Honorable Treachery: A History of U.S. Intelligence, Espionage, and Covert Action from the American Revolution to the CIA 277 (1991). One person, for example, was sentenced to ninety days imprisonment for calling the president a "damned fool."

13. *See* Gary R. Wills, A Necessary Evil: A History of American Distrust of Government (135–40).

14. Debs v. United States, 249 U.S. 211 (1919); *see also* Frohwerk v. United States, 249 U.S. 204 (1919) (upholding Frohwerk's conviction for conspiracy to publish an antiwar pamphlet); Schenck v. United States, 249 U.S. 47 (1919) (*affirming* Schenck's conviction for sending antiwar literature via U.S. mail and holding that the Espionage Act of 1917 did not violate the First Amendment).

15. Korematsu v. United States, 323 U.S. 214 (1944).

16. President George W. Bush, Remarks by the President and Prime Minister Kjell Magne Bondevik of Norway in Photo Opportunity (Dec. 5, 2001) transcript, available at www.whitehouse.gov/news/releases/2001/12/20011205-11.html.

17. Panel I of a Senate Judiciary Committee Hearing: Preserving Freedoms While Defending against Terrorism, Federal News Service, Dec. 4, 2001 (comments of Senator Session). Attorney General Ashcroft stated that "foreign terrorists who commit war crimes against the United States . . . are not entitled to and do not deserve the protection of the American Constitution." Nightline (ABC television broadcast, Nov. 14, 2001).

18. Press Secretary Ari Fleischer, Press Briefing at the James S. Brady Briefing Room (Oct. 1, 2001) transcript, available at www.whitehouse.gov/news/releases/2001/10/200111001-4.html.

19. *See generally* Matthew Rothschild, *The New McCarthyism*, The Progressive, Jan. 1, 2002, at 18.

20. Laurence H. Tribe, *Trial by Fury*, The New Republic, Dec. 10, 2001, at 20 (arguing that it may be right in normal times to allow a hundred guilty defendants to go free rather than convict an innocent one, but we must reconsider that arithmetic when one of the guilty may blow up the rest of Manhattan).

21. Linda Greenhouse, *In New York Visit, O'Connor Foresees Limits on Freedom*, N.Y. Times, Sept. 29, 2001, at B5.

22. Ronald Dworkin, *The Threat to Patriotism*, N.Y. Review of Books, Feb. 28, 2002, at 41; Uniting and Strengthening America by Providing Appropriate Tools Required to Intercept and Obstruct Terrorism (USA PATRIOT) Act of 2001: Hearing on H.R. 3162 before the Subcommittee on the Constitution, Federalism and Property Rights of the Senate Judiciary Committee, 107th Cong. (2001) (statement of Professor David Cole).

23. *See* Jules Lobel, *Emergency Power and the Decline of Liberalism*, 98 Yale L.J. 1385, 1389–91 (1989).

24. Joan M. Jevsen, Army Surveillance in America 1775–1980 178 (1991).

25. *See* Banks and Bowman, *supra* note 10, at 24–27; S. Rep. No. 94-755, at 24 (1976) [hereinafter Church Committee].

26. *See, e.g.*, Dean Acheson, This Vast External Realm 19 (1973), in which the former Secretary of State argued that our national survival was facing a grave danger

from Communism. President Kennedy also utilized the survival imagery in his inaugural address when he asserted that "we shall pay any price, bear any burden, meet any hardship . . . to assure the survival and success of liberty." To Turn the Tide 6–7 (John W. Gardner ed., 1962) (quoting President Kennedy's inaugural address Jan. 20, 1961).

27. Constitutional Questions Concerning Emergency Powers: Hearings before the Senate Spec. Comm. on the Termination of the Nat'l Emergency, 93rd Cong., 1st Sess. 83 (1973) (statement of Professor G. Casper) [hereinafter Natl. Emergency Hearings, J. William Fulbright, *American Foreign Policy in the Twentieth Century under an Eighteenth-Century Constitution*, 47 Cornell L.Q. 1, 7 (1961). *See also* Arthur M. Schlesinger, Jr., The Imperial Presidency 163–64 (1973).

28. J. William Fulbright, *American Foreign Policy in the Twentieth Century under an Eighteenth-Century Constitution*, 47 Cornell L.Q. 1, 7 (1961). *See also* Arthur M. Schlesinger, Jr., The Imperial Presidency 163–64 (1973).

29. Proclamation No. 2914, 15 Fed. Reg. 9029 (Dec. 19, 1950).

30. S. Rep. No. 93-1170, at 2 (1974).

31. *See* S. Rep. No. 93-1170, at 2–3 (1974).

32. Internal Security Act of 1950, Pub. L. No. 81-831, 103, 64 Stat. 987, 1021 (1950) (repealed in 1971). Robert J. Goldstein, Political Repression in Modern America: From 1870 to the Present 322–24 (1978). Congress appropriated $775,000 in 1952 to set up six detention camps in Arizona, Florida, Pennsylvania, Oklahoma, and California. *Id.* at 324. The emergency detention provision of the Internal Security Act was drawn up with the aid of ACLU attorneys and supported by Senate liberals such as Hubert Humphrey, Wayne Morse, and Paul Douglas. *Id.* at 366. Indeed, the Act, as repressive and dangerous as it might seem in retrospect, caused concern to the FBI, which had been maintaining a list of persons to arrest under a more flexible Justice Department plan that could be invoked in a time of "threatened invasion" against "dangerous persons," a practice that continued after the Act was passed. Although the ISA was finally repealed in 1971, forms of emergency detention aided the FEMA plan. Ben Bradlee, Jr., Guts and Glory: The Rise and Fall of Oliver North 132 (1988) (A draft of an executive order proposed by the FEMA plan is said to have contained a provision for "alien control" and "detention of enemy aliens"); *see also* United States v. Salerno, 481 U.S. 739, 748 (1987) (dictum on constitutionality of aliens' internment during wartime).

33. *See* Natl. Emergency Hearings, *supra* note 27, at 256 (statement of Mr. Miller).

34. United States v. Curtiss-Wright Export Corp., 299 U.S. 304, 320 (1936).

35. Korematsu v. United States, 323 U.S. 214, 218–19 (1944); Hirabayashi v. United States, 320 U.S. 81, 95 (1943) (holding that the standard is whether the government has "reasonable ground for believing that the threat is real"). *But cf.* Duncan v. Kahanamoku, 327 U.S. 304, 336 (1946) (Stone, J., concurring) ("But executive action is not proof of its own necessity, and the military's judgment here is not conclusive that every action taken pursuant to the declaration of martial law was justified by the exigency.").

36. *See, e.g.,* Sardino v. Fed. Reserve Bank of N.Y., 361 F.2d 106, 109 (2d Cir. 1966); United States v. Yoshida Int'l Inc., 526 F.2d 560, 579, 581 n.32 (C.C.P.A.

1975) (stating that the court will not review presidential judgment that a national emergency exists, although it will review whether the president's acts are within statutory authority); Beacon Prod. Corp. v. Reagan, 633 F. Supp. 1191, 1194–95 (D. Mass. 1986), *aff'd*, 814 F.2d 1 (1st Cir. 1987) (deciding whether a national emergency as defined by statute existed with respect to Nicaragua in 1984 presents a nonjusticiable political question); *see also* Perpich v. United States Dep't. of Def., 66 F. Supp. 1319 (D. Minn. 1987), *reh'g en banc granted*, 880 F.2d 11, 30 (8th Cir. 1989) (finding the determination of existence of national emergency involves "central political question"). *See generally* Christopher N. May In the Name of War: Judicial Review and the War Powers Since 1918 256–64 (1989) (discussing judicial reluctance to adjudicate cases involving Executive emergency powers since 1918).

37. Yoshida, 526 F.2d at 573.

38. Youngstown Sheet & Tube v. Sawyer, 343 U.S. 579 (1952).

39. Harold Hongju Koh, *Why the President (Almost) Always Wins in Foreign Affairs: Lessons of the Iran-Contra Affair*, 97 Yale L.J. 1255, 1282–85, 1309 (1988) (stating that *Youngstown* assumes dialogue and general consensus between Congress and the President about substantive foreign policy ends); Jules Lobel, *The Limits of Constitutional Power: Conflicts between Foreign Policy and International Law*, 71 Va. L. Rev. 1071, 1119–20 (1985) (arguing *Youngstown* requires congressional approval of executive action in violation of international law); Michael J. Glennon, *The War Power Resolution: Sad Record, Dismal Promise* 17 Loy. L.A. L. Rev. 657, 661 (1984) (arguing that *Youngstown* supports the War Powers Resolution).

40. *See* Gerhard Casper, *Constitutional Constraints on the Conduct of Foreign and Defense Policy: A Non-Judicial Model*, 43 U. Chi. L. Rev. 463, 465–66 (1976). *See also* Myres S. McDougal and Asher Lans, *Treaties and Congressional-Executive Agreements: Interchangeable Instruments of National Policy*, 54 Yale L.J. 181, 212, 221 (1945) (arguing against mechanical or formalistic view of Constitution); Eugene V. Rostow, *Response to "A More Effective System" for Foreign Relations: The Constitutional Framework*, 61 Va. L. Rev. 797, 798 (1975); Zbigniew Brzezinski, *Forging a Bipartisan and Strategic Approach to Foreign Affairs*, 43 U. Miami L. Rev. 5, 6 (1988) (President Carter's national security adviser argues, "the Constitution does not hand down clear cut guidelines for the process of shaping national security policy[,]" leaving legislative and executive powers "blended" in an "inevitably . . . fluid" relationship).

41. For example, Secretary of State Williams Rogers opposed the War Powers Resolution as unconstitutional because "it would attempt to fix in detail, or 'freeze' the allocation of power between the president and Congress." S. Rep. No. 93–220, at 18 (1973). *See also* Edwin Meese III, *Constitutional Fidelity and Foreign Affairs*, 43 U. Miami L. Rev. 223, 224 (1988) (arguing that ambiguity regarding limits and congressional versus executive authority makes struggle to define these limits "more political than constitutional"). Advocates of a forceful assertion of U.S. power abroad have also eschewed the strict, formal rules restraining the use of force contained in the U.N. Charter in favor of a more fluid, "realistic" perspective. As Ambassador Jeane Kirkpatrick argued in defending the United States invasion of Grenada, "the prohibitions against the use of force in the UN Charter are contextual, not absolute."

Ved P. Nanda, *The United States Armed Intervention in Grenada—Impact on World Order*, 14 Cal. W. Int'l L.J. 395, 418 (1984).

42. Dames and Moore v. Regan, 453 U.S. 654, 668 (1981).

43. S. Rep. No. 94-755 (1976); H. Rep. No. 95–459 (1977), S. Rep. No. 94-1168 (1976).

44. Oscar Hammerstein II, *Ol' Man River*, in Showboat (1927).

45. War Powers Resolution, Pub. L. No. 93–148, 87 Stat. 555 (1973) (codified at 50 U.S.C. § 1541–1548 (1994)).

46. National Emergencies Act, Pub. L. No. 94-412, 90 Stat. 1255 (1976) (codified at 50 U.S.C. § 1601 (1994)).

47. International Emergency Economic Powers Act, Pub. L. No. 95-223, 91 Stat. 1625 (1977) (codified at 50 U.S.C. Supp. V § 1701 (1994)).

48. As Defense Secretary Donald H. Rumsfeld stated, the war against terrorism will be "a marathon . . . not a sprint." Defense Secretary Donald H. Rumsfeld, Department of Defense News Briefing (Sept. 20, 2001) transcript, available at www .defenselink.mil/news/Sep2001/t092001_t920ruma.html. See also Rumsfeld's statement that "This is not something that begins with a significant event or ends with a significant event. It is something that will involve a sustained effort over a good period of time." Defense Secretary Donald H. Rumsfeld, Department of Defense Briefing (Sept. 25, 2001) transcript, available at www.defenselink.mil/news/Sep2001/ t09252001_t095sd.html.

49. George Orwell, 1984 (1949).

50. David Von Drehle, *World War, Cold War Won. Now, the Gray War*, Wash. Post, Sept. 12, 2001, at A9.

51. Robert S. Dudney, *Verbatim Special,* Air Force Mag., Nov. 2001, at 42 (quoting Colin Powell, State Dep't Briefing, 9-12-01).

52. Bruce Cumings, *Reflections on "Containment,"* The Nation, Mar. 4, 2002, at 19.

53. David Shribman, *State of the Nation Address,* Boston Globe, Jan. 30, 2002, at A1.

54. Herb Keinon, *Sharon Declares Day of Mourning*, Jerusalem Post, Sept. 12, 2001, at 1.

55. Amnesty International, United States of America Amnesty International's Concerns Regarding Post–September 11 Detentions in the USA (Mar. 2002), available at www.aiusa.org/usacrisis/9.11.detentions2.pdf ("By mid-February, 327 people picked up in the post 9.11 sweeps were reported to be still in INS custody."). Cf. Reuters, Hundreds of Arabs Still Detained in U.S. Jails (Mar. 13, 2002), available at www.reuters.com/printerfriendly.jhtml?type=search&StoryID=696703 (on file with the University of Pittsburgh Law Review) (Arab American Institute Chairman James Zogby believes that 327 detainees are from original detentions just after September 11, but that the real number of detainees as of March was as high as two thousand).

56. *See, e.g.,* Amy Goldstein, *"I Want to Go Home"; Detainee Tony Oulai Awaits End of Four-Month Legal Limbo*, Wash. Post., Jan. 26, 2002, at A1.

57. *Id.*

58. *See* Amnesty International, *supra* note 55.

59. *See, e.g.,* Goldstein, *supra* note 56. *See generally* Amnesty International, *supra* note 55, on conditions of detention.

60. Hanna Rosin, *Groups Find Way to Get Names of INS Detainees; Presentations on Rights Planned in NJ Facilities*, Wash. Post, Jan. 31, 2002, at A16.

61. *See* Ali al-Maqtari, Testimony before the Senate Judiciary Committee (Dec. 4, 2001), available at http://judiciary.senate.gov/te120401F-al-Maqtari.htm (on file with author).

62. *Id.*

63. Amy Goldstein, *No Evidence in Pilot's Case; West African Still Held as Material Witness in Attack Probe*, Wash. Post, Feb. 2, 2002, at A20.

64. *See* Christopher Drew and Judith Miller, *Though Not Linked to Terrorism, Many Detainees Cannot Go Home*, N.Y. Times, Feb. 18, 2002, at A1.

65. *Id.*

66. Goldstein, *supra* note 56.

67. Interim Rule with Request for Comment, 66 Fed. Reg. 48334–35 (Sept. 17, 2001) (to be codified at 8 C.F.R. § 287).

68. *Id.* at 48334.

69. Amnesty International, *supra* note 55, at 11 ("In 36 out of 718 cases, the individuals were charged twenty-eight days or more after their arrest.").

70. *See* Executive Office for Immigration Review; Review of Custody Determinations, 66 Fed. Reg. 54910 (Oct. 31, 2001).

71. *Id.*

72. *Id.*

73. This policy was set forth in a memorandum from Chief Immigration Judge Michael J. Creppy (Sept. 21, 2001), see Amnesty International, *supra* note 55, at 7.

74. James X. Dempsey and David Cole, *Terrorism and the Constitution: Sacrificing Civil Liberties in the Name of National Security* 149 (2d ed. 2002).

75. Amnesty International, *supra* note 55, at 7 ("This restriction on information includes confirming or denying whether such a case is on the docket or scheduled for a hearing.").

76. William Glaberson, *Judge Rejects Long Prison Term for Arab Caught in Terror Sweep*, N.Y. Times, Feb. 16, 2002, at A8.

77. *Id. See also* Katherine E. Finkelstein, *Sept. 11 Shadow Lingers as Egyptian's Trial Begins*, N.Y. Times, Jan. 14, 2002, at A9.

78. Glaberson, *supra* note 76.

79. *See, e.g.,* Mark Fineman et al., *Alleged "Trainer" of Sept. 11 Attackers is Granted Bail*; *Terrorism: Britain Frees Algerian Pilot after U.S. Fails to Produce Concrete Evidence against Him*, L.A. Times, Feb. 13, 2002, at A1 (suggesting U.S. law enforcement officials have made detaining individuals to prevent another attack their top priority, paying less attention to evidence-gathering techniques used to build a criminal case); Goldstein, *supra* note 56 (detailing how an African was detained for months when his only violation was of an FAA regulatory rule, which an FAA spokesman says is "not something that you put somebody in custody for").

80. National Security; Prevention of Acts of Violence and Terrorism, 66 Fed. Reg. 55062-63 (Oct. 30, 2001) (to be codified at 28 C.F.R. § 501.3(d)).

81. *See* United States v. Harrelson, 754 F.2d 1153, 1168–69 (5th Cir. 1985). *See generally* Nadine Strossen, Testimony of Nadine Strossen, President of the American

Civil Liberties Union, before Congressman John Conyers' Forum on Nat'l Security and the Constitution, available at www.aclu.org/congress/l012402a.html.

82. The new regulation requires that notice be provided to the individual whose conversations are monitored, so it is unlikely to yield any information about terrorist acts, but will only have the effect of interfering with the attorney–client relationship.

83. National Security; Prevention of Acts of Violence and Terrorism, 66 Fed. Reg. 55065 (Oct. 30, 2001) (to be codified at 28 C.F.R. 501.2(c)). The old regulation limited the period of time to 120 days, which could be extended.

84. *See* Anne-Marie Cusac, *You're in the Hole: A Crackdown on Dissident Prisoners*, The Progressive, Dec. 2001, at 31.

85. Strossen, *supra* note 81.

86. *Id.*

87. *See* David Rosenbaum, *When Government Doesn't Tell*, N.Y. Times, Feb. 3, 2002, 4, at 1.

88. Dana Milbank, *In War, Its Power to the President; In Aftermath of Attacks, Bush White House Claims Authority Rivaling FDR's*, Wash. Post, Nov. 20, 2001, at A1 (quoting David Walker, director of the General Accounting Office (GAO)).

89. Heidi Przybyla, *Bush to Ignore Rule on Written Notices of Intelligence*, Bloomberg News, Dec. 28, 2001.

90. Anne E. Kornblut, *Bush's Stance on Secrecy Draws a Number of Critics: Papers, Pretzel Cited as Instances Lacking Disclosure*, Boston Globe, Feb. 11, 2002, at A3.

91. Jim McGee, *Ex-FBI Officials Criticize Tactics on Terrorism; Detention of Suspects Not Effective, They Say*, Wash. Post, Nov. 28, 2001, at A1.

92. Strossen, *supra* note 81.

93. Military Order of November 13, 2001 — Detention, Treatment, and Trial of Certain Non-Citizens in the War Against Terrorism, 66 Fed. Reg. 57833–57836 (Nov. 16, 2001).

94. *Id.*

95. Authorization for Use of Military Force, Pub. L. No. 107–40, 115 Stat. 224 (2001).

96. *See, e.g.*, Letter from the Inter-American Commission on Human Rights (Mar. 13, 2002) (available at www.oas.org) (on file with author) (adopting precautionary measures to require the U.S. to submit detainee status to a decision by a complete international tribunal.

97. *See* Secretary of Defense Donald H. Rumsfeld, Testimony Before the Senate Armed Forces Committee "Military Commissions" (Dec. 12, 2001) (transcript on file with the University of Pittsburgh Law Review).

98. *See* American Arab Anti-Discrimination Comm. v. Reno, 70 F.3d 1045 (9th Cir. 1995).

99. The Uniting and Strengthening of America by Providing Appropriate Tools Required to Intercept and Obstruct Terrorism Act, Pub. L. No. 107–56, 115 Stat. 272, 345 (2001) [hereinafter USA PATRIOT Act].

100. *See* Harisiades v. Shaughnessy, 342 U.S. 580 (1952).

101. USA PATRIOT Act, *supra* note 99, at 411(a) (*amending* 8 U.S.C. 1182(a)(3)).

102. *See* Nancy Chang, *The USA PATRIOT Act: What's So Patriotic about Trampling on the Bill of Rights?*, Center for Constitutional Rights, Nov. 2001, available at www.ccr-ny.org/whatsnew/usa_patriot_act.asp.

103. USA PATRIOT Act, *supra* note 99, at 412(a).

104. Church Committee, *supra* note 25.

105. *Id.* at 151–53, 169–70, 183–92, 198–202, 290. The executive branch utilized approximately 7,000 warrantless wiretaps and 2,200 microphone installations between 1940 and the mid 1960s in investigations concerning foreign intelligence agents and Communist Party leaders, as well as major criminal activities. See Electronic Surveillance Within the United States for Foreign Intelligence Purposes: Hearings on S. 3197 Before the Subcommittee on Intelligence and the Rights of Americans of the Senate Select Comm. on Intelligence, 94th Cong., 2d Sess. at 25 (1976) (statement by Attorney General Levi). *See* Americo R. Cinquegrana, *The Walls (and Wires) Have Ears: The Background and First Ten Years of the Foreign Intelligence Surveillance Act of 1978*, 137 U. Pa. L. Rev. 793 (1989).

106. Church Committee, *supra* note 25, at 299, 302, 327–28.

107. Foreign Intelligence Surveillance Act, 50 U.S.C. 1801 et seq. (1978).

108. *Id.* at § 1804(a)(7)(B), 1823(a)(7)(B).

109. *See* Michael Ratner, *Moving Toward a Police State (Or Have We Arrived?) Secret Military Tribunals, Mass Arrests and Disappearances, Wiretapping and Torture, Counter Punch*, Nov. 20, 2001, available at www.counterpunch.org/ratner5.html. See also Cinquegrana, supra note 105, at 814–15 (stating that no government request for electronic surveillance has been denied by the court during its first ten years).

110. 50 U.S.C. 1804(a)(7)(B) (1978) (emphasis added).

111. *See* United States v. Truong Dinh Hung, 629 F.2d 908, 915 (4th Cir. 1980); United States v. Duggan, 743 F.2d 59, 77 (2d Cir. 1984). *See generally* Congressional Research Service, Terrorism: Section by Section Analysis of the USA PATRIOT Act 14, 15 n.6.

112. USA PATRIOT Act, *supra* note 99, at 218 (amending 50 U.S.C. § 1804(a)(7)(B), 1823(a)(7)(B)).

113. *Denver Police Files Raise Rights Concerns*, N.Y. Times, Mar. 14, 2002, at A25; Sean Kelly, *Cities Share Protester Files, Police Departments Call Practice Proactive*, Denver Post, Mar. 13, 2002, at A1

114. *See* Congressional Research Service, *supra* note 111, at 14.

115. USA PATRIOT Act, *supra* note 99, at 203.

116. Chang, *supra* note 102, at 2.

117. *Id.*

118. USA PATRIOT Act, *supra* note 99, at 213 (amending 18 U.S.C. 3103a).

119. *See* Electronic Frontier Foundation, *EFF Analysis of the Provisions of the USA Patriot Act that Relate to Online Activities* (Oct. 31, 2001), available at www.eff.org/Privacy/Surveillance/Terrorism_ilitias/20011031_eff_usa_patriot_analysis.html.

120. USA PATRIOT Act, *supra* note 99, at 802 (amending 18 U.S.C. 2331).

121. USA PATRIOT Act, *supra* note 99, at 224.

4

Politics and Principle: An Assessment of the Roosevelt Record on Civil Rights and Civil Liberties

Peter Irons

Franklin D. Roosevelt did little to advance the cause of civil rights and liberties during his twelve years in the White House. Admittedly, there is a whiff of sacrilege in this retrospective judgment of a man whose place in the pantheon of national leadership is secure. When he took office in 1933, Roosevelt faced the awesome task of rebuilding a shattered economy. That his success in this monumental endeavor was imperfect, frustrated at first by a recalcitrant judiciary and later by electoral setbacks, is less a measure of Roosevelt's presidential greatness than is his success in mending the shattered hopes and dreams of those who suffered the ravages of the Great Depression. Once the nation turned from domestic reconstruction to meet the challenge of fascist aggression, Roosevelt led a virtually united people to the brink of military victory. His death in 1945 came at a time of unprecedented American power and prestige in the world community.

Notwithstanding this ineradicable legacy, the fact remains that Franklin Roosevelt displayed a consistent lack of leadership in the area of civil rights and liberties. This is not to say that he did not, on the appropriate occasion, mouth the rhetoric of concern and support for the constitutional rights of those racial, religious, and ethnic minorities that were subjected to prejudice or repression. Undoubtedly sincere, such expressions of concern were colored both by Roosevelt's greater concern with the economic problems that consumed his presidential energies and by his patrician outlook and privileged background. The combined impact of these factors is evident in his Constitution Day speech of 1937. "Tolerance and concern for fair play are virtues which do not flourish in the stony soil of economic want and social distress," he told his audience at the Antietam battlefield in Maryland. "Those of us whose circumstances have been cast in fortunate lots are too prone to bear with fortitude the hardships of a goodly portion of our fellow countrymen and women."[1]

Roosevelt's view of "fair play" as the core value of the constitutional system bore the marks of his Groton chapel lessons and of exhortations on its playing fields. But his commitment to the "rules of the game" as a guiding principle of public behavior gave little solace to the victims of official lawlessness. Not once in his speech at Antietam, an occasion and place that called for a forthright statement, did Roosevelt defend the rights of the black Americans over whose status as slaves the Civil War had been waged. Speaking in a state that bordered the symbolic Mason–Dixon line and that held its black citizens in the grip of Jim Crow laws, the President voiced the code words of segregation. "The Bill of Rights is precious to all of us," he first stated in a ritual nod to the constitutional decalogue. "The reserved powers of the States to deal with matters of purely local concern are also precious," he immediately assured those who might fear any federal assault on their local "customs" and laws.[2]

Singling out this speech as being representative of Roosevelt's public statements on civil rights and liberties is not unfair. In such remarks he rarely ventured beyond the safe redoubt of platitude, in sharp contrast to his pointed and often personal barbs at those who disputed the wisdom of the New Deal recovery program.[3] Partisanship offers a partial explanation for this rhetorical disparity. Critics on economic issues were largely, although by no means exclusively, Republicans, and Roosevelt seemed to revel in excoriation of the GOP minority in Congress and its big-business backers.[4] His habitual avoidance of specific reference to racial and civil liberties issues reflected, at least in part, the political reality of Dixiecrat domination of the Congress.[5]

Partisan factors alone, however, cannot fully explain Roosevelt's continuing failure to confront directly the civil rights and liberties issues that persisted throughout his presidential tenure. Compassion for the poor and powerless he had in full measure, and as chief executive he did not shrink from pursuing the maximum exertion of federal power on behalf of this "forgotten" constituency. Uppermost in the minds of those who framed the Bill of Rights, Roosevelt told his Antietam audience, was the conviction that fulfillment of these rights required "a central government, strong enough to avert economic chaos."[6] But at the same time, he believed firmly in states' rights, and in particular in the responsibility of state and local government for law enforcement. The concept of a federal mandate for the protection of racial and political minorities was simply outside his Jeffersonian notion of the proper allocation of federal and state powers.

This brief sketch of Roosevelt's basic conception of the constitutional structure of the American governmental system is intended as a prologue to the discussion in this article of several of the more significant civil rights and liberties issues and episodes during the period from 1933 to 1945. The definitional problem in such an undertaking is complex. For the sake of brevity, this article will deal primarily with issues arising from claims of abridgment of rights protected by the first amendment and the Civil War amendments, and will stress those rights arguably protected by federal statute or by direct constitutional proscription. However, the concepts of civil rights and liberties are fluid and subject to considerable debate over their scope and content. Thus, a more practical rule of thumb will be employed: this article will focus on episodes that prompted an organization such as the American Civil Liberties Union (ACLU) or the National Association for the Advancement of Colored People (NAACP) to complain that the Roosevelt administration was derelict in protecting what these groups viewed as civil rights and liberties.[7] These outcries, after all, focused the attention of the public, the press, and government officials on a case or problem and gave historical import to the issues involved.

The central focus of this article is on the role played in these episodes by the U.S. Department of Justice, the primary federal agency entrusted with law enforcement duties and powers. In particular, the role of the attorney general as the department's titular head and as the personification of federal enforcement of civil rights and liberties provides this article with its analytic framework. A recent press commentary put this crucial cabinet post in perspective: "More than anyone but the President himself, it is the Attorney General who sets the moral tone of an administration, symbolizing its commitment or lack of commitment to impartial justice."[8] The four men who served Franklin Roosevelt in this post—Homer Cummings, Frank Murphy, Robert Jackson, and Francis Biddle—spanned the spectrum in the "moral tone" that each imposed on the department's approach to civil rights and liberties, from the virtual unconcern shown by Cummings to the passionate moralism and activism with which Murphy invested his office.

President Roosevelt allowed his attorneys general to function with considerable autonomy. Although the President took an active interest in federal judicial appointments[9] and in candidates for the patronage post of United States Attorney in the federal districts, he rarely intervened in the litigation decisions of the Justice Department.[10] Roosevelt and his White House staff were kept informed of developments in significant or politically sensitive cases, but with the Justice Department Roosevelt displayed less of his penchant for meddling in the affairs of cabinet agencies than with most others.[11] Within the context of the President's ultimate responsibility for the acts and policies of his subordinates, the Roosevelt record in civil rights and liberties is, then, more properly viewed as the separate records of his four attorneys general.

LYNCH MOBS AND LABOR VIOLENCE:
THE ERA OF HOMER CUMMINGS

Homer S. Cummings became attorney general by accident. Roosevelt had named Senator Thomas Walsh, a progressive Montana Democrat, to this post, but Walsh died two days before the presidential inauguration.[12] Rather than leave the cabinet incomplete while he searched for a distinguished replacement, Roosevelt hastily reached into the ranks of his political allies and tapped Cummings, who had been slated for the post of governor-general of the Philippines.[13]

Roosevelt was not the first and certainly not the last President to appoint an attorney general as a reward for faithful party service. Sixty-one at the time he took office, Cummings was a Yale Law School graduate who had combined private practice in Stamford, Connecticut, with an active career in public service and party politics.[14] He played a key role as Roosevelt's floor manager at the 1932 Democratic convention and worked hard in the election campaign. As[15] a former county prosecutor, Cummings brought a law-and-order perspective to the Justice Department, tempered with a genuine concern for due process and the rights of defendants.[16] But he was, at heart, a genial, gregarious politician more at home in smoke-filled rooms and on the golf course than with the angry advocates of civil rights and liberties.

During his six years as attorney general, Cummings pursued one objective, crime control, with an obsessive zeal. At a time when the automobile and telephone made it easy for criminals to travel and operate across state lines, Cummings moved quickly and with great success in persuading Congress to expand vastly his department's law enforcement powers. In his official report for 1934, he boasted of his lobbying prowess and its results "in curbing the activities of notorious murderers, kidnappers, gangsters, bank robbers and extortionists engaged in disparate interstate enterprises."[17]

In his anti-crime crusade, Cummings was more than willing to press the department's existing powers to their limits and to seek even more authority over matters that were traditionally state and local concerns. But he retreated to the states' rights argument when confronted with demands that he take action against lynching. Roosevelt's election had given hope to those groups, led by the NAACP, which had vainly sought for years the enactment of a federal anti-lynching law.[18] The campaign for the law became a crusade in 1933, spurred by national revulsion at a wave of brutal lynchings (twenty-eight during the year). Its proponents united behind a bill introduced by Senators Edward Costigan of Colorado and Robert Wagner of New York.[19]

While the anti-lynching coalition organized its lobbying effort, and sought Roosevelt's aid in breaking the expected Southern filibuster in the Senate, three black youths were lynched in Alabama in August 1933. This crime prompted civil rights leaders to demand federal prosecution of the Tuscaloosa County sheriff for turning the victims over to the mob.[20] A delegation headed by Walter White, the NAACP's executive secretary, met with Attorney General Cummings on August 24. The delegation pointed out to Cummings a federal statute which made it a criminal offense for a person acting "under color of any law" to deprive another "of any rights, privileges, or immunities secured or protected by the Constitution and laws of the United States . . . ."[21] The visitors reminded the attorney general that the sheriff's action had deprived the lynched youths of their lives, in violation of the fourteenth amendment.

The demand for prosecution in this case was largely symbolic, in view of the maximum penalty provided under the statute, a one-year prison term or $1000 fine. What the delegation undoubtedly hoped, rather than to obtain the sheriff's indictment, was to sensitize Cummings to the issue and to enlist his support for the Costigan-Wagner bill. Cummings' response left Walter White with a feeling of outrage: "The attorney general was suave; he would make no commitment; he called for a brief."[22] As Cummings had asked, the civil rights groups prepared and sent to him a lengthy brief which argued the applicability of the federal statute, section 52 of the criminal code, to state and local officials dealing with lynch mobs. According to White, the attorney general simply informed the delegation several months later that "the department did not intend to take any action" in the Tuscaloosa case.[23]

President Roosevelt genuinely abhorred lynching, which he denounced in 1933 as "a vile form of collective murder."[24] But he put no political muscle behind his verbal support for the Costigan-Wagner bill, limiting his effort to the marshmallow statement that "the President will be glad to see the bill pass and wishes it passed."[25] The Dixiecrats who controlled the Senate quite predictably ignored this exhortation and killed both this bill and its successors.[26] Attorney General Cummings took his cues on this issue from the White House and matched Roosevelt in verbal evasion. In August 1938 he told the sponsor of a House bill that would direct the FBI to investigate lynching that he viewed the crime "with loathing," but that "the responsibility, so far as legislation is concerned, is primarily and unmistakably with Congress."[27] Like the president, Cummings stayed on the sidelines as the battles over lynching raged during his six years in office, an ineffective cheerleader in this one-sided contest with enormous human and moral stakes.

The second major civil rights and liberties issue that arose during the Cummings era in the Justice Department was that of violence and legal repression directed at labor organizers and strikers. Backed by local police, National Guard troops, and the courts, employers had virtually crushed the labor movement in the decade that preceded the New Deal.[28] Heartened by the promise of federal legislation to ensure their rights to organize and bargain collectively, millions of unorganized workers voted for Roosevelt and, after his election, plastered factory gates with appeals that "The President Wants You to Join the Union."[29] Congress responded to labor pressure by inserting into the National Industrial Recovery Act (NIRA), passed in 1933, the requirement in section 7(a) that employers permit workers to "organize and bargain collectively through representatives of their own choosing" over issues of wages, hours, and working conditions.[30]

Hailed as "Labor's Bill of Rights," section 7(a) triggered an intense but short-lived labor organizing campaign that foundered on the rocks of employer resistance. Along with competition from company unions, the discharge of union members, infiltration by labor spies, and the widespread refusal of employers to recognize unions, those who tried to "organize the unorganized" encountered Justice Department reluctance to seek judicial enforcement of section 7(a).[31] Francis Biddle, whose initial New Deal post was chairman of the first National Labor Relations Board, often bickered with Attorney General Cummings over Justice Department foot-dragging in enforcement cases.[32] Cummings found fault with every case prepared by Biddle's board and took only a handful before the conservative federal judges who struck down New Deal statutes with undisguised hostility.[33]

Justice Department obstruction was only one of the factors that made section 7(a) a victim of the business counteroffensive against unions in the 1933–1936 period.[34] State and local officials proved to be equally unwilling to protect organizers and striking workers, and were often eager to intervene on the side of the employers. The clashes of strikers and policemen at picket lines resulted in more than eighteen thousand arrests between 1933 and 1936, and over one hundred strikers were killed in labor disputes during this period.[35] Only a year after Roosevelt took office, the ACLU had shifted from praise of his labor program to bitter criticism and condemnation of federal officials for siding with employers.[36]

The bloody 1934 San Francisco general strike put the Roosevelt administration to the first real test of its labor sympathies. Led by Harry Bridges, the longshoremen, whose waterfront strike spread across the city, fought battles with the police, leaving two strikers dead and hundreds injured.[37] Employer groups appealed to the federal government for National Guard intervention. General Hugh Johnson, the bombastic National Recovery Administration director, supported military force to break the strike and rushed to San Francisco. There he likened the situation to "civil war" and urged conservative union leaders, who backed the general strike but also feared Bridges as a radical, to "run these subversive influences out from their ranks like rats."[38]

Although the Justice Department played no direct role in the San Francisco strike, Attorney General Cummings advised Roosevelt that the president had federal statutory authority to employ Army troops against the strikers and to declare martial law in the area. Frances Perkins, the Labor Secretary whose moderate counsel ultimately prevailed, met with Cummings and "pleaded that this was in no way an alarming situation" that required a military response. "I thought it unwise," she reported telling Cummings, "to begin the Roosevelt administration by shooting it out with working people who were only exercising their rights . . . to organize and demand collective bargaining."[39] Federal troops remained in their barracks and the general strike fizzled out when craft union leaders withdrew their support from Bridges and his longshoremen.[40]

Though Cummings was willing to dispatch armed forces against striking workers in San Francisco, he was reluctant to dispatch Justice Department lawyers to investigate claims of civil rights and liberties violations around the nation. One case in which he did order an inquiry involved charges that sharecroppers and tenant farmers on the cotton plantations of eastern Arkansas were held in peonage and subjected to violent reprisals for striking against planters.[41] The sharecroppers and tenants were members of the biracial Southern Tenant Farmers Union (STFU). Repeated complaints by STFU leaders and their northern liberal allies prompted Cummings in June 1936 to order an investigation of allegations that striking cotton choppers were being fined for vagrancy and then "forced to work at the point of guns to pay off these fines."[42]

Cummings authorized the Arkansas investigation with an eye toward enforcement of the federal Antipeonage Act, the modern version of a Reconstruction statute designed to protect former slaves from a form of forced labor that resulted from perpetual indebtedness.[43] As early as 1914, the Supreme Court had held that certain state laws violated the Antipeonage Act.[44] Nonetheless, the Justice Department had rarely taken advantage of the Antipeonage Act to pursue widely alleged abuses, and the STFU and its supporters hailed Cummings' announcement. The special assistant he dispatched to Arkansas, Sam Whittaker, not only investigated the peonage charges but also the claims that members of the STFU staff had been beaten and flogged.[45] The outcome of the federal inquiry disheartened the STFU and its supporters. The Whittaker investigation, Cummings announced to the press in August 1936, "failed to reveal any violation of Federal statutes."[46] The facts uncovered by Whittaker, added the attorney general, would be turned over to Arkansas officials for possible state action. Not surprisingly, no state prosecutions were forthcoming.

The Arkansas turmoil had one result that later prompted Cummings to initiate the only major prosecution under federal civil rights laws during his tenure in office. Dismayed by the ineffective Arkansas probe, Gardner Jackson, an untiring activist who organized support for the STFU and other liberal causes, turned his efforts from the executive to the legislative branch of the federal government. Jackson persuaded Senator Robert LaFollette, Jr., the Wisconsin Progressive, to introduce a resolution to authorize a congressional investigative body with jurisdiction over civil liberties issues.[47] The Senate passed the resolution in June 1936 and Senator Hugo Black, who chaired the Committee on Education and Labor, appointed LaFollette to head a three-member subcommittee that became popularly known as the LaFollette Civil Liberties Committee.[48]

The LaFollette Committee devoted its first year to exposure of the "labor spy" network that spread across the country and was funded by anti-union employers to the tune of several million dollars a year.[49] In 1937, LaFollette turned his attention to labor violence in Harlan County, Kentucky, where for the past six years coal miners had fought for recognition of their union, the United Mine Workers of America.[50] Coal operators in "Bloody Harlan" owned the county sheriff, Theodore Middleton, whose deputies patrolled the mining camps with machine guns. Between 1934 and 1937 thirty-seven of Middleton's deputies were convicted of felonies and sixty-four were indicted at least once.[51]

LaFollette began hearings on the Harlan County situation in April 1937, just two weeks after the Supreme Court upheld the National Labor Relations Act in the *Jones & Laughlin* case.[52] The combination of the well-publicized hearings and judicial approval of labor's rights to organize free of employer interference had an obvious impact on the Justice Department. On May 19, 1937, Attorney General Cummings issued a press release that announced his dispatch of FBI agents to Harlan County with orders to investigate complaints of "violence and terrorism" in the troubled area. "If the investigation discloses offenses under Federal jurisdiction," Cummings stated, "vigorous and prompt prosecution will follow."[53]

Based on evidence collected by the FBI and presented to the LaFollette Committee, Cummings authorized the prosecution of more than fifty defendants, including sixteen coal companies, eighteen company operators, and twenty-two deputy sheriffs.[54] They were indicted under the Reconstruction-era statute that made it a crime for two or more persons to conspire to deprive any citizen of rights secured by the Constitution or federal law.[55] Tried in

1938, the Harlan County cases ended in a mistrial after a hung jury. The defendants were not retried, but Justice Department and other federal officials persuaded coal operators to end their reign of terror against the miners and the union organizing campaign.[56]

It seems clear that Cummings bowed to public and political pressure in approving federal prosecution in the Harlan County case. Still, his reluctant use of the federal civil rights laws did set a precedent that his successors followed with more vigorous action. The Cummings era in the Justice Department spanned six years marked by widespread violence and official oppression visited on blacks and union members. The statutory enforcement tools available to federal prosecutors were weak and lacked firm judicial sanction. Nonetheless, Cummings made no move to strengthen these tools and failed almost totally to set a "moral tone" of support for civil rights and liberties. The "accidental" attorney general left his post in 1939 with a record of failed opportunity.

BRUTALITY AND BIGOTS TURNING THE SCREWS OF ENFORCEMENT

Each of the three men who followed Homer Cummings as attorney general in the Roosevelt administration proclaimed a determination to enforce the civil rights laws to their fullest extent. A number of political factors—the rightward turn of Congress, looming war clouds and the ensuing global conflict, and the concomitant fear of "subversive" and "disloyal" groups in American society—placed obstacles in the path of impartial enforcement. The impact of these factors produced lapses in the records of Cummings' successors that cannot be ignored or excused.[57] But on the whole, the final six years of the Roosevelt era were marked by a vastly improved Justice Department record in the area of civil rights and liberties.

It is impossible to say whether President Roosevelt selected Frank Murphy to succeed Cummings with the intention to restore the "moral tone" that could be set by the attorney general. Murphy was a loyal New Deal politician who needed a job, having been defeated for reelection as governor of Michigan in the 1938 electoral debacle of Democrats in both Congress and the states.[58] Murphy was rewarded, as Cummings had been, for faithful party service. But this was the only characteristic the two men shared. More than any attorney general in American history, Murphy brought to the post a crusading spirit and a passionate moralism that reflected his former membership on the NAACP board of directors and his hatred of racial and religious prejudice.[59]

Murphy wasted no time in charting a new course for the Justice Department. On February 3, 1939, less than a month after he assumed office, he created a new departmental body, first called the Civil Liberties Unit and later retitled and more widely known as the Civil Rights Section (CRS). In announcing this move, Murphy stressed that "an important function of the law enforcement branch of government is the aggressive protection of fundamental rights inherent in a free people." He promised to "pursue a program of vigilant action in the prosecution" of those who infringed constitutional and federal statutory rights.[60] The small but dedicated group of lawyers assigned to the CRS immediately began to review the existing body of federal law with the aim of finding a solid basis for enforcement. They also began selecting cases for prosecution from the backlog of complaints that had piled up in the department, and from the wave of complaints that flowed in after the publicity given to Murphy's statement.[61]

The new attorney general had an acute perception, as a veteran of local and state service during the Depression decade, of the fact that civil rights and liberties were most often infringed by officials at these lower levels of government. Taking the stump at the May 1934 meeting of the United States Conference of Mayors, Murphy combined an impassioned plea for cooperation with a chiding lecture to his former colleagues. Noting that his department had received "a steady deluge of letters complaining that civil liberties have been abridged" by local police and officials, Murphy summed up these informal petitions as an indictment of his listeners:

> They indicate clearly that some public officials have used their power arbitrarily; that ordinances have been passed and invoked that are oppressive and unjust and violate common right; that citizens have been denied the right to express freely their opinions and to worship as they please; and that some have been prevented from petitioning their government for the redress of grievances.[62]

Murphy did not need to remind his audience that each count of this indictment was leveled particularly at one mayor who was conspicuously absent from the meeting, Frank Hague of Jersey City. Determined to keep labor organizers out of his fiefdom, Hague's compliant city council had enacted ordinances that gave city officials unbridled discretion to ban picketing on city streets. Jersey City police had arrested hundreds of those who defied the ordinances. This volatile situation gave a special emphasis to Murphy's statement that "the first battleground of civil liberties is the local communities."[63] The mayors could hardly have missed the point when the Supreme Court, in an opinion handed down just three weeks after Murphy spoke, struck down the Jersey City ordinances as an infringement of constitutional rights secured by the Fourteenth Amendment and protected by federal statute.[64]

Although the Justice Department had not been a party to the Jersey City case, the Supreme Court decision gave heart to lawyers in the CRS and prompted them to press for federal prosecution of local officials who acted "under color of law" in denying protected civil rights. Given the lead-time required for the preparation of such cases, only a handful were brought during the year that Murphy served as attorney general. Conscious of the depth of black frustration at the failure of the anti-lynching campaign, CRS lawyers decided to focus on police brutality cases. As their first target, they selected an Atlanta policeman, William Sutherland, accused of extracting a confession from a black prisoner with an electric "tacking iron," a third-degree method that left the victim severely burned.[65]

Revulsion at the torture inflicted by Sutherland led the local United States Attorney to recommend federal prosecution, despite the policeman's earlier acquittal in state court. In March 1940 a federal grand jury issued an indictment based on section 52 of the criminal code, charging the defendant with acting "under color of law" in depriving the victim of his rights to due process and equal protection of the laws. Justice Department lawyers won a legal victory when the federal judge overruled a demurrer to the indictment based on the argument that a policeman who had clearly exceeded his statutory authority acted without official sanction and was thus beyond the reach of federal law. The federal prosecutors failed, however, to gain a conviction in two trials because of jury disagreement; they finally dropped the case.[66] Justice Department lawyers were not unsuccessful in all of the early police brutality cases. Another prosecution begun in 1940, against an Arkansas deputy sheriff charged with brutality against prisoners, ended with a conviction in 1942. CRS lawyers were especially heartened in this case by an appellate decision that sanctioned the use of section 52 in police brutality cases.[67]

Federal civil rights prosecutions began in earnest when Frank Murphy became attorney general. The "moral tone" he set in this area continued under the two men who next held this post, although they lacked his fervent commitment. Upon Murphy's nomination to the Supreme Court in January 1940, President Roosevelt replaced him with Robert H. Jackson, an upstate New York lawyer who had campaigned vigorously for Roosevelt in 1932. Rewarded with the office of general counsel in the Bureau of Internal Revenue, Jackson later moved to the Justice Department and became solicitor general in 1938, serving under both Cummings and Murphy.[68] During his tenure as attorney general, Jackson supported the civil rights enforcement program with considerably less fervor than Murphy.[69]

Jackson did approve one notable prosecution in a voting rights case, providing Justice Department lawyers with a long-sought judicial sanction. This case did not involve disenfranchised blacks, but rather a scandal within the lily-white Louisiana Democratic party. Members of the party's reform faction, in their zeal to oust the entrenched Long machine, were caught stealing ballots during the bitter primary election and were indicted under sections 51 and 52 of the federal criminal code. When the federal district judge sustained demurrers to these charges, the government appealed directly to the Supreme Court.[70] The significance of the Court's ruling in the *Classic* case,[71] a narrow four-to-three decision handed down in March 1941, did not lie in its reversal of the trial judge on the section 51 charge. This part of the opinion merely extended to congressional primaries an earlier ruling that dealt with fraudulent practices in general elections.[72] The Court broke new ground, however, in holding that state officials who committed acts outside the scope of their authority could be prosecuted under section 52, which did not require proof of a conspiracy to infringe constitutional rights.[73]

With their most potent enforcement tool sharpened by the Supreme Court, lawyers in the CRS wielded section 52 in a new round of police brutality prosecutions. When Robert Jackson followed Frank Murphy to the Supreme Court in June 1941, responsibility for this campaign fell on Francis Biddle, the fourth and last attorney general to serve under Roosevelt. Like his immediate predecessor, Biddle was elevated from the post of solicitor general and was also a veteran of New Deal legal service.[74] Underneath the "casual" exterior noted by friends, Biddle had a core of toughness and closely matched Murphy in his commitment to civil rights and liberties.

Biddle later wrote proudly of his record in bringing prosecutions against state officials "who had misused the power of office under 'color of law' to deprive individuals of their rights."[75] He took a personal interest in the case brought in 1943 against Claude Screws, a rural Georgia sheriff who, joined by a deputy and a local policeman, beat to death a handcuffed black prisoner arrested on a forged warrant.[76] After conviction by a federal jury, Screws and his co-defendants received three-year prison sentences. Biddle expressed pleasure that jury members "were not deflected from doing their sworn duty by the usual charge of 'Yankee interference.'"[77]

The conviction of the homicidal officers proved to be a pyrrhic victory. After the verdicts were upheld by the Fifth Circuit Court of Appeals,[78] the Supreme Court agreed to review the cases and proceeded to blunt the utility of section 52. Six justices supported the constitutionality of the statute, but a five-member majority held that the trial judge had erred in his jury instructions and ordered a new trial. Writing for the Court, Justice William O. Douglas stated that the law required the jury to find that the defendants had "willfully" deprived their victim of a right "made specific either by the express terms of the Constitution or laws of the United States or by decisions interpreting them."[79] The import of Douglas's opinion seemed to be that the jury must find that the defendants had in mind the due process rights of their victim when they bludgeoned him to death. Not surprisingly, Screws and his fellow officers were acquitted on retrial, which led Biddle to complain that the results of the *Screws* decision "was greatly to lessen the value of Section 52 in punishing atrocities of this character where the state refused to take action."[80]

The Supreme Court also complicated the task of providing federal protection to members of the Jehovah's Witnesses sect, whose street-corner preaching and door-to-door proselytizing had provoked hundreds of arrests and the passage of many restrictive local ordinances. In June 1940 the Court upheld the action of a Pennsylvania school board in expelling two young Witnesses who refused to salute the American flag.[81] Victor Rotnem, a Civil Rights Section lawyer who headed the unit while Biddle was attorney general, described the violent consequences of the Court's opinion: "Between June 12 and June 20, 1940, hundreds of attacks upon the Witnesses were reported to the Department of Justice. Several were of such violence that it was deemed advisable to have the Federal Bureau of Investigation look into them."[82]

One of these violent reprisals against the Witnesses led to a successful prosecution under section 52. When seven members of the sect arrived in Richwood, West Virginia, in June 1940, they visited the mayor's office to seek police protection. They were promptly seized by a deputy sheriff, forced to drink large doses of castor oil and taken out to face a mob of 1,500 hostile people. The deputy, who had removed his badge, then ordered the Witnesses to salute the flag, after which they were tied to a rope, marched through the streets, and finally told to leave the town and not to return.[83] Lawyers in the CRS brought charges against the deputy sheriff and chief of police and secured convictions that were upheld by the Fourth Circuit Court of Appeals.[84]

Overall, the Justice Department compiled a creditable record over the last six years of the Roosevelt administration in cases that dealt with racial and religious minorities. Needless to say, the CRS was unable to bring prosecutions in more than a handful of the cases referred to it.[85] Many of these complaints were factually weak, many were settled without prosecution, some did not pass grand jury scrutiny, and others that resulted in indictments were lost when juries refused to convict. The Supreme Court's backing-and-filling in its statutory interpretation of section 52 complicated the enforcement program. Institutional factors also affected the work of CRS lawyers. "Certain career lawyers in the upper echelons of the Justice Department were hostile to the program," one of the CRS lawyers recently stated.[86] Resistance to civil rights enforcement at lower levels, particularly within the FBI, additionally hampered efforts to secure evidence against local officials and policemen.[87] Notwithstanding these hobbles, CRS lawyers did their best to protect and enforce constitutional rights.

COMMUNISM AND CONCENTRATION CAMPS:
CIVIL RIGHTS IN CRISIS

Balanced against the Roosevelt administration's efforts to protect the civil rights and liberties of oppressed minorities are its egregious failures. Among the episodes in which the Justice Department capitulated to political pressure, three in particular stand out as examples of subordination of the Constitution to the politics of paranoia. Each of these episodes—the campaign to deport Harry Bridges, the prosecution of "seditious" critics of American wartime policies, and the internment of Japanese Americans—illustrate the dominance of politics over law when the two institutions battle.

Harry Bridges was the victim of a unique political and legal vendetta which lasted more than two decades. His troubles began in 1934, when Bridges directed the San Francisco waterfront strike that spread across the city and split the Roosevelt administration into hard-line and more moderate factions.[88] Members of the Communist Party supported the strike and made up a vocal and influential minority in the longshoremen's union that Bridges headed. These connections, along with his openly radical views, made Bridges the target of West Coast shipping interests and their allies among local, state, and federal officials. Charges that the union leader was a communist became a staple of hostile press comments and denunciation by conservative politicians.[89]

As an alien, Bridges was especially vulnerable to legal attack. (Although Bridges had twice taken out naturalization papers after his arrival in the United States from his native Australia in 1920, he had let them lapse each time before the deadlines set for formal application for American citizenship.) The first official move to seek his deportation began in 1937 on the initiative of the Seattle director of the Immigration and Naturalization Service (INS), an agency then part of the Labor Department.[90] The INS official bombarded his Washington headquarters with affidavits and police reports that alleged that Bridges was a communist. Labor Secretary Frances Perkins sought Roosevelt's advice on whether to bring deportation proceedings against Bridges under federal law. According to Perkins, Roosevelt dismissed the idea on civil liberties grounds.[91]

Despite this presidential directive, mounting political pressure finally forced Perkins to issue a deportation warrant against Bridges in March 1938. Her distaste for the crusade to deport Bridges was reflected in her selection of James Landis to serve as trial examiner in the fact-finding hearings mandated by INS regulation. Then the dean of Harvard Law School, Landis upheld his reputation as a New Deal liberal in finding, after an eleven-week hearing that produced a 152-page report submitted in December 1939, that the evidence presented had not shown that Bridges was currently either a member of or "affiliated" with the Communist Party.[92]

The conservative reaction to the Landis report took several forms. One was an impeachment resolution filed against Perkins in the House of Representatives, which scared the Secretary but went nowhere.[93] More important was the successful campaign to transfer the INS to the Justice Department, which bypassed Perkins. The next move in the congressional crusade involved a classic bill of attainder. This legislative billy-club directed Attorney General Robert Jackson to deport Bridges "forthwith to Australia" on the ground that his "presence in this country the Congress deems hurtful."[94] Jackson responded with a public letter denouncing this bill as unconstitutional and noting that Bridges "had been accused, investigated, and tried at great length, and judgment has been rendered that he had not been proved guilty of the charges made against him."[95]

Jackson's success in blocking passage of the bill of attainder proved to be illusory. In June 1940, Bridges' leading congressional opponent, Sam Hobbs, added to the Alien Registration Act—better known as the Smith Act—a provision directing the deportation of aliens who "at any time" after their arrival in the United States had been members of or "affiliated" with the Communist Party.[96] Hobbs thus circumvented Landis's interpretation of the earlier statute and opened the door for renewed proceedings against Bridges.[97] Jackson promptly ordered the FBI to reopen its investigation of the outspoken union leader, whose opposition to the growing "preparedness" campaign put him at odds with the attorney general's interventionist sentiments.[98] Announcing in February 1941 that a 2,500-page FBI report contained "new and additional evidence" in the case, Jackson issued a second deportation warrant and chose Charles B. Sears, a retired New York State judge, to conduct a second round of hearings.[99] Based largely on the testimony of two witnesses who had not appeared at the prior hearings, both of them bitter union foes of Bridges, Sears concluded after the ten-week session, in a 185-page report submitted in September 1941, that Bridges was a Communist Party member and should be deported to his native country.[100]

The timing of the Sears report placed the burden of decision on Francis Biddle, who had recently replaced Jackson as attorney general. Political factors complicated Biddle's task. Three months before he received Sears' deportation recommendation, Germany had invaded the Soviet Union and Bridges had shifted to fervent support of the Allied cause.[101] Conscious of the pressures to overrule Sears and dismiss the warrant, Biddle nonetheless decided—despite the unanimous opinion of the Board of Immigration Appeals that the testimony accepted by Sears was suspect—to order Bridges' deportation.[102] This decision upset President Roosevelt, for whom politics almost always took precedence over law. "I'm sorry to hear that," Roosevelt responded when Biddle informed him of the decision. But the president knew that the judicial wheels turned slowly. "I'll bet," he told Biddle, "that the Supreme Court will never let him be deported. And the decision is a long way off."[103]

Roosevelt's prediction was accurate on both counts. Three years elapsed between the time Bridges was served with the deportation order and the Supreme Court's decision in June 1945—two weeks after the German surrender—to vacate the order. Writing for the five-member majority, Justice Douglas cut a narrow path of statutory interpretation, holding that Judge Sears had relied on unsworn testimony and had misconstrued the term "affiliation" in his report.[104] This evasion of the central issue, that of the vendetta against Bridges for his labor militance and political views, provoked an acidulous concurrence from Justice Murphy, directed both at Douglas and Biddle: "The record in this case will stand forever as a monument to man's intolerance of man. Seldom if ever in the history of this nation has there been such a concentrated and relentless crusade to deport an individual because he dared to exercise the freedom that belongs to him as a human being and that is guaranteed to him by the Constitution."[105]

The crusade to deport Harry Bridges left a lasting stain on the record of the Roosevelt administration. Despite his ultimate success in gaining American citizenship, made possible after the Supreme Court reversed a perjury conviction obtained by Truman's Justice Department,[106] Bridges spent the better part of two decades before inquisitorial bodies and in court. Political in motivation, the charges against him were nonetheless cast by successive attorneys general into legal form and pursued in the face of clear judicial precedent. Bridges survived the "communist" charges, but his ordeal left the Justice Department with an unhealed wound.

It is ironic that the Smith Act, largely intended to force the deportation of Harry Bridges, failed in its primary purpose but succeeded in establishing, almost without debate, the first peacetime sedition law since 1798.[107] It is equally ironic that the Justice Department, during the Roosevelt administration, avoided prosecuting Communist Party leaders under the provisions designed to punish advocates of revolutionary doctrine. The congressional sponsors of these provisions had directly aimed them at the "Bolshevik" allies of the Soviet Union.[108] The German invasion of Russia in June 1941, however, changed the erstwhile revolutionaries into ardent patriots and immunized the party's leaders from prosecution until Cold War politics gripped the Truman administration.[109]

The final irony of the Smith Act is that its first victims were members of the miniscule Socialist Workers Party (SWP), a Trotskyite group that detested the Communist Party and its Stalinist policies. The SWP's vocal opposition to Roosevelt's wartime alliance with Stalin made its leaders obvious targets for federal surveillance. Domestic political factors, however, had a greater impact on the decision to bring Smith Act indictments against SWP leaders. The party's bastion was in Minneapolis, among members of the Teamsters Union. In June 1941, the SWP-led Teamsters local withdrew from the American Federation of Labor and joined the Congress of Industrial Organizations. This threat to his leadership prompted Dan Tobin, the Teamsters president and a Roosevelt ally, to appeal for federal action against the SWP apostates. Tobin's request brought immediate action. On June 28, federal marshals raided the SWP's Minneapolis office and twenty-nine party leaders were subsequently indicted for Smith Act violations.[110]

Francis Biddle authorized the SWP prosecutions as acting attorney general and publicly trumpeted the indictments as the opening shot in a national drive against radicals and communists.[111] Eighteen of the defendants were convicted and sentenced to prison. Although the SWP leaders refused to disavow the "revolutionary aims" of the party, none of the documents submitted as evidence at the trial went beyond advocacy of "mass action, propaganda and mass agitation" as complements of the party's participation in trade union work and electoral campaigns. Nonetheless, the federal appellate court that upheld the convictions professed no doubt that "force was the ultimate means" intended in the party's campaign against capitalism.[112] Ruling in 1943, the Supreme Court refused to review the convictions and the SWP leaders served their sentences.[113]

Much later, writing in his memoirs, Biddle confessed that "I have since come to regret that I authorized the prosecution" of the vocal but isolated Trotskyites. He admitted that "by no conceivable stretch of a liberal imagination" had the defendants ever posed a "clear and present danger" to the government they were charged with conspiring to overthrow.[114] Wartime pressures also prompted another sedition prosecution intended to balance the political scales. Responding to a flurry of notes from Roosevelt that were attached to "scurrilous attacks on his leadership" in the publications of American fascists, Biddle approved in June 1942 the indictment of twenty-six Nazi propagandists. The resulting trial, which Biddle described as a "shockingly dreary and degrading experience," ended in a mistrial when the trial judge died. The indictments were ultimately dismissed, and Biddle admitted his embarrassment but not remorse at this second use of the Smith Act.[115]

No single episode more dishonored the civil rights and liberties record of the Roosevelt administration than the forced evacuation from the West Coast of 110,000 Americans of Japanese ancestry.[116] The travail of this friendless and frightened minority began eleven weeks after the Japanese attack on

Pearl Harbor, when Roosevelt signed Executive Order 9066 on February 19, 1942.[117] Predicated on the need to protect military installations from the threat of espionage and sabotage, this presidential edict resulted in the internment of Japanese Americans in concentration camps—euphemistically called "Relocation Centers"—scattered from the California desert to the swamps of Arkansas. Before those camp residents certified as "loyal" by federal officials were released from confinement, they spent an average of 900 days under armed guard, imprisoned without charge or trial.[118]

Historians and legal commentators have since condemned the evacuation decision and internment program with virtual unanimity.[119] More disturbing than these retrospective judgments is the fact that those who framed the "military necessity" rationale for the incarceration of Japanese Americans were conscious at the time of its falsity. Nonetheless, over the ineffectual protests of two Justice Department lawyers, military claims that Japanese Americans had committed acts of espionage were presented to the Supreme Court in the test cases that challenged the constitutionality of the internment program.[120]

Responsibility for the treatment of Japanese Americans rests with high-ranking officials in each branch—executive, legislative, and judicial—of the federal government. The evacuation decision, which resulted largely from political pressure applied on the War Department by California officials and members of the West Coast congressional delegation,[121] was framed by a military officer who admitted that "no one has justified fully the sheer military necessity for such action."[122] Secretary of War Henry L. Stimson, who approved the executive order sent to the White House for Roosevelt's signature, privately confessed his conviction that "it will make a tremendous hole in our constitutional system."[123] Attorney General Francis Biddle also swallowed his doubts about the necessity for the executive order. Justice Department lawyers had strenuously argued to Biddle that evacuation of a single racial group would be unconstitutional.[124] Biddle later explained his capitulation to Stimson on the grounds that "I was new to the Cabinet, and disinclined to insist on my view to an elder statesman whose wisdom and integrity I greatly respected."[125]

More than any other government official, Assistant Secretary of War John J. McCloy assumed the responsibility for guiding the executive order to Roosevelt's desk. Determined to overcome Stimson's constitutional qualms and Biddle's objections to evacuation, McCloy prevailed in a dramatic showdown with the objecting Justice Department lawyers, who were distressed to learn that the attorney general had bowed to Roosevelt's entreaties and McCloy's insistence.[126] McCloy wasted no time in directing the West Coast military commander, General John L. DeWitt, to begin the evacuation of Japanese Americans from their West Coast homes.[127] McCloy also took the initiative in pushing through Congress the legislation that placed criminal penalties behind Dewitt's curfew and exclusion orders, the initial steps in the internment program.[128]

Given the unenviable choice between barbed-wire compounds and prison bars, it is hardly surprising that only a handful of Japanese Americans challenged DeWitt's orders in the courts. Three young men appealed their criminal convictions to the Supreme Court. Minoru Yasui, a lawyer and reserve Army officer who had been turned down for active service, brought a test case against the curfew in Portland, Oregon. Gordon Hirabayashi, a college senior and Quaker pacifist, deliberately violated the curfew and exclusion orders in Seattle. Fred Korematsu, a shipyard welder, had been arrested for violating an exclusion order in San Leandro, California. The final case to reach the Supreme Court involved a young woman, Mitsuye Endo, who filed a habeas corpus petition after reporting for internment in California.[129]

Confining its initial rulings to the curfew issue, the Supreme Court unanimously affirmed in June 1943 the convictions of Yasui and Hirabayashi.[130] Chief Justice Harlan Fiske Stone, in the *Hirabayashi* opinion, cited the Army's claim that the "racial attachments" to their ancestral homeland made reasonable the suspicion that Japanese Americans posed a danger of espionage and sabotage. Refusing to question the judgment of military officials, Stone wrote that "it is not for any court to sit in review of the wisdom of their action or substitute its judgment for theirs."[131] At the time, Justice Department lawyers were aware that military intelligence reports contradicted the Army's "disloyalty" claim. The Court, however, was not aware of this when it decided these first cases, because Solicitor General Charles Fahy rebuffed Justice Department lawyers' efforts to bring these reports to the Court's attention, despite objections that failure to do so "might approximate the suppression of evidence."[132]

Eighteen months passed before the Supreme Court ruled on the two remaining internment cases. During this time President Roosevelt paid more attention to partisan factors than to the plight of Japanese Americans. Secretary of War Stimson informed Roosevelt in May 1944 of the Army's opinion that the internment program could be safely ended. Concerned about the potential electoral consequences of such a move, the President brushed aside this request.[133] Despite the urgings of military leaders and Cabinet members, Roosevelt held the Japanese Americans hostage to political concerns until the Supreme Court forced his hand in the *Endo* case. Decided in December 1944, this decision finally opened the gates of the internment camps.[134]

Though the Court held unanimously in *Endo* that Congress had not authorized an indefinite internment program, the Justices split over the constitutionality of the military orders that preceded and led to internment. The

Supreme Court's bitter division in the *Korematsu* case reflected two factors: the shifting tides of war toward the United States and its allies; and recognition that racism had motivated the internment. With ultimate wartime victory in sight, the Court's unanimity in *Hirabayashi* and *Yasui* eroded. The *Korematsu* opinion, written by Justice Hugo Black for a six-member majority, was defensive in tone and narrowly circumscribed in upholding the exclusion orders.[135] General DeWitt's public comment that "a Jap's a Jap,"[136] and the claim in his official report on the internment program that Japanese Americans belonged to "an enemy race,"[137] clearly embarrassed Black.[138] Asserting that Korematsu had not been ordered to leave his home town "because of hostility to him or his race," Black rested his opinion on unspecified "evidence of disloyalty" among the Japanese Americans.[139] Justice Frank Murphy, the most outraged of the three dissenters, found no such evidence in the record and retorted that internment represented nothing more than the "legalization of racism."[140]

Perhaps the most disturbing aspect of the *Korematsu* case was the high-level decision to prevent the Supreme Court from learning of the existence of official reports that refuted the "military necessity" rationale for internment. In his Final Report to the War Department on the program, General DeWitt had charged Japanese Americans with the commission of acts of espionage, including the transmission of visual and radio signals to Japanese submarines off the West Coast.[141] Two Justice Department lawyers, suspicious of DeWitt's claims, persuaded Attorney General Biddle to order investigations by the FBI and the Federal Communications Commission. The reports of these agencies to Biddle conclusively refuted DeWitt's unsupported allegations.[142]

Convinced that the "lies" and "intentional falsehoods" in the DeWitt report should be brought to the attention of the Supreme Court, the two lawyers added a footnote to the government's *Korematsu* brief that alluded to the countering reports and disavowed any reliance on the espionage claims. But after the last-minute intervention of Assistant Secretary of War John McCloy, Solicitor General Charles Fahy pulled the brief from the printing press and excised the confessional footnote from it.[143] Bureaucratic politics thus prevailed over professional ethics and the integrity of the judicial system.

POLITICS AND PRINCIPLES—
THE ROOSEVELT RECORD IN RETROSPECT

Any fair assessment of the Roosevelt record on civil rights and liberties must balance accomplishments with failures. More importantly, such an assessment must judge Roosevelt's record against those of the presidents who pre-

ceded and followed him, in particular those who share the "progressive" man-
tle that historians have draped over his shoulders. Woodrow Wilson, another
wartime president, permitted his attorney general to unleash a "Red Scare"
that led to the imprisonment or deportation of hundreds of political dissidents.
Harry Truman, who displayed a genuine commitment to the civil rights of
black Americans, approved an "employee loyalty" program that paved the
way for the excesses of McCarthyism.[144] More conservative presidents have
devised "enemies' lists" and have pressured the Justice Department to support
tax credits for racially segregated private schools.[145] In truth, no twentieth-
century president has displayed a consistent and unbending commitment to
principles of civil rights and liberties. Political factors, often affected by foreign policy crises, have diminished the support given by even the most progressive presidents to constitutional principles.

Franklin D. Roosevelt was no exception to this pattern, although the balance sheet of his administration includes some positive accomplishments. After six years of neglect under the direction of Homer Cummings, the Justice
Department turned its attention to such problems as police brutality against
blacks and the repression of religious sects. Those who succeeded Cummings
as attorney general during the Roosevelt administration brought a number of
significant prosecutions under the civil rights statutes, which had gathered
dust since their passage after the Civil War. However constrained by inadequate funding and the lack of judicial precedent to back up effective enforcement, the efforts of the CRS cannot be dismissed.

In the final analysis, however, the debits on this ledger outweigh the credits. The persecution of Harry Bridges and the Smith Act prosecutions evidenced both a capitulation to political pressures and a disregard for the dictates of due process. Politics and prejudice combined to bring about the
wartime internment of Japanese Americans, the ugliest blot on the Roosevelt
record. In addition, later administrations based assaults on civil liberties on
programs initiated by Roosevelt; he authorized the Justice Department to engage in the warrantless wiretapping of suspected "subversives," and permitted the FBI to compile a "Security Index" of persons targeted for summary
arrest and imprisonment during times of "national emergency."[146] The "Hus-
ton Plan" of the Nixon administration, which proposed "surreptitious entries"
and other illegal practices as part of a domestic intelligence program,[147] had
its origins in FBI activities that Roosevelt had approved.

This article has placed great emphasis on the role of the men who served
under Roosevelt as attorney general in setting the "moral tone" for the Justice
Department in its task of enforcing the laws intended to protect civil rights
and liberties. The contrast between Homer Cummings and Frank Murphy, in
particular, illustrates the importance of this fundamentally personal factor.

But the men who direct the Justice Department are chosen by the president and serve at his pleasure. When politics and principles clash in significant cases, the resulting conflicts are most often resolved in the Oval Office of the White House. The "moral tone" set by Franklin D. Roosevelt in the crucial area of civil rights and liberties was, regrettably, one more of disdain than determination.

NOTES

1. *Quoted in* Roosevelt and Frankfurter 415–16 (M. Freedman ann. 1967). The only reference in this speech to the problem of "non-discrimination against minorities" came in Roosevelt's profession that he was "most happy at the effectiveness" of current judicial protection of "minority rights." *Id.* at 414.

2. *Quoted in id.* at 416. Roosevelt also assuaged the states' rights sentiments of his listeners by denouncing the Reconstruction-era Congress as a "callous majority" that had been responsible for "the agony of our Southern States in the period after the War between the States." *Id.* at 414. This evocation of Confederate terminology and mythology could hardly have heartened those who looked to Roosevelt for leadership on civil rights.

3. In his Antietam speech, for example, Roosevelt barely masked his criticism of "the Supreme Court Odd Man" who had held that "state minimum wage laws for women were unconstitutional." *Id.* at 410. In this clear reference to Supreme Court Justice Owen Roberts, Roosevelt noted that Roberts had recently confessed that for "twenty years he had been wrong" on this issue. *Id.* at 410. This was an obvious reminder of Roberts' "switch-in-time-that-saved-nine" vote in West Coast Hotel Co. v. Parrish, 300 U.S. 379 (1937).

4. During his first presidential term, Roosevelt had in fact courted business support and muted his attacks on congressional critics. When this strategy failed to muster GOP support for his recovery program, Roosevelt lashed out in the 1936 election campaign against the "economic royalists" who sought a "new industrial dictatorship." *Quoted in* William Leuchtenburg, *Franklin D. Roosevelt and the New Deal* 183–84 (1963); *See also* Arthur Schlesinger, Jr., *The Politics of Upheaval* 638–39 (1960).

5. *See* Harvard Sitkoff, *A New Deal for Blacks* 40–45, 284, 286–88, 292–94 (1978). This is the best existing treatment of relations between blacks and the Roosevelt administration. Chapter 11 deals with the campaign for an antilynching bill and chapter 9 deals with the National Association for the Advancement of Colored People (NAACP) and its legal strategy to end segregation.

6. *Quoted in* Roosevelt and Frankfurter, *supra* note 1, at 415.

7. Facts about civil rights and liberties violations, and expressions of the views of these organizations, can be found in the annual reports of the ACLU and in *The Crisis*, the monthly publication of the NAACP.

8. Taylor, *Ties of Attorneys General to Chief,* N.Y. Times, Jan. 30, 1984, at A14, col. 3.

9. Francis Biddle, In Brief Authority 192–204 (1962) (Attorney General Biddle describes many instances of Roosevelt's involvement in decisions about judicial nominations.).

10. *Id.* at 191. Roosevelt did, on occasion, take a personal interest in cases that affected his economic recovery program, meeting with government lawyers to discuss litigation decisions. *See* Peter Irons, *The New Deal Lawyers* 39 (1982).

11. *See* Biddle, *supra* note 9, at 191.

12. N.Y. Times, Mar. 3, 1933, at 1, col. 3.

13. *Dictionary of American Biography* 137 (Supp. 6, 1980). There is no full-length biography of Cummings. In his book about the Justice Department, Homer Cummings and Carl McFarland, Federal Justice (1937), he made no reference to civil rights and liberties problems during his tenure as attorney general. The most important of his writings and official documents are collected in *Selected Papers of Homer Cummings* (C. Swisher ed. 1939).

14. Cummings had been a three-term mayor of Stamford, an unsuccessful candidate for the United States House and Senate, and a Democratic national committeeman from 1900 to 1925. Dictionary of American Biography, *supra* note 13, at 137.

15. *Id.*

16. In 1924, when Cummings was state's attorney for Fairfield County, Connecticut, a vagrant was indicted for the murder of a Catholic priest. Despite a confession in the case, Cummings became convinced of the defendant's innocence after a scrupulous investigation, and in a "gripping courtroom scene" gained dismissal of the indictment. *Id.*

17. *Quoted in* N.Y. Times, Jan. 2, 1935, at 10, col. 6.

18. Sitkoff, *supra* note 5, at 279–80.

19. *Id.* at 280–88; *See also Hearings on S. 1978 Before the Senate Judiciary Committee*, 73d Cong., 2d Sess. (1934).

20. White, *U.S. Department of (White) Justice*, The Crisis, Oct. 1935 at 309.

21. Civil Rights Act of 1870, ch. 114, § 17, 16 Stat. 144 (codified at 18 U.S.C. § 52 (1946)) (current version at 18 U.S.C. § 242 (1982)). For the history of this crucial statute, and an exhaustive discussion of its use during the Roosevelt administration, *See* Robert Carr, Federal Protection of Civil Rights (1947). Carr notes that this statute had its origins in the Civil Rights Act of April 9, 1866, and that prior to the Roosevelt administration it "had been involved in only two reported cases, both in federal district courts." *Id.* at 70–71. Carr's invaluable book, which focuses on the activities of the Civil Rights Section of the Justice Department, *see infra* text accompanying notes 60–85, is based on access to Justice Department case files.

22. White, *supra* note 20, at 309.

23. *Id.* White noted with scorn that Cummings did not reply directly but passed the message through his executive assistant, William Stanley. White was also distressed that Cummings refused to place the topic of lynching on the agenda of the National Crime Conference in December 1934, despite Roosevelt's denunciation of lynching in his conference speech. *Id.* at 310.

24. *Quoted in* Sitkoff, *supra* note 5, at 280. Roosevelt was responding to the November 1933 lynching of two white men in San Jose, California, which "set off a

nation-wide protest that the NAACP used to launch its campaign" for the Costigan-Wagner bill. *Id.* It is an ironic historical parallel that thirty years later, President Lyndon Johnson did not pressure Congress for passage of the Voting Rights Act of 1965 until two white civil rights workers were murdered in Alabama. Robert Evans & Robert Novak, Lyndon B. Johnson: The Exercise of Power, 493–97 (1966).

25. *Quoted in id.* at 283.

26. *Id.* at 284–97. After Congress adjourned in 1934 without voting on the Costigan-Wagner bill, presidential assistant Louis Howe wrote a note on his copy of the bill: "Not favored at this time—may create hostility to other crime bills." *Quoted in Id.* at 284.

27. *Quoted in* N.Y. Times, Aug. 3, 1938, at 38, col. 5. This bill would not have made lynching a federal crime but would merely have provided for investigations at the direction of the attorney general.

28. Robert Goldstein, *Political Repression in Modern America* 183–91 (1978). Spanning the period from the 1870s to the 1970s, this book exhaustively documents private and public repression against labor, political dissidents, and the members of racial and religious minorities. Goldstein notes that the 1920s were the heyday of the antistrike injunction; more than nine hundred were issued by state and federal courts during this decade. *Id.* at 183; *See also* I. Bernstein, The Lean Years (1960). This book about the labor movement in the 1920s is another excellent source of data.

29. *Quoted in* Irons, *supra* note 10, at 203. The antiunion campaign succeeded in reducing the strength of organized labor from four million members in 1920 to less than half that number in 1933. *Id*

30. National Industrial Recovery Act (NIRA), ch. 90, § 7(a), 48 Stat. 195, 198 (1933) (current version at 29 U.S.C. § 157 (1982)). Roosevelt had opposed the inclusion of § 7(a) in the NIRA, and agreed to it only after labor leaders threatened to call a general strike if he resisted. *See* P. Irons, *supra* note 10, at 204.

31. Irons, *supra* note 10, at 208–10.

32. *Id.* at 221–25.

33. *Id.* at 218–20.

34. A well-financed legal campaign against both the NIRA and the National Labor Relations Act (NLRA), organized by the American Liberty League, crippled enforcement of both statutes until the Supreme Court upheld the NLRA in NLRB v. Jones & Laughlin Steel Corp., 301 U.S. 1 (1937). P. Irons, *supra* note 10, at 81, 243–48.

35. Goldstein, *supra* note 28, at 218.

36. In its 1933–1934 annual report the ACLU complained that "the New Deal administration has refused to interfere in this industrial strife to make good its implied support of trade unionism." American Civil Liberties Union, Liberty under the New Deal 3 (1934). Two years later, the ACLU saw little improvement in the record of the Roosevelt administration, citing "the resort to force and violence by employers" as one of the greatest threats to labor and civil liberties. American Civil Liberties Union, How Goes the Bill of Rights? 5 (1936).

37. A lengthy account of the strike is found in Charles Larrowe, Harry Bridges 62–94 (1972); *See also infra* text accompanying notes 88–106 for a discussion of the later effort to deport Bridges.

38. Larrowe, *supra* note 37, at 85. Johnson was in San Francisco to give a speech and barged into the volatile situation without any official role.

39. Frances Perkins, The Roosevelt I Knew 314 (1946). Perkins reports that Roosevelt deliberately avoided taking sides in the strike or making any public statement about it. *Id.* at 312–15.

40. *See* Larrowe, *supra* note 37, at 62–94 (discussing generally the developments of the strike).

41. For an account of the early years of the Southern Tenant Farmers Union (STFU), *see* Donald H. Grubbs, Cry from the Cotton (1971). The efforts of lawyers in the Agricultural Adjustment Administration, the federal agency with jurisdiction over labor relations between growers and farmworkers, to aid the STFU and Southern sharecroppers are discussed in Irons, *supra* note 10, at 164–73.

42. N.Y. Times, June 4, 1936, at 4, col. 6. The strikers demanded wages of $1.50 for a ten-hour day, rather than the 75 cents they were receiving. *Id.*

43. 18 U.S.C. § 444 (1935) (current version at 18 U.S.C. § 1581 (1982)). This revision of the Reconstruction-era Peonage Abolition Act imposed a fine of not more than $5000, or not more than five years in prison, or both, for holding any person in "a condition of peonage." *Id.* In 1905, the Supreme Court upheld the constitutionality of the act in Clyatt v. United States, 197 U.S. 207 (1905). The Court defined peonage as "a status or condition of compulsory service, based upon the indebtedness of the peon to the master." *Id.* at 215. For a discussion of the statute's history and use by the Roosevelt administration, *See* Carr, *supra* note 21, at 77–80, 180–82.

44. United States v. Reynolds, 235 U.S. 133 (1914) (invalidating Alabama laws allowing a person fined upon conviction for a misdemeanor to confess judgment with a surety in the amount of the fine and agree with the surety, in consideration of the surety's payment of the fine, to reimburse him by working for him).

45. N.Y. Times, June 19, 1936, at 15, col. 1.

46. *Quoted in* N.Y. Times, Aug. 13, 1936, at 19, col. 6.

47. Jerold S. Auerbach, *Labor and Liberty* 43–47, 62–73 (1966). Auerbach's book provides a thorough and sympathetic history of the LaFollette Committee. He notes as well the contributions of Heber Blankenhorn, an investigator for the NLRB, in pressing for the Senate investigating committee. *Id.* at 59–73.

48. *Id.* at 75. Senators Elbert Thomas and Louis Murphy were also named to the subcommittee; Murphy died shortly after his appointment and was not replaced until 1939. *Id.*

49. *Id.* at 97–115. For a list of reports issued by the LaFollette Committee, *see id.* at 221.

50. *Id.* at 115–20. Violence against the Harlan County miners reached such levels that a special commission, appointed by Governor A. B. Chandler in 1935, reported that it was "almost unbelievable that anywhere in a free and democratic Nation . . . conditions can be found as bad as they are in Harlan County. There exists a virtual reign of terror . . . ." *Id.* at 116.

51. *Id.* at 117–18.

52. NLRB v. Jones & Laughlin Steel Corp., 301 U.S. 1 (1937).

53. *Quoted in* N.Y. Times, May 20, 1937, at 3, col. 5. Cummings attributed his move to the revelations of the LaFollette Committee and to complaints by John L. Lewis, president of the United Mine Workers and chairman of the Committee for Industrial Organization. *Id.*

54. *See* Carr, *supra* note 21, at 27.

55. The Enforcement Act of 1870, ch. 114, § 6, 16 Stat. 141 (codified at 18 U.S.C. § 51 (1946)) (current version at 18 U.S.C. § 241 (1982)). This law was designed to enforce the Thirteenth Amendment. The statute provided a stiff maximum penalty of ten years in prison and a fine of not more than $5000, in contrast to the one-year term and $1000 fine provided for violation of 18 U.S.C. § 52, *See infra* note 21. *See* Carr, *supra* note 21, at 57–70 for a discussion of the history of § 51 and its use by the Roosevelt administration.

56. Carr, *supra* note 21, at 27–28. Justice Department pressure led the coal operators to sign a contract with the United Mine Workers in order to avoid a retrial. Auerbach, *supra* note 47, at 120. The report of the LaFollette Committee on the Harlan County situation is in Senate Committee on Education and Labor, Private Police Systems, S.Rep. No. 6, Part 2, 76th Cong., 1st Sess. (1939).

57. *See supra* text accompanying notes 88–143 for discussion of these issues.

58. Murphy, born in 1893, gained "a lasting hatred for 'industrial slavery'" during his boyhood work in a starch factory. *Current Biography* 610 (M. Block ed. 1940). He served for three years as an assistant United States attorney and sat as a municipal judge before his election as mayor of Detroit in 1930. Roosevelt appointed him as governor general of the Philippines (the post for which Homer Cummings had been slated) in 1932. During his term as governor of Michigan, his refusal to employ troops to oust the General Motors "sitdown" strikers cost him conservative support, while his early threat to use force cost him labor votes in 1938. *Id.*; *See also* Sidney Fine, Frank Murphy; *The Detroit Years* (1975); J. Howard, Mr. Justice Murphy (1968).

59. Sitkoff, *supra* note 5, at 66. Murphy's status as an Irish Catholic affected his views on civil rights and liberties. John Pickering, who served as law clerk to Murphy on the Supreme Court, recently stated that Murphy "had a terrible streak of religious fervor in him, and felt very strongly about religious freedom and race." *Quoted in* Peter Irons, *Justice at War* 243 (1983).

60. *Quoted in* Carr, *supra* note 21, at 1.

61. *Id.* at 33–34, 56–57; *See also* Henry Schweinhaut, *The Civil Liberties Section of the Department of Justice*, 1 Bill of Rts. Rev. 206 (1941). Henry Schweinhaut headed the CRS from 1939 to 1941, followed by Victor Rotnem from 1941 to 1945.

62. *Quoted in* N.Y. Times, May 16, 1939, at 16, col. 2. The Times, which editorially commended Murphy for his speech, professed an inability to "put as much confidence as Mr. Murphy does" in the prospect of effective federal and state enforcement of civil liberties, noting the prevalence of state criminal syndicalism laws and similar repressive statutes. N.Y. Times, May 17, 1939, at 22, col. 2.

63. *Quoted in id.*, May 16, 1939, at 16, col. 2. The ACLU, in its 1938 annual report, singled out Jersey City as the only large city where "practically all meeting places [are] closed to organizations opposed by the authorities." American Civil Liberties Union. *Eternal Vigilance!* 43 (1938).

64. Hague v. Committee for Indus. Org., 307 U.S. 496 (1939). The Court based its ruling on the Civil Rights Act of April 20, 1871, which subjected "any person" who acted "under color of any law" to deprive another of rights protected under the Constitution to a suit for damages or equitable relief. Civil Rights Act of 1871, ch. 22, § 1, 17 Stat. 13 (codified at 8 U.S.C. § 43 (1941)) (current version at 42 U.S.C. § 1983 (Supp. V 1981)). This judicial approval of the civil counterpart to § 52 of the federal criminal law obviously strengthened the hand of Justice Department lawyers in bringing criminal prosecutions against state and local officials.

65. Carr, *supra* note 21, at 151–52.

66. *Id.* at 152–54. Carr, whose account of this case is based on the Justice Department file, noted "a strong reluctance by the FBI" to conduct an investigation of a local police department. Unnamed "higher authorities" in the Department sided with the FBI until CRS lawyers complained loudly. *Id.* at 152–53; *see infra* note 87.

67. *Id.* at 154–55; Culp v. United States, 131 F.2d 93 (8th Cir. 1942).

68. Jackson, born in 1892, spent twenty years in trial practice in Jamestown, N.Y., and became "widely esteemed for his salty independence of mind and clear courtroom presentation." Dictionary of American Biography 357 (Supp. V 1977); *See also* Eugene Gerhardt, *Robert H. Jackson: Country Lawyer, Supreme Court Justice, America's Advocate* (1958). Roosevelt, while governor of New York, appointed Jackson in 1930 to a state commission to reform the judicial system. *Id.* Jackson also gained Roosevelt's favor with his vigorous 1937 Senate testimony in defense of the President's "court-packing" plan. *Id.*

69. Albert E. Arent, a CRS lawyer who served under both Murphy and Jackson, recently stated that Jackson "paid very little attention to our work and the old guard [in the Department] made it frustrating for us." Letter from Arent to author (January 31, 1984) (copy on file with the Washington Law Review).

70. *See* Carr, *supra* note 21, at 85–94.

71. United States v. Classic, 313 U.S. 299 (1941).

72. United States v. Mosley, 238 U.S. 383 (1915). *See* Carr, *supra* note 21, at 65 66, for a discussion of this case.

73. "Misuse of power, possessed by virtue of state law and made possible only because the wrongdoer is clothed with the authority of state law, is action taken 'under color of' state law." United States v. Classic, 313 U.S. 299 at 326 (1941).

74. Francis Biddle, born in 1886, graduated from Harvard Law School and served a clerkship with Justice Oliver Wendell Holmes. He spent twenty-three years in corporate practice in Philadelphia before Roosevelt appointed him in 1934 as chairman of the first NLRB. Biddle also spent an unhappy year as a federal circuit judge at Roosevelt's insistence. Unlike his predecessors as attorney general in the Roosevelt administration, Biddle had been a Republican before his New Deal service and had had no involvement in party politics. Francis Biddle, *In Brief Authority* (1962) (Biddle recounts his experiences in public service and as attorney general); *See also* Irons, *supra* note 10, at 221.

75. Biddle, *supra* note 74, at 156.

76. *Id.* at 156–59. Robert Hall, the black victim, owned a pearl-handled pistol that one of Screws' deputies coveted and took from Hall. On Hall's complaint, the county

grand jury ordered the pistol returned. In retaliation, Screws forged a warrant that charged Hall with theft of an automobile tire. The officers who beat Hall to death were drunk and "boasted they were going to 'get' a Negro who had 'lived too long' and got too smart." *Id.* at 157.

77. *Id.* at 157.

78. Screws v. United States—Final (5th Cir. 1944), *rev'd.* 325 U.S. 91 (1945); *See also* Carr, *supra* note 21, at 106–15.

79. Screws v. United States, 325 U.S. 91, 104 (1945).

80. Biddle, *supra* note 74, at 159.

81. Minersville School Dist. v. Gobitis, 310 U.S. 586 (1940). This decision was *overruled* in West Virginia St. Bd. of Educ. v. Barnette, 319 U.S. 624 (1943).

82. Victor W. Rotnem & F. G. Folsom, Jr., *Recent Restrictions upon Religious Liberty*, 36 Amer. Pol. Sci. Rev. 1053, 1061 (1942). This article recounts several of the instances of church burnings and mob violence to which witnesses were subjected.

83. For an account of this case, *see* Carr, *supra* note 21, at 134–35, 143–44, 155–59.

84. Catlette v. United States, 132 F.2d 902 (4th Cir. 1943). Finding that "the failure of Catlette to protect the victims from group violence or to arrest the members of the mob who assaulted the victims constituted a violation of his common law duty," the court placed his "dereliction . . . squarely within the provisions" of § 52. *Id.* at 907.

85. "More than eight thousand complaints that reached the CRS in 1942 resulted in only seventy-six prosecutions; in 1943, over thirteen thousand complaints produced prosecutive action in only sixty-one cases; and, in 1944, the twenty thousand complaints culminated in only sixty-four prosecutions." Carr, *supra* note 21, at 129.

86. Letter from Arent to author (January 31, 1984) (copy on file with the Washington Law Review).

87. *See* Carr, *supra* note 21, at 152–53. Carr noted, however, that the FBI and CRS "worked together reasonably well" in later cases. *Id.* at 153

88. *See infra* text accompanying notes 37–40.

89. *See* Larrowe, *supra* note 37, at 32–35, 56–59. Bridges recently admitted his political affinity with Communist Party positions. "I agreed with the party 95 percent of the time. But I never joined. They never asked me, and I never volunteered." Interview with Harry Bridges in San Francisco (January 8, 1984).

90. *See* Larrowe, *supra* note 37, at 138–42; Perkins, *supra* note 39, at 316–17.

91. Perkins, *supra* note 39, at 317–18. Secretary Perkins related her meeting with Roosevelt to discuss the pressure to deport Bridges. The President asked if Bridges had "done anything to overthrow the Government." Perkins said he had not. "'Then why in the world,' asked the President, 'should a man be punished for what he thinks, for what he believes? That's against the Constitution.'" *Id.* at 318. This account strikes me as somewhat disingenuous.

92. U.S. Department of Labor, In the Matter of Harry R. Bridges (1939).

93. Perkins, *supra* note 39, at 218–19; *See* 84 Cong. Rec. 702–11 for the text of the impeachment resolution, offered by J. Parnell Thomas, a New Jersey Republican. The House Judiciary Committee, controlled by the Democrats, reported unfavorably (and unanimously) on the resolution and it was tabled by the House without debate on March 24, 1939. *Id.* at 3273.

94. 86 Cong. Rec. 8203.

95. N.Y. Times, June 20, 1940, at 12, col. 3. Although Jackson carefully stated that he did "not now consider" whether the proposed legislation constituted a bill of attainder, was an ex post facto law, or violated the due process clause of the fifth amendment, the tone of his letter left no doubt of his position on these issues. *Id.*

96. Immigration Act of 1917, ch. 439, § 23, 54 Stat. 673 (1940).

97. Hobbs did not conceal his intention. "It is my joy to announce that this bill will do, in a perfectly legal and constitutional manner, what the bill specifically aimed at the deportation of Harry Bridges seeks to accomplish." 86 Cong. Rec. 9031.

98. Jackson had recently, in August 1940, drafted an opinion for Roosevelt defending the legality of the so-called destroyers-for-bases deal, which involved the transfer of fifty American destroyers to Great Britain, despite the seeming prohibition of the Neutrality Act of 1917. *See* Philip Goodhart, *Fifty Ships That Saved the World* 60, 187–88 (1965).

99. N.Y. Times, Feb. 13, 1941, at 1, 15. Bridges responded that "this new attack amounts to persecution. How many times must a man be cleared of the same charge before they leave him alone?" *Id.* at 15.

100. U.S. Department of Justice, Memorandum of Decision in the Matter of Harry Renton Bridges (1941); *See also* Larrowe, *supra* note 37, at 226–37, for an account of the Sears hearing.

101. *See* Biddle, *supra* note 74, at 299.

102. *Id.* at 297–302. Biddle confessed that the evidence in the Sears report on the question of Bridges' alleged Communist Party membership "was not overwhelming." But he professed "little doubt" that Bridges was a Communist, and placed great emphasis in explaining his decision on "the effect on the war effort that the removal of Bridges might have." *Id.* at 300; *See also* Larrowe, *supra* note 37, at 238–42.

103. Biddle, *supra* note 74, at 302.

104. Bridges v Wixon, 326 U.S. 135, 141–49, 150–56 (1945).

105. *Id.* at 157.

106. Bridges v. United States, 346 U.S. 209 (1953). *See also* Larrowe, *supra* note 37 for an account of Bridges' perjury trial and subsequent judicial proceedings.

107. Act of July 14, 1798, ch. 74, 1 Stat. 596 (1798).

108. *See, e.g.,* 86 Cong. Rec. at app. 4085–88 (remarks of Rep. Leland Ford).

109. The Supreme Court upheld the Smith Act convictions of eleven Communist Party leaders in Dennis v. United States, 341 U.S. 494 (1951). For an account of the Smith Act prosecutions, *see* Michael R. Belknap, Cold War Political Justice (1977).

110. *See* Goldstein, *supra* note 28, at 252–53; Pahl, *G-String Conspiracy, Political Reprisal or Armed Revolt? The Minnesota Trotskyite Trial*, 8 Labor History 30 (1967).

111. Pahl, *supra* note 110, at 44–45.

112. Dunne v. United States, 138 F.2d 137 (8th Cir. 1943), *cert. denied,* 320 U.S. 790 (1943). The court based its conclusion that "force was the ultimate means to be used by the Party in the overthrow of the Government" on the finding that "Defense Guards" made up of union members were designed "to use force in protection of the unions." *Id.* at 149 (emphasis added).

113. Dunne v. United States, 320 U.S. 790 (1943) *(writ of certiorari denied)*.

114. Biddle, *supra* note 74, at 152.

115. *Id.* at 235–43. Biddle admitted that pressure from Roosevelt had directly influenced his decision to secure the sedition indictments. *Id.* at 238.

116. The account below is based largely on Peter Irons, *Justice at War* (1983). This book, which discusses the evacuation decision and the political and bureaucratic forces that produced it, is primarily concerned with the four test cases that reached the Supreme Court as challenges to various elements of the internment program. These cases are discussed infra in text accompanying notes 129–43.

117. 7 Fed. Reg. 1407 (1942). *See also* Irons, *supra* note 116, at 3–63 for discussion of the pressures that led to the evacuation decision and of the internal debate within the government that preceded issuance of the executive order.

118. Irons, *supra* note 116, at 64–74.

119. *See, e.g.*, Roger Daniels, *Concentration Camps USA: Japanese Americans and World War II* (1972); Morton Grodzins, *Americans Betrayed* (1949); Jacobus Ten Broek, Edward N. Barnhart, and Floyd W. Matson, *Prejudice, War, and the Constitution* (1954); Dembitz, *Racial Discrimination and the Military Judgment*, 45 Colum. L. Rev. 175 (1945); Rostow, *The Japanese American Cases—A Disaster*, 54 Yale L.J. 489 (1945); *See also* Commission on Wartime Relocation and Internment of Civilians, Personal Justice Denied (1983). This report of a congressional commission established in 1980, based on the testimony of some 750 witnesses and review of thousands of government documents, concluded that the internment was not justified by "military necessity" but resulted from a combination of "race prejudice, war hysteria, and a failure of political leadership." *Id.* at 18.

120. *See* Irons, *supra* note 116, at 278–92. The espionage claims were made in U.S. Department of War, Final Report: Japanese Evacuation from the West Coast, 1942, at 8 (1943).

121. *See* Irons, *supra* note 116, at 38–44, 50–53.

122. *Id.* at 50. This officer, Colonel Karl R. Bendetsen, was on the staff of the judge advocate general and worked closely with, and under the direction of, Assistant Secretary of War John J. McCloy. Bendetsen was later appointed to direct the evacuation and internment program under General John L. Dewitt, commander of the Western Defense Command.

123. *Id.* at 55.

124. *Id.* at 44–45, 52–56, 61–63.

125. Biddle, *supra* note 74, at 226. Biddle also noted that Roosevelt was not troubled that evacuation of Japanese Americans would constitute a basic violation of civil rights and liberties. "If anything, he thought that rights should yield to the necessities of war." *Id.*

126. Irons, *supra* note 116, at 61–63. When Biddle announced his agreement with the War Department, his two assistants at the meeting, Edward J. Ennis and James H. Rowe, Jr., were devastated. "Ennis almost wept," Rowe later said, "I was so mad that I could not speak at all myself." *Id.* at 62.

127. *Id.* at 64.

128. *Id.* at 64–68. The statute passed by Congress to enforce Roosevelt's executive order, Pub. L. No. 77-503, provided a maximum one-year sentence for violation of

any military orders issued under authority of Executive Order 9066. Ch. 191, 56 Stat. 173 (1942).

129. Irons, *supra* note 116, 75–103.

130. Hirabayashi v. United States, 320 U.S. 81 (1943); Yasui v. United States, 320 U.S. 115 (1943).

131. Hirabayashi, 320 U.S. at 93, 96–98.

132. Irons, *supra* note 116, at 202–06.

133. *Id.* at 268–77.

134. Ex Parte Endo, 323 U.S. 283 (1944). Justice William O. Douglas, who wrote for a unanimous Court, confined his opinion to the narrow question of whether Congress had expressly authorized the internment camps, finding it had not. Douglas did, however, hold that "initial detention in Relocation Centers" was lawful. *Id.* at 301

135. Korematsu v. United States, 323, U.S. 214 (1944).

136. Irons, *supra* note 116, at 193.

137. *Id.* at 58, 336.

138. *Id.* at 336–37.

139. Korematsu, 323 U.S. at 223.

140. *Id.* at 242 (Murphy, J., *dissenting*). The other dissenters were Justices Owen Roberts and Robert Jackson.

141. U.S. Department of War, *supra* note 120, at 4, 8.

142. Irons, *supra* note 116, at 278–84.

143. *Id.* at 284–92. McCloy, in his 1981 testimony before the Commission on Wartime Relocation and Internment of Civilians, doggedly defended the internment program, characterizing it as "retribution" for the Japanese attack on Pearl Harbor. *Id.* at 351–54.

144. *See* Goldstein, *supra* note 28, at 298–306.

145. The crimes of the Nixon administration and its assaults on civil liberties have been exhaustively documented. *See, e.g.,* Richard Ben-Veniste and George Frampton, Jr., *Stonewall: The Real Story of the Watergate Prosecution* (1977); Leon Friedman, *United States v. Nixon* (1974); U.S. government. Watergate Special Prosecution Force, Final Report (1975). For the adverse decision by the Supreme Court on the tax credit policy of the Reagan administration, *see* Bob Jones University v. United States, 103 S.Ct. 2017 (1983) (nonprofit private schools that employ racially discriminatory admission standards on the basis of religious doctrine do not qualify as tax-exempt organizations under the Internal Revenue Code, nor are contributions to such schools deductible as charitable contributions).

146. *See* Goldstein, *supra* note 28, at 298–306.

147. *Id.* at 485–86.

II

THE AFTERMATH OF 9/11

5

Indefinite Material Witness Detention without Probable Cause: Thinking outside the Fourth Amendment

Michael Greenberger

Every day I tell the staff at the Justice Department: "Think anew. The world is changing. What are the ways we can safeguard the American people against attack?" . . . I say, "Think outside the box," but I always say, "think inside the Constitution."

—Attorney General John Ashcroft, speaking to the Associated Press[1]

The media,[2] legal academics,[3] and the organized bar[4] have quite rightly focused considerable attention on an array of extraordinary law enforcement actions by the Bush administration in waging its "War on Terrorism." As of this writing, at the beginning of January 2004, these high-profile issues have been and are being considered, inter alia, by the various United States Courts of Appeals and by the United States Supreme Court on petitions for certiorari and on the merits. They include: (1) whether a U.S. citizen unilaterally declared by the executive branch to be an "enemy combatant" has a right to consult counsel and to judicial review of his status;[5] (2) whether aliens detained indefinitely by the Department of Defense outside the United States as "unlawful enemy combatants" (and thus without the humanitarian protections afforded "prisoners of war" under the Geneva Convention) are forever barred from exercising their treaty right to challenge that punitive status in the United States or elsewhere;[6] (3) whether the Freedom of Information Act obliges the Department of Justice to identify resident aliens secretly arrested and detained in the United States in post–September 11 dragnets;[7] (4) whether the Department of Justice may, by general order, require the otherwise open deportation hearings of such secretly arrested aliens to be held in secret;[8] and (5) whether the president, acting pursuant to, inter alia, his Article I War Powers, may deprive a defendant, accused in a federal court of capital terrorism crimes, access to exculpatory evidence to which he would otherwise be entitled under the Sixth Amendment.[9]

There is yet another important constitutional issue recently addressed by the U.S. Court of Appeals for the Second Circuit that has not received the widespread attention of the issues identified above. It arises out of Attorney General Ashcroft's announcement shortly after the terrorist attacks of September 11, 2001, that the "aggressive detention of material witnesses [was] vital to preventing, disrupting, or delaying new attacks."[10] Since that time, the Department of Justice has used the federal material witness statute[11] to arrest numerous individuals and detain them indefinitely in the general prison population for the ostensible purpose of securing future grand jury testimony. These individuals, while held pursuant to the statute, are not charged with any crime; nor, upon their detention, is there any probable cause that they have committed a crime.[12] While the Justice Department's aggressive use of the federal material witness statute may reflect the attorney general's directive to "think outside the box," the "box" at issue may very well be the Constitution of the United States. Described immediately below are the factual findings, which were uncontested on appeal, in one of the two leading federal district court cases addressing the Justice Department's material witness detention activities. These facts serve to illustrate the constitutionally questionable nature of this practice.

GRAND JURY MATERIAL WITNESS DETENTION

The Detention of Osama Awadallah

The following factual findings surrounding Osama Awadallah's initial detention and interrogation were made by Judge Shira Scheindlin of the U.S. District Court for the Southern District of New York.[13] On September 20, 2001, Awadallah—a Jordanian citizen, lawful permanent resident of the United States, and Muslim[14]—woke up and made his way to class at Grossmont College in San Diego, California.[15] In 1999, he had come to the United States at age eighteen to be near his father, three brothers, and stepmother.[16] Since his arrival, he had held many part-time jobs and attended classes.[17] He planned to become a United States citizen like his father and oldest brother.[18]

In the wake of the September 11 terrorist attacks on the World Trade Center and the Pentagon, FBI agents had found the name "Osama" and a phone number written on a slip of paper in the car of one of the hijackers, which was parked in a Dulles Airport parking lot in Northern Virginia.[19] Through a search of phone listings, the FBI matched the number to Osama Awadallah.[20]

Awadallah had not used that phone number in over a year.[21] Nevertheless, no fewer than eight FBI agents arrived at Awadallah's San Diego apartment on September 20, 2001, to question him regarding his knowledge of the attacks.[22]

When the FBI arrived at Awadallah's apartment around 10:15 a.m., no one was home.[23] A little over an hour later, Awadallah's roommate returned.[24] FBI agents approached his roommate and asked if they could question him and search the apartment. He consented to both requests.[25] At about 2:00 p.m., Awadallah arrived home from class to rest and pray and was greeted by two FBI agents.[26] They asked him if they could question him briefly.[27] He agreed, but when he tried to enter his apartment, the agents prevented him from doing so.[28] Awadallah insisted on getting access to his apartment bathroom "because, as a devout Muslim, he prays five times a day including once at midday," and "[b]efore each prayer, [he] washes his mouth, nose, face, head, hands, and feet."[29] After consulting with each other and checking the apartment first, the FBI agents relented and permitted Awadallah to enter.[30]

Upon entering, "Awadallah realized for the first time that his roommate . . . was being interviewed."[31] Awadallah then tried to use the bathroom in his apartment, but FBI agents "ordered him to leave [the door] open" while they watched him urinate and wash before prayer.[32] Awadallah and his roommate, also a Muslim, managed to pray, but under the watchful eye of the FBI agents.[33] After Awadallah and his roommate finished praying, the FBI agents asked him to sign a consent form giving the FBI the ability to search his apartment and car.[34] The agents told Awadallah that if he did not sign the consent form, they would get a warrant and would "tear up the home."[35]

Although Awadallah asked if the agents could interview him in his apartment, the agents insisted that he go to the FBI San Diego office in an FBI vehicle.[36] Awadallah got into the FBI vehicle, but quickly realized he had left his watch in the apartment.[37] He tried to get out of the vehicle, but found the doors were locked.[38] Seeing this, he decided not to ask the agents if he could retrieve his watch.[39]

The agents told him that the questioning would take about a half hour and assured him that they would "do their best" to get him back in time for his 6:00 p.m. class.[40] He "repeatedly expressed that he did not want to miss his computer class."[41] In spite of their assurances, FBI agents kept him in a locked room at their offices from 3:10 p.m. until 11:00 p.m., questioning him for over six of those hours.[42] Awadallah was "very, very cooperative," and answered all their questions.[43] The agents told him that "they believed him," but "'to clear the table,' they wanted him to take a lie detector [polygraph] test," which he agreed to do the next morning.[44] The FBI agents then drove him home.[45]

Sometime after 11:00 p.m., he went to the mosque, where he told his brothers what had happened.[46] His brothers advised him not to return for a polygraph test until they had secured a lawyer for him.[47] The next morning, Awadallah called the FBI and told them that he wanted to wait to take the polygraph test until he had a lawyer.[48] The FBI agent, however, persuaded Awadallah to go through with the test, advising Awadallah that "there [was] no need for anybody to come with [him]."[49] They also told him they "would not bother him anymore" after he took the test.[50] After Awadallah agreed to take the test, FBI agents returned to his apartment and transported him to their offices.[51]

The FBI questioned Awadallah for approximately an hour and a half to two hours, during which they were in communication (outside of Awadallah's presence) with their legal counsel, an assistant United States attorney in New York.[52] After questioning Awadallah during the polygraph test on his knowledge of the September 11 hijackers, the FBI agents accused Awadallah of lying.[53] When Awadallah tried to leave, the FBI agents ordered him not to move.[54] Awadallah requested a lawyer, but the agents refused this request and continued questioning him, stating that they were going to take him to New York and "detain him 'for one year' so that they could 'find out' more about him."[55] Awadallah again demanded a lawyer, but the agents responded, "Here you don't have rights. When you go [to the San Diego Metropolitan Correctional Center] or you go to New York, then you [can] ask whatever you want."[56] After his questioning, he was arrested as a material witness pending a grand jury investigation of the September 11 terrorist attacks.[57] He was not informed of any constitutional rights at this time.[58]

Awadallah was then sent to the San Diego Metropolitan Correctional Center (SDMCC).[59] Because Awadallah's allegations of abuse during his incarceration—that is, post–September 21, 2001—were "not material to the issues before the court," Judge Scheindlin did not make factual findings on disputed matters regarding his confinement.[60] However, she noted that "many" of his allegations regarding treatment during detention were uncontested.[61] Furthermore, a series of widely publicized United States Department of Justice, Office of the Inspector General reports issued in 2003 fully corroborated allegations of abuse by September 11 detainees in nearby detention facilities quite similar to the one in which Awadallah was imprisoned.[62] Even reading Awadallah's claims regarding the conditions of his confinement in a light most favorable to the government, Judge Scheindlin wrote, "Awadallah bore the full weight of a prison system designed to punish convicted criminals," when he was only a material witness.[63]

Upon his detention in SDMCC, Awadallah's family hired a lawyer, Randall Hamud, who went to the SDMCC on September 21 to speak with his client.[64]

The lawyer was denied access to Awadallah, and Awadallah was never informed that his lawyer was at the prison.[65] Hamud was not able to see Awadallah until the next day.[66] While at the SDMCC, Awadallah was kept in solitary confinement. He was also denied the use of the showers for four days and soap and toilet paper for two days.[67] When the toilet in his cell backed up and flooded his cell floor, "the correctional facility did not fix the problem for at least two days."[68] Awadallah could not eat while at SDMCC because "the correctional facility only served him non-*halal* meals," food that does not comply with Muslim dietary law.[69]

On September 27, Awadallah was transferred to the San Bernardino County Jail (SBCJ) for one day.[70] While at the SBCJ, Awadallah was forced to strip naked before a female officer.[71] A guard "twisted his arm, forced him to bow, and pushed his face to the floor."[72] The SBCJ provided him only one meal, and it did not satisfy his dietary requirements; thus, Awadallah "only ate an apple the entire day" he was detained at the SBCJ.[73] The next day, September 28, the government transferred Awadallah to a federal facility in Oklahoma City.[74] There, "a guard threw shoes at his head and face, cursed at him, and made insulting remarks about [Islam]."[75]

On October 1, 2001, U.S. marshals transported Awadallah, shackled in leg irons, to New York City.[76] While in transit, the "marshals threatened to get Awadallah's brother and cursed 'the Arabs.'"[77] Once at the Metropolitan Correctional Center in New York (NYMCC), he was placed in a room "so cold that his body turned blue."[78] After a doctor examined him, a guard "push[ed] him into a door and a wall while he was handcuffed, kicked his leg shackles and pulled him by the hair to force him to face an American flag."[79] This manhandling caused Awadallah's hand to bleed.[80] When the marshals transported Awadallah, hands cuffed behind his back and bound to his feet, to court the next day, they grabbed his upper arms so hard they bruised.[81] The marshals kicked his left foot until it bled, and "the supervising marshal threatened to kill him."[82] In the NYMCC, he was "kept in solitary confinement and shackled and strip-searched whenever he left his cell."[83] He was never assured that his food complied with his dietary needs for the first few weeks of his confinement; therefore, he "refrained from eating any meat, or any food that touched the meat," which resulted in eating little or no food all day.[84] As he was not permitted to use the phone or receive family visitors either at the Oklahoma facility or the NYMCC, Awadallah's attorney, Hamud, did not know where his client was located until October 1.[85]

Nineteen days after he was first detained in San Diego, Awadallah, while shackled to his chair, finally testified before a grand jury in New York on October 10, 2001,[86] and October 15, 2001.[87] In his first grand jury testimony, he denied knowledge of the name of one of the hijackers, Khalid Al-Mihdhar.[88]

He was then shown one of his college exam booklets in which he had written the name "Khalid" in answer to an exam question asking him to describe in English people he had met.[89] During his second grand jury testimony he tried to recant and explain his confusion on October 10.[90] Eight days later—twenty-seven days after he was first detained as a material witness—the United States filed a complaint against him alleging that he committed perjury by falsely testifying at the grand jury that he did not know the name of one of the hijackers.[91] He was "arrested" on the perjury complaint on October 21 and was indicted on October 31, 2001.[92] Awadallah requested bail three times before being granted it on November 21, 2001.[93] He posted bail on December 13, 2001, and was released after spending a total of eighty-three days in jail.[94] Over two years later, with his perjury charges still in effect, Awadallah remains free and has fully satisfied his release conditions.[95]

Protection of a Legitimate Government Interest or Pretext?

It is quite clear that the post–September 11 Justice Department's detention of individuals under the federal material witness statute, without probable cause of having committed a crime, to secure grand jury testimony is now widely practiced within the United States.[96]

The Justice Department argues that the plain language of the federal material witness statute, 18 U.S.C. § 3144, authorizes its lengthy detention of material witnesses pending future grand jury testimony. The statute provides "if . . . the testimony of a person is material in a criminal proceeding, and . . . it may become impracticable to secure the presence of the person by subpoena, a judicial officer may order the arrest of the person."[97] The government points in particular to the breadth of the term "criminal proceeding" under section 3144 to argue that the authority extends not only to arresting and imprisoning material witnesses for criminal trials, but also for grand jury investigations. The government justifies the practice as protecting a legitimate and compelling government interest in the investigation, disruption, and prevention of terrorism, and as necessary to ensure the presence of important witnesses who are likely to flee the jurisdiction or even the country.[98]

Section 3144 has been widely recognized as applicable to the detention of witnesses pending a criminal trial, a practice that generally has been constitutionally sanctioned.[99] However, the legitimacy of holding an innocent material witness pending trial is tempered by section 3144's provision of two ameliorative options: release of the material witness on bail, or in the absence of granting bail, a prompt deposition in lieu of detention. Section 3144 provides, "No material witness may be detained because of inability to comply with any condition of release if the testimony of such witness can adequately be secured by deposition, and if further detention is not necessary to prevent a failure of justice."[100] Therefore, a material witness detained pending trial may have his or her deposition taken "within a reasonable period of time" pursuant to Federal Rule of Criminal Procedure 15 (hereinafter Rule 15) in exchange for his or her release.[101] The government, up until the time it reversed its position before the Second Circuit, contended that Rule 15's express terms do not apply to grand jury proceedings,[102] and therefore, a material witness in a grand jury investigation may be held indefinitely pending the convening of a grand jury, if he or she was not afforded bail.[103]

The fundamental purpose of a grand jury is to protect the accused from "hasty, malicious, and oppressive persecution," and to ensure that charges are grounded on reason, not malice or ill will.[104] Yet, if the government can obtain material witness warrants to detain and imprison grand jury material witnesses indefinitely, it can easily sidestep the Fourth Amendment's probable cause requirement. It is clear that the Ashcroft Justice Department detains grand jury material witnesses under harsh and coercive conditions.[105] Facts surrounding the recent arrests of other grand jury material witnesses illustrate that these indefinite and often harsh detentions are part of a tactic to coerce incriminating statements.[106]

The case of Abdallah Higazy has become a classic illustration of this technique. Higazy, an Egyptian national, was detained on a material witness warrant pending the convening of a grand jury.[107] He was an engineering student attending classes at Brooklyn Polytechnic.[108] On September 11, 2001, he was staying at the Millennium Hilton Hotel across from the World Trade Center (WTC) in New York City when he was forced to evacuate with the other guests soon after the terrorist attacks on the WTC.[109] Several weeks after the attacks, management conducted an inventory of the still vacant hotel.[110] A security guard for the hotel reported finding a radio transceiver together with Higazy's passport and a copy of the Koran in Higazy's room.[111] The guard claimed that all of these items were in the room's safe, which is provided for guests' valuables.[112] The radio could be used for air-to-air and air-to-ground communication.[113] Consequently, FBI questioned Higazy when he returned to the hotel on December 17, 2001, to obtain the belongings he left behind.[114] Higazy denied the transceiver was his, but admitted that he was familiar with such radios because he had previously served in the Egyptian Air Corps.[115] Hearing this, the government detained Higazy and petitioned for a material witness warrant pending his testimony before a grand jury.[116] The court granted the petition on December 18, 2001, on the basis of the hotel security guard's assertion that the radio was left behind with Higazy's possessions and ordered that Higazy be held "for up to ten days for the purpose of securing his appearance before the grand jury."[117]

To clear himself, Higazy offered to take a polygraph test, to which the government agreed.[118] However, the polygraph test, given on December 27, 2001, quickly metamorphosed into an interrogation without the presence of counsel.[119] The FBI pressured and threatened Higazy to the point that he believed he had no choice but to confess to owning the radio.[120] At a hearing on December 28, 2001, to review the continued detention of Higazy as a material witness, the government presented the confession as evidence that continued detention was necessary.[121] The court ordered material witness detention until January 14, 2002.[122] However, the government never presented Higazy to a grand jury, but charged him with making material false statements on January 11, 2002, presumably based on his polygraph admission.[123] However, the detention order was vacated on January 14, 2002—the same day an American pilot went to the Millennium Hilton Hotel to claim his belongings, of which the transceiver was one.[124] This revelation prompted the FBI to investigate further.[125] Upon finding that the hotel security guard had lied repeatedly, the government dropped the charges against Higazy and released him on January 16, 2002, after having detained him in the general prison population for thirty days.[126]

Conflicting District Court Interpretations of Section 3144

Prior to the Second Circuit's resolution of the meaning and validity of section 3144,[127] two federal district court judges in the Southern District of New York had issued seemingly inconsistent rulings on the Justice Department's use of the federal material witness statute to hold a witness indefinitely for grand jury proceedings: *United States v. Awadallah* (*Awadallah III*) and *In re the Application of the United States for a Material Witness Warrant*.[128] Because the Second Circuit draws heavily from the two lower court decisions, each is discussed immediately below.

The facts underlying *Awadallah III* have already been discussed at length above. It is important to note for this chapter's discussion, however, that several district court opinions have been issued in this case. In *Awadallah I*, Judge Scheindlin granted bail to Awadallah, subject to certain conditions, after he had been indicted on perjury charges.[129] In *Awadallah II*, Judge Scheindlin denied Awadallah's motion to dismiss his perjury charge, but granted his request for an evidentiary hearing on the admissibility of, inter alia, his grand jury testimony.[130] In *Awadallah III*, the court held that Awadallah was unlawfully detained pending his grand jury appearance because the federal material witness statute does not allow for the arrest of material witnesses pending grand jury proceedings and, therefore, his purportedly incriminating grand jury testimony was not admissible as the fruit of the unlawful detention.[131] The court suggested that if the statute permitted indefinite detention of grand jury material witnesses, it would not survive Fourth Amendment scrutiny.[132] In *Awadallah IV*, the court suppressed virtually all of the government's evidence for use at Awadallah's perjury trial on grounds that it was seized in violation of the Fourth Amendment.[133] Consequently, Awadallah's eighty-three days in jail resulted in the dismissal of the indictment[134] until the Second Circuit reversed and remanded the trial court's decision.[135] This chapter focuses heavily on the legal rationale in *Awadallah III* and its treatment on appeal in the Second Circuit, but some information also is drawn from each of the four *Awadallah* district court cases.

Less than three months after Judge Scheindlin's decisions in *Awadallah III* and *IV*, Chief Judge Michael Mukasey of the Southern District of New York declined to follow his colleague's reasoning in *In Re the Application of the United States for a Material Witness Warrant ("In Re Material Witness Warrant")*.[136] In denying the defendant's motion for release or in the alternative, for a deposition in lieu of detention, the court held that the federal material witness statute does in fact apply to grand jury witnesses and is otherwise constitutional.[137] Neither party appealed Chief Judge Mukasey's ruling.

HISTORY OF THE FEDERAL MATERIAL WITNESS STATUTE

A material witness is a nonparty who has particular information about a crime that could be helpful to the defense or prosecution.[138] At common law and in courts of equity, a person designated as a witness was viewed as having a duty to appear in court and could be served with process or a subpoena.[139] The philosophy behind material witness detention has its roots in English law, where every citizen owed a duty to his king.[140] That has evolved in the United States as a duty to the courts.[141] Thus, the policy behind these statutes is to ensure the appearance of material witnesses at trial for the swift and fair administration of justice.[142]

The laws that form the basis of the material witness statute are the Judiciary Act of 1789 and the Bail Reform Act. The Judiciary Act[143] formally recognized the duty of witnesses to appear and testify, and required recognizance from material witnesses in criminal proceedings.[144] An 1846 amendment to the Judiciary Act of 1789 further clarified the federal courts' authority to arrest and requires assurances that a witness would appear in a trial for "any criminal cause or proceeding."[145] If a material witness failed to give such assurances, he or she could be confined until his or her testimony was given.[146]

Congress enacted the Bail Reform Act of 1966[147] to "modernize the pretrial release system in [the] federal courts."[148] The Act continued to authorize courts to set bail for material witnesses, but with the added caveat that a material witness unable to post bail could not be detained if his or her testimony could be adequately secured by deposition.[149] However, Congress disallowed the detention of material witnesses if their testimony could "adequately be secured" by deposition, and "further detention [was] not necessary to prevent a failure of justice."[150] Congress amended the Bail Reform Act again in 1984 to clarify the authority of the courts in making pretrial release decisions.[151] The Federal Rules of Criminal Procedure also were amended in 1966 and 1984 to reflect the Bail Reform Act and subsequent amendments thereto.[152] With the exception of a change that restored the explicit power to arrest material witnesses, the federal material witness statute was virtually unmodified in 1984.[153] In passing the 1984 amendments to the Bail Reform Act, Congress made it clear that "whenever possible" material witnesses should not be detained, even those so unreliable that bail could not be granted, if his or her testimony could be secured by deposition.[154]

Although detention of material witnesses has been practiced in the United States since 1789, the federal government engaged in the practice before September 11 primarily for detaining witnesses for criminal trials. In that long history, the federal material witness statute has never been challenged under the Fourth Amendment to the U.S. Constitution.[155] One critical reason that the statute has escaped a Fourth Amendment unreasonableness analysis may very well be that any arrests and imprisonments made pursuant to the statute have been tempered by granting bail, or in lieu of bail, taking a prompt deposition to preserve the witness' testimony for trial.[156] The relatively rare use[157] of the federal material witness statute to detain a witness pending the convening of a grand jury is evidenced by the fact that there is only one pre–September 11 case, *Bacon v. United States*,[158] that meaningfully addresses the constitutionality of imprisoning a grand jury material witness in the absence of probable cause under the Fourth Amendment.

BACON V. UNITED STATES

Facts and Procedural History

On April 22, 1971, a United States District Judge for the Western District of Washington issued a material witness arrest warrant for Leslie Bacon solely on the basis of the prosecution's affidavit that summarily alleged she would not respond to a subpoena to testify before a grand jury and would try to flee the court's jurisdiction.[159] The warrant set bail for $100,000.[160] Pursuant to the warrant, FBI agents arrested her and served her with a grand jury subpoena in the District of Columbia on April 27.[161] At the removal hearing before the U.S. District Court for the District of Columbia on April 28, she moved to quash the arrest warrant or, in the alternative, to reduce bail.[162] The district court denied her motion and ordered her transfer to the state of Washington.[163] Although she appeared before a grand jury in the state of Washington on April 30, May 1, and May 2, Bacon refused to answer questions and a contempt order was entered against her.[164] Bacon filed a petition for a writ of habeas corpus on the grounds, inter alia, that her arrest and incarceration without probable cause and the imposition of $100,000 bail were invalid.[165] The court in the Western District of Washington denied the petition and Bacon appealed to the Ninth Circuit.[166]

Ninth Circuit's Holding and Reasoning

Grand Jury Proceedings as Criminal Proceedings

After first establishing as a general matter that an uncooperative material witness may be arrested and detained under the then-extant federal material witness statute and Rule 46(b) (governing release from custody), the Ninth Circuit addressed the more specific question of whether the statute's and rule's reference to "criminal proceedings" included grand jury proceedings within their scope. The *Bacon* court answered affirmatively by first reasoning that the authorizing legislation for the Federal Rules of Criminal Procedure stated "[t]he Supreme Court of the United States shall have the power to prescribe, from time to time, rules of pleading, practice, and procedure with respect *to any or all proceedings prior to and including verdict* . . . in criminal cases," and therefore, the term "criminal proceedings" must include grand jury proceedings.[167] The court then concluded that, in promulgating the Rules, the Supreme Court expressly exercised its authority to the fullest based on Rule 2, which states, "these rules are intended to provide for the just determination of *every criminal proceeding.*"[168] Finally, the Ninth Circuit noted that other rules expressly apply or have been interpreted to apply to grand jury proceedings.[169] Specifically, Rule 6 "authorizes the summoning of grand juries and establishes procedures to govern their operation," and Rule 17 provides for subpoena power in both criminal trials and grand jury investigations.[170] Accordingly, it concluded that the term "criminal proceedings" as used throughout the Rules must apply to grand jury proceedings.[171]

Constitutionality of Bacon's Arrest and Detention

Ms. Bacon argued that even if, as a general matter, the federal material witness provision's reference to "criminal proceedings" includes grand jury matters, the statute and accompanying rule are unconstitutional on their face because, inter alia, imprisoning a material witness without probable cause violates the Constitution.[172] However, the Ninth Circuit refused to decide the facial attack on these provisions because Ms. Bacon had not properly briefed the issue.[173]

Validity of the Arrest Warrant and Custody Order

Although the Ninth Circuit did not address the facial constitutionality of arresting and detaining material witnesses pursuant to the federal material witness statute or Rule 46(b), it did rule that the issuance of a material witness arrest warrant *on the facts of that case* violated the Fourth Amendment.[174] In so doing, the Ninth Circuit determined that *any* material witness arrest and detention, whether for trial or for grand jury, must be supported by evidence of impracticability—that is, "sufficient facts must be shown to give the judicial officer probable cause to believe that it may be impracticable to secure the presence of the witness by subpoena. *Mere assertion will not do.*"[175] The court found the summary evidence presented by the government in its affidavit seeking the arrest of Ms. Bacon was not sufficient to conclude that she would be likely to flee.[176] Thus, the Ninth Circuit held that the warrant and subsequent arrest were unreasonable under the Fourth Amendment, and therefore, invalid *as applied* to the specific circumstances of Bacon's case.[177]

UNITED STATES V. AWADALLAH

Awadallah III is the first case since *Bacon* to address whether the federal material witness statute applies to grand jury witnesses. Like the Ninth Circuit, the *Awadallah III* court had to determine whether the term "criminal proceeding" in the statute included grand jury proceedings.[178] Also like the Ninth Circuit, Judge Scheindlin acknowledged that the term on its face created "some uncertainty."[179] However, unlike the Ninth Circuit, Judge Scheindlin declared that the structure of the statute itself clarifies any ambiguity found in section 3144.[180] She stated: "When construed in context, the phrase 'criminal proceeding' in section 3144 could not be clearer,"[181]—that is, it does *not* apply to grand juries.

The Bail Reform Act and the Material Witness Statute

Language and Structure

To develop the statutory context on which she relied, Judge Scheindlin focused on the federal material witness statute's key words: "If it appears from

an affidavit filed by a *party*, that the testimony of a person is *material* in a *criminal proceeding*, and it is shown" that it could be "impracticable" to secure his testimony via subpoena, the witness may be detained according to "the provisions of *section 3142*."[182] The court initially concentrated on the word "party," a term that Judge Scheindlin concluded plainly relates to an adversarial process where at least two opposing parties exist.[183] She reasoned further that because grand jury proceedings are investigative in nature and not adversarial, no "party" exists until the grand jury has completed its investigation and returned an indictment.[184] Therefore, Judge Scheindlin concluded that section 3144's reference to a "party" makes clear that it is not applicable to grand jury proceedings.[185]

She also found section 3144's applicability to "material" witnesses instructive.[186] She noted that, in a trial context, a court may easily determine "materiality" by examining all the evidence presented.[187] However, she explained that a "materiality" determination cannot be made in the context of grand jury investigations because they are secretive in nature.[188] Courts usually cannot make inquiries into such proceedings.[189] Consequently, to determine whether a grand jury witness was "material," a judge would simply have to rest on the bald assertions of a government agent, thereby essentially abdicating a judicial responsibility.[190] Therefore, she found that section 3144's reference to a "material witness" made it clear that the statute did not address grand jury matters.[191]

Furthermore, Judge Scheindlin noted that section 3144 expressly incorporates section 3142.[192] Section 3142 governs "release or detention of a defendant *pending trial*."[193] Indeed, she noted that factors listed in section 3142 be weighed when making detention determinations do not apply to grand jury witnesses.[194] Section 3142 requires an inquiry into the "nature and circumstances" of the charges; the "weight of the evidence" against the person charged; the accused's "history and characteristics"; and the type and degree of danger posed if the court released the person charged.[195] She concluded that applying these factors to a grand jury context would be like trying "to a square peg into a round hole."[196] Clearly, the first, second, and fourth factors do not apply to a material witness because a witness has not been charged with any crime—he or she has only *observed* the commission of a crime. A judge cannot apply three of the four factors to a material witness in grand jury context, so Judge Scheindlin found yet another interpretive "clue" showing that section 3144 does not apply to grand jury proceedings.[198]

Finally, the judge noted that the federal material witness statute is encompassed within the entire Bail Reform Act,[199] and she found no reference grand jury proceedings within the entirety of that Act.[200] While examining tion 3141, a part of the Bail Reform Act that governs the release of individ

the court stated the "only two situations" where a judicial officer could release or detain a person was "pending trial" or "pending sentence or appeal."[201] The court concluded that neither situation was broad enough to include grand jury proceedings.[202] Section 3146, another pertinent section of the Act, punishes those who fail to appear in court as a defendant or material witness,[203] but the court noted a grand jury has "never been viewed as a 'court.'"[204] Again, Judge Scheindlin concluded that, when section 3144 was construed as a part of the much larger Bail Reform Act, the federal material witness statute could not apply to grand jury proceedings.

Legislative History

Turning to legislative history of the Bail Reform Act, the "bedrock of the current material witness statute,"[205] the *Awadallah III* court recognized that virtually all legislative references to the federal material witness statute focused on how to secure the appearance of material witnesses for trial, not for grand jury proceedings.[206] Judge Scheindlin noted that the only legislative reference to the application of the material witness statute to grand jury proceedings is found in a report submitted to the Senate criticizing the entire federal material witness statute as unconstitutional.[207] She also noted that the commentaries published on the material witness statute before and after its enactment in 1966 discussed only the practice of detaining material witnesses pending trial, not for grand jury proceedings.[208]

The court was further impressed by the fact that when the Bail Reform Act was amended in 1984, only two changes were made to the federal material witness statute: judicial officers gained the explicit authorization to issue arrest warrants for material witnesses, and they could order the detention of a material witness if no conditions of release would ensure the witness' appearance.[209] Neither change, she concluded, gave the government authority to apply the federal material witness statute to grand jury witnesses.[210]

Federal Rules of Criminal Procedure

The *Awadallah III* court also reviewed the two rules, as they were worded at the time of Awadallah's detention, expressly relating to the federal material witness statute: Rule 15 (governing depositions) and Rule 46 (controlling the release from custody prior to trial).[211] If a deposition is sought by the material witness and the judge allows it, section 3144 demonstrates a strong bias for the release of a material witness after the government takes the deposition[212]—unless, of course, probable cause develops through the deposition to arrest the witness on criminal charges. However, the government argued be-

fore Judge Scheindlin that it was not required to take Mr. Awadallah's deposition under the statute and could detain him indefinitely because Rule 15 expressly applies to depositions in the pretrial *and not the grand jury context*.[213] Agreeing with the government's reading of the plain language of Rule 15,[214] she reasoned that, by applying its deposition reference exclusively to the pretrial context, Congress could not have intended the material witness statute to apply to grand jury witnesses.[215] She said the differences between grand juries and pretrial proceedings were too "critical" and too "obvious" for Congress to have meant otherwise.[216] As for Rule 46, the court viewed this rule's express reference to "release prior to trial" as further convincing evidence that the statute only applies to witnesses held for trial, not for grand jury proceedings.[217]

Bacon Distinguished

The *Awadallah III* court acknowledged that the only interpretive authority for the proposition that the federal material witness statute can be used to detain grand jury material witnesses is the Ninth Circuit's decision in *Bacon*.[218] The court noted, however, that *Bacon*, as a Ninth Circuit decision, was not binding on the Southern District of New York.[219] Second, the *Awadallah III* court concluded that *Bacon*'s discussion about whether the federal material witness statute applies to grand jury witnesses was dicta[220] because it was wholly unnecessary to *Bacon*'s ultimate holding that her arrest was unconstitutional under the circumstances of that case.[221] Furthermore, the *Bacon* court's reliance on the fact that Rules 2, 6, and 17 specifically apply to grand juries necessitates a finding that Rule 46 must also apply to grand juries[222] was "preposterous because it would lead to the conclusion that [every Federal] Rule[] of Criminal Procedure . . . extend[s] to grand juries."[223] Indeed, she noted that, while making its own contextual argument based on, inter alia, Rules 2, 6, and 17, the Ninth Circuit failed to conduct a contextual analysis of critical words within the federal material witness statute itself, such as "party" and "material," which strongly suggest it does not apply to grand juries.[224]

Constitutional Considerations

The *Awadallah III* court held that even if a possible reading of the federal material witness statute suggested applying it to grand jury witnesses, the dubious constitutional result would preclude the court from that interpretation.[225] Noting that the test for reasonableness of a seizure under the Fourth Amendment requires balancing the nature and quality of the intrusion against the importance of the governmental interest at stake,[226] the *Awadallah III* court

pointed out that a grand jury witness who is detained loses the right to liberty
in order to aid an ex parte investigation of criminal activity, which could be
triggered by mere "tips" or "rumors."[227] In the context of arresting and detaining a material witness prior to criminal trial, the court explained that the
statute is objectively reasonable because, in the absence of bail, the deposition provision in the federal material witness statute achieves a reasonable
balance between society's interest in enforcing the law, the defendant's Sixth
Amendment right to confront witnesses against him, and the material witness' liberty interest.[228] That is, the government can detain a witness who
might otherwise flee long enough to conduct a prompt deposition, as long as
the deposition will adequately capture the material witness' testimony, and release would not cause a "failure of justice."[229] However, this balance is evis-
cerated when the material witness statute is applied to grand jury witnesses.[230]
Because she agreed with the government that Rule 15, as it existed at the time
of Awadallah's arrest,[231] did not afford a grand jury material witness the right
to a deposition in lieu of incarceration, she concluded that there is no coun-
terbalancing factor.[232] Under *Bacon*'s reading, grand jury witnesses can be
held indefinitely, like regular prisoners on the basis of a "tip" or "rumor."[233]
The court determined that this lack of a reasonable balance would make the
federal material witness statute unconstitutional if applied to grand jury witnesses.[234]

The court emphasized that the unreasonableness of the seizure was aggra-
vated by the harsh nature of the detention in *Awadallah III*.[235] Judge
Scheindlin focused on the Supreme Court's explanation in *Terry v. Ohio*[236]
that the government has an interest in "effective crime prevention and detection" that may justify temporary seizure, but a detention must be "reasonably
related in scope to the circumstances which justified the interference in the
first place."[237] In *Awadallah III*, she found that Awadallah's austere imprisonment as a high-security inmate was well outside the scope of the necessities of the investigation.[238] The court further observed that "'in our society
liberty is the norm and detention without trial is the carefully limited exception,'" but interpreting section 3144 to apply to grand jury witnesses would
make "detention the norm and liberty the exception."[239]

IN RE: MATERIAL WITNESS WARRANT

Chief Judge Mukasey of the Southern District of New York parted company
with Judge Scheindlin in *In re Material Witness Warrant* by holding that the
federal material witness statute does apply to grand jury witnesses.[240] In ana-
lyzing Chief Judge Mukasey's decision, it must be noted that the facts were

not as well developed as those in *Awadallah III*. The record in *In re Material Witness Warrant* was sealed pursuant to Rule 6(e), which provides for secrecy of grand jury proceedings.[241] However, Judge Mukasey revealed that the material witness in his case was already being held by the Immigration and Naturalization Service on a deportation order when the federal prosecutors obtained a material witness warrant and took custody of him.[242] Thus, unlike Awadallah, the material witness before Chief Judge Mukasey had not been removed from his regular civilian routine to be incarcerated pending the convening of a grand jury.[243] Citing the recent ruling in *Awadallah III*, the material witness sought to quash his warrant before Chief Judge Mukasey and enforce his deportation order principally by arguing that section 3144 does not apply to grand jury witnesses.[244] In the alternative, the material witness requested that his deposition be taken pursuant to section 3144 and Rule 15 in lieu of incarceration pending the convening of a grand jury.[245]

Bacon Analysis

In finding that the federal material witness statute applies to grand jury proceedings, Chief Judge Mukasey disagreed with the *Awadallah III* court's assessment that *Bacon*'s discussion of the scope of the federal material witness statute was merely dictum.[246] He ruled that the Ninth Circuit's application of the federal material witness statute applied to grand juries was a critical step in its ultimate finding that the government failed to make a sufficient showing of impracticability to support the warrant for grand jury testimony.[247] Chief Judge Mukasey reasoned: "If the statute did not authorize issuance of a warrant for the arrest of a grand jury witness, there would have been no occasion for the *Bacon* Court to consider whether the government had made the required showing that it was impracticable to secure petitioner's attendance before the grand jury without such a warrant."[248]

In the Bail Reform Act Amendments' legislative history, Chief Judge Mukasey also found what he believed to be dispositive evidence that the federal material witness statute applied to grand jury proceedings.[249] He noted that the *Awadallah III* court had overlooked a footnote in a Senate Judiciary Committee report for the enactment of the Bail Reform Act Amendments in 1984 that expressly cited *Bacon* for the proposition that the statute applies to grand jury proceedings.[250] The court stated, "Generally, when Congress enacts a statute that has been interpreted by the courts, it is 'presumed to be aware of . . . judicial interpretation of a statute and to adopt that interpretation when it re-enacts a statute without change.'"[251] The court found this legislative footnote to be conclusive evidence of Congress' intent to extend the federal material witness statute to grand jury witnesses.[252]

Plain Meaning of Section 3144

Having concluded that *Bacon*'s ruling, and the congressional reference to it, was dispositive, Chief Judge Mukasey went on to attack the notion that the statute's reference to the term "criminal proceeding" was ambiguous.[253] He read the term "criminal proceeding" as self-evidently comprehensive enough to include grand jury proceedings.[254] To support this conclusion, he cited the fact that the federal material witness statute appears in Title 18 of the United States Code, which also contains the statutory provisions governing grand jury proceedings.[255] The court also found dispositive (as had the Ninth Circuit in *Bacon*) that Rule 2 provides "the rules are 'intended to provide for the just determination of *every* criminal proceeding.'"[256] Finally, based on a plain reading of the statute, Chief Judge Mukasey concluded that the reach of Rule 46, which expressly refers to section 3144, is not limited to trial witnesses only.[257] The court also supported its broad reading of the term "criminal proceeding" by noting that other similar criminal statutes using that term have been read to include grand jury proceedings.[258] The court noted that cases reaching the opposite result involved statutes wholly different from the federal material witness statute.[259]

Chief Judge Mukasey also challenged *Awadallah III*'s reading of the terms "party" and "material" within section 3144 to find "criminal proceedings" do not include grand jury proceedings.[260] He argued that the word "party" in the federal material witness statute can apply self-evidently to "*any* party of interest," *not* just a party to an adversarial proceeding.[261] The court took further issue with the *Awadallah III* court's conclusion that a materiality determination cannot be made by a judge exclusively on the basis of the prosecution's description of the secret grand jury proceeding.[262] He cited three decisions determining that evidence or a witness' testimony were material based on the representation of the prosecutor alone.[263] He also noted that judges commonly make materiality evaluations when deciding whether to issue subpoenas based on one party's representation.[264]

The Federal Rules of Criminal Procedure

Most important for resolving the constitutional conundrum raised by arresting and indefinitely detaining material witnesses without probable cause pending a grand jury proceeding is Chief Judge Mukasey's handling of the question whether such a witness is entitled to a prompt deposition in lieu of incarceration. Again, section 3144 expressly provides that a deposition pursuant to Rule 15 is available to a material witness whose appearance at the "criminal proceeding" may otherwise be "impractical."[265] As shown above,

Judge Scheindlin agreed with the government's argument before her and found that Rule 15's express terms make it applicable only to a pretrial (and not a grand jury) setting.[266] Chief Judge Mukasey equivocates on this issue, finding that the language in Rule 15 points in both directions:

> [The] text [of Rule 15], referring as it does to taking a deposition to preserve testimony "for use at trial," to a "written motion of the witness . . . upon notice to the parties," to the defendant's attendance, and to "examination and cross-examination" shows that those who drafted the rule contemplated use of the deposition at a trial or in some hearing attended by both parties. *On the other hand, just as section 3144 refers to section 3142 as the standard for setting bail for material witnesses, even though several of the provisions of section 3142 plainly apply only to criminal defendants, it is not inconceivable that a deposition in aid of a grand jury proceedings might be taken pursuant to Rule 15, using those provisions of the Rule that would apply.*[267]

Indeed, elsewhere in the opinion, Chief Judge Mukasey reasons that the very rule dealing with bail eligibility—Rule 46(g)—applies to grand jury witnesses subject to arrest, and it therefore "*suggests that the remedy of testimony by deposition might be available to a grand jury witness when, for example, the grand jury before whom the witness is to testify cannot convene promptly.*"[268]

Despite his tantalizing suggestions that Rule 15 may be read to afford a grand jury witness the right to a deposition in lieu of incarceration, Chief Judge Mukasey, for a whole host of reasons, concluded, "I need not decide whether Rule 15 is elastic enough to authorize a deposition in aid of a grand jury investigation."[269] Perhaps the most convincing of those reasons was that the material witness in his case had never sought to be released on bail, thereby not squarely raising the issue whether his detention could be shortened by taking his deposition.[270] The failure to seek any release is wholly understandable because the material witness before Chief Judge Mukasey was otherwise properly detained subject to his deportation.

Constitutional Analysis

Unlike the *Awadallah III* court, Chief Judge Mukasey perceived no serious constitutional impediments with the federal material witness statute as applied to grand jury witnesses.[271] He found two flaws in the *Awadallah III* court's Fourth Amendment analysis of the statute as applied to grand jury witnesses. First, he reasoned that the *Awadallah III* court's Fourth Amendment concerns about the reasonableness of detaining grand jury witnesses under the material witness statute would not disappear if grand jury witnesses were excluded from the reach of the statute. In other words, material witnesses held for trial without probable cause would still have a Fourth Amendment claim.[272] However, this analysis fails to recognize that in a criminal trial setting, the material witness has the clear option of being deposed in lieu of detention, whereas in a grand jury investigation, the government's position at that time was that a material witness did not have this option. Again, in the history of the federal material witness statute, there has been no occasion to review lengthy material witness incarcerations pending the convening of a grand jury under the Fourth Amendment, probably because of the "safety valve" of affording a prompt deposition of the material witness to secure their trial testimony. As noted above, Judge Scheindlin found that the deposition option was not open to a grand jury material witness, and so her constitutional analysis confronted the constitutionality of a lengthy material witness incarceration in its starkest form.[273] Indeed, Chief Judge Mukasey's ruling that the deposition issue as applied to grand jury witnesses was not properly before him meant that he issued his Fourth Amendment ruling in the context of a detainee who, for all intents and purposes, had not challenged his incarceration. Under these circumstances, it was easier to find no Fourth Amendment violation.

Second, Chief Judge Mukasey supported his reading of section 3144 as being consistent with the Fourth Amendment by citing case law supporting the reasonableness of detaining a witness to secure his or her testimony.[274] Citing Supreme Court precedent, he stressed the importance placed on grand jury testimony in federal jurisprudence and noted the duty of every citizen "to disclose knowledge of crime."[275] He also pointed out that the Second, Sixth, Eighth, and Ninth Circuits have not found a constitutional problem with the detention of grand jury witnesses.[276] Yet, none of these cases squarely address the constitutionality of the federal material witness statute under the Fourth Amendment. Chief Judge Mukasey noted that several decisions have applied the federal material witness statute to grand jury witnesses.[277] The problem with these cases is that they do not squarely address the issue of whether section 3144 applies to grand jury witnesses, nor do they address Fourth Amendment concerns under these circumstances. Because *In re Material Witness Warrant* was not appealed, a division remained within the Second Circuit until that appellate court decided Awadallah's appeal.

SUMMARY AND ANALYSIS OF "CONFLICTING" DISTRICT COURT OPINIONS

It is tempting to conclude, as have many commentators, that Judge Scheindlin's decision in *Awadallah III* and Chief Judge Mukasey's decision in *In re Material Witness Warrant* are irreconcilably in conflict and that the Second Circuit would have to choose the approach in one of these cases over the other.[278] After all, Judge Scheindlin found that the federal material witness statute does not apply to grand jury proceedings.[279] Chief Judge Mukasey found that it did.[280]

Judge Scheindlin also found the Ninth Circuit's *Bacon* ruling that the federal material witness statute applied to grand jury proceedings to be unpersuasive because it was dictum—that is, unnecessary to *Bacon*'s ultimate holding that the grand jury material witness arrest warrant did not show with requisite constitutional specificity the likely unavailability of the witness in that case.[281] Chief Judge Mukasey, on the other hand, found *Bacon*'s pronouncement that the federal material witness statute applied to grand jury proceedings to be vital to the Ninth Circuit's holding that the grand jury material witness warrant there lacked constitutional specificity.[282] He further found *Bacon* to be "controlling" in some significant sense because, even though decided by the Ninth Circuit, it was later cited approvingly by a Senate Judiciary Committee report during the 1984 amendment to the very statute at issue.[283]

Judge Scheindlin further concluded that, if the federal material witness statute were to apply to grand jury proceedings, it would violate the Fourth Amendment because it would allow lengthy incarceration without a showing of probable cause that a crime had been committed.[284] In so doing, she determined, in agreement with the government's argument before her, that the statute's ameliorative reference to a deposition in lieu of incarceration did not apply to the investigative ex parte grand jury process.[285] Chief Judge Mukasey found no such constitutional problem but was considerably aided in that result, inter alia, by not closing the door on the prospect of considerably shortening the detention of an otherwise innocent grand jury witness through a deposition.[286] He thought that Rule 15 could plausibly be read, especially in light of Rule 46(g), to afford a grand jury material witness the right to a deposition tailored to the peculiar nature of the grand jury context.[287] However, he avoided a determination on the issue by stating that it had not been properly raised in his case.[288]

Yet, if Chief Judge Mukasey was right about the availability of a prompt, court-ordered deposition under Rule 15 to ameliorate an otherwise lengthy and possibly coercive detention of a grand jury material witness, that would resolve an otherwise seemingly irreconcilable conundrum between the legitimate interests of the material witness and the government. On the one hand, the lengthy imprisonment of what might very well be otherwise innocent persons pending the convening of a grand jury raises, as Judge Scheindlin found on the facts of *Awadallah III*, serious Fourth Amendment questions.

Conversely, the government's concern that a grand jury material witness might flee the jurisdiction (or the country) before the grand jury testimony can be secured is also worthy of consideration. These conflicting tensions could be resolved in the context of holding a material witness without probable cause for purposes of a grand jury by the express availability of securing that testimony by a prompt deposition appropriately tailored to the peculiarities of grand jury proceedings under Rule 15.

If a prompt deposition had been available to Awadallah, the prospect of his lengthy and almost certainly coercive imprisonment as a material witness would have been eliminated. Leaving to the side the strength of his perjury charge, if Awadallah had testified at a prompt deposition in the same allegedly untruthful manner he testified before the grand jury, the government could have criminally charged and detained him on the basis of his deposition testimony. Moreover, the deposition testimony would not have been tainted by a highly questionable incarceration, which in the final analysis was the principal basis for Judge Scheindlin's suppression of the evidence of, inter alia, perjury that the government wished to use against him.

The question of whether the federal material witness statute's reference to "criminal proceedings" includes grand jury proceedings is doubtless one of substantial ambiguity. The attempts of the *Bacon*, *Awadallah III*, and *In re Material Witness Warrant* courts to resolve that ambiguity by reference to statutory "context" and legislative history was based on well-established rules of statutory construction, but the use of those rules was clearly wielded in a highly result-oriented fashion. In terms of real-world practicalities, Judge Scheindlin's decision is doubtlessly correct on the abhorrent facts of that case, but it does not, as a general matter, accommodate what may be a legitimate and compelling governmental concern: that a grand jury material witness may flee the jurisdiction or the country if his or her testimony is not secured. Under her holding that section 3144 never applies to grand jury proceedings, the government can never secure the testimony of a witness whose appearance at the grand jury proceeding is questionable. If Rule 15, however, allows for a pre-grand jury deposition, as Chief Judge Mukasey suggested, then "fear of flight" can be accommodated by the taking of a deposition.

In resolving whether a material witness may be deposed to secure testimony for a grand jury under Rule 15, two points should be dispositive. First, if, as Chief Judge Mukasey argued, legislative reports underlying the federal material witness statute are to be given great weight,[289] the emphatic language in the relevant Senate Committee Report that the availability of deposition in lieu of incarceration is a central component of that statute should be controlling. Second, if the statute is otherwise somehow ambiguous on this point, even Chief Judge Mukasey contended that Rule 15 can be reasonably read to provide "the remedy of testimony by deposition . . . to a grand jury witness when, for example, the grand jury before which the witness is to testify cannot convene promptly."[290] It is well settled that an ambiguous statute must be given a reading that avoids constitutional difficulties. The Supreme Court has stated, "If an otherwise acceptable construction of a statute would raise serious constitutional problems, and where an alternative interpretation of the statute is 'fairly possible,' [courts] are obliged to construe the statute to avoid such problems."[291] As Chief Judge Mukasey contends, there is at the very least a "fairly plausible" reading of Rule 15 that would provide a material witness deposition tailored to the pre-grand jury setting. Otherwise, the stark constitutional issue Judge Scheindlin confronted concerning indefinite incarceration without the availability of a deposition would raise the specter of a Fourth Amendment violation.

On appeal to the Second Circuit, one would have hoped that the *Awadallah* court would have followed what appears to have been the logical extension of Chief Judge Mukasey's reasoning, and would have held that detaining a material witness for twenty days without bail or a deposition violates section 3144 or constitutes an illegal seizure under the Fourth Amendment. The Second Circuit traveled part way down that path by finding that section 3144 and Rule 15 do make depositions available in the grand jury context.[292] It also noted, "It would be improper for the government to use § 3144 for other ends, such as the detention of persons suspected of criminal activity for which probable cause has not yet been established."[293] However, the Second Circuit surprisingly concluded that even though a deposition is available for grand jury material witnesses under section 3144, a deposition need not be taken if the detainee is offered a bail hearing, even if bail is denied.[294] Therefore, rather than properly balancing both parties' competing interests, the Second Circuit's rationale abandoned the best parts of Judge Scheindlin and Chief Judge Mukasey's opinions and reached a result that implicitly endorsed the government's indefinite and coercive detentions of grand jury material witnesses. Nowhere did the Second Circuit explain how such an indefinite detention without probable cause of having committed a crime would not run afoul of its warning, in dictum, that the federal material witness statute should not be abused by making arrests without probable cause.

AWADALLAH ON APPEAL TO THE SECOND CIRCUIT

On appeal to the Second Circuit, the government did not challenge Judge Scheindlin's factual findings, and the Second Circuit approved and adopted them in all but one limited circumstance.[295] With regard to the abusive and coercive conditions of Awadallah's confinement, the Second Circuit said that those allegations were immaterial to the issues before the district court,[296] a conclusion that obviously aided the appellate court in ultimately finding that Awadallah's confinement did not violate the Fourth Amendment. By largely ignoring his conditions of confinement, the Second Circuit also was able to avoid mentioning that "many" of Awadallah's allegations regarding treatment during his harsh detention were uncontested by the government.[297] Furthermore, the Second Circuit failed to take judicial notice of a widely publicized, contemporaneous United States Department of Justice, Office of the Inspector General report criticizing the abusive conditions of confinement faced by September 11 detainees in similar New York detention facilities.[298]

The Reach of Section 3144

The Second Circuit reviewed Judge Scheindlin and Chief Judge Mukasey's decisions as they pertained to the question of whether grand jury proceedings were included within the term "criminal proceeding" in section 3144. In so doing, it looked at the plain language of the statute, interpretations of "proceeding" or "criminal proceeding" in other contexts, and the statutory context of section 3144 itself.[299] The court agreed with Judge Scheindlin and disagreed with Chief Judge Mukasey regarding the textual clarity of section 3144.[300] It found the plain language of section 3144 to be highly ambiguous, and concluded that "we must look beyond the text of § 3144 to discern the meaning of 'criminal proceeding.'"[301]

In that regard, the court examined section 3144's legislative history for an interpretive clue.[302] The Second Circuit fully endorsed Chief Judge Mukasey's reliance on the footnote of a Senate Judiciary Committee report accompanying the Bail Reform Act of 1984,[303] which cited *Bacon* to support the committee's summary statement that the term "criminal proceeding" in section 3144 includes grand jury proceedings.[304] The appellate court found the Senate Judiciary Committee's express ratification of *Bacon* dispositive on the question of the drafters' intent, and concluded, "[A] grand jury proceeding is a 'criminal proceeding' for purposes of § 3144."[305]

In order to fully support the conclusion that section 3144 applied to grand juries, the Second Circuit still had to contend with Judge Scheindlin's ruling that Rule 15 (governing depositions) did not apply in the grand jury context. Her finding in this regard was consistent with the government's reading of the rule at the time.[306] Obviously recognizing that its assertion before the district court undercut the argument that section 3144 (which references Rule 15) does apply to those bodies, the government switched its position on appeal and argued that a grand jury material witness can receive a deposition in lieu of detention under Rule 15 and section 3144.[307] The government explained this awkward reversal by stating it was now persuaded by the expansive reading of Rule 15 suggested by Chief Judge Mukasey.[308] While openly troubled by this "change of heart" on appeal, the Second Circuit reluctantly accepted the government's justification and agreed that Rule 15 is flexible enough to allow the testimony of grand jury material witnesses to be secured by deposition.[309] However, the switch in the government's position forced the Second Circuit to face the much more difficult question of whether the Fourth Amendment allowed the government to imprison Awadallah for as long as it did without probable cause of having committed a crime and without affording him either of section 3144's two ameliorative options for release: bail or a deposition in lieu of continued detention.

Constitutional Analysis

In setting the stage for its determination that section 3144 survived constitutional analysis, even as applied to Awadallah's predicament, the Second Circuit explored the canon of constitutional avoidance by which a court refrains from reading an ambiguous statute to be unconstitutional if a plausible, constitutionally satisfactory interpretation exists.[310] The court explained that the canon comes into play only if the statute is ambiguous and "there are serious concerns about the statute's constitutionality."[311]

The Second Circuit found that Awadallah's twenty-day detention as a material witness prior to his grand jury testimony did not raise "serious concerns" by surprisingly and inexplicably concluding that Awadallah's two failed bail hearings while he was incarcerated made his detention reasonable.[312] In this regard, the Second Circuit offered findings from the unsuccessful bail hearings that concluded Awadallah was a flight risk and that his detention was "reasonable under the circumstances."[313] In so ruling, the appellate court failed to address the text of section 3144, which expressly states that, except where it would cause a "failure of justice," a deposition was to be afforded to an arrested material witness who could not make bail. The appellate court also completely ignored the entire tenor of the Senate Judiciary Committee report accompanying section 3144, which stated: "The committee stresses that whenever possible, the depositions of such witnesses should be obtained so that they may be released from custody."[314] It also ignored that report's emphatic instruction to the judiciary, that when material witnesses cannot meet the conditions of bail, "the judicial officer is *required* to order the witness' release after the taking of the deposition if this will not result in a failure of justice."[315] Finally, the Second Circuit ignored the fact that section 3144 was originally derived from an integral part of the Bail Reform Act of

1966—an Act whose entire purpose was "to assure that all persons, regardless of their financial status, shall not needlessly be detained pending their appearance to answer charges, to testify, or pending appeal, when detention serves neither the ends of justice nor the public interest."[316] Disregarding these fundamental mandates from the legislative history was especially surprising given the Second Circuit's dispositive deference to a single *footnote* within the Senate Judiciary Committee report summarily stating that section 3144 applied to grand juries.[317]

The Second Circuit also defended its finding that no serious constitutional concerns exist by citing several supposedly supportive decisions,[318] all of which were inapposite. First and foremost, none of the cases construed the constitutionality of section 3144, or its predecessor section 3149. Other decisions relied on by the Second Circuit in *Awadallah* did not contain constitutional challenges to any material witness statute. The musings over material witness statutes in those cases were irrelevant to the holdings—that is, they were dicta.[319] A separate case did uphold the constitutionality of a state material witness statute under the Privileges and Immunities Clauses of Article IV and the Fourteenth Amendment, but *not* the Fourth Amendment.[320]

Although two of the cited cases, *United States* ex rel. *Glinton v. Denno* (*Glinton II*) and *United States* ex rel. *Allen* v. *La Vallee*—both decided in the 1960s—did involve Fourth Amendment challenges, they concerned a New York state material witness statute significantly different than section 3144. In those two cases, the New York statute *required* that material witnesses be released or given conditions of bail, and it did not prohibit the use of a deposition as one of those conditions.[321] The defendants in those cases could not satisfy their respective bail requirements.[322] Awadallah had been flatly denied bail and the chance to offer his testimony via deposition.[323] Ironically, of course, he was ultimately afforded bail after being charged, and his reliability as a material witness is evidenced by the fact that, even as of this writing (over two years after his initial arrest), he is still free on bail, satisfying the conditions of his release, and awaiting trial.[324]

Furthermore, the 1969 *Allen* decision acknowledged that the then-recent expansion of Fourth and Fifth Amendment rights may have dictated a different result in *Allen* if recent precedent could be applied retroactively to the facts of that case.[325] The clear implication of *Allen* was that, in future cases, the circumstances faced by Allen and Glinton would be found unconstitutional. As additional evidence of the statute's questionable nature, the New York legislature added further procedural protections to that state's material witness statute in the year following *Allen*.[326] Because of the expansion of constitutional rights since the mid 1960s, the Second Circuit's reliance in *Awadallah* on opinions over thirty-five years old to support the continuing validity of indefinitely detaining a federal grand jury material witness without probable cause is, at the very least, highly questionable.

The Impact of the Second Circuit's Ruling for Awadallah

In the end, the Second Circuit reversed and remanded *Awadallah* to the district court with instructions to reinstate the perjury charges,[327] even though Awadallah had been coercively detained in prison for twenty days as a material witness in a prison designed for convicted criminals, without probable cause of having committed a crime, or the opportunity to free himself through bail or a deposition in lieu of further detention. This holding represents nothing less than a wholehearted endorsement of the Justice Department's material witness policies put in place after September 11, 2001. Moreover, recent press reports indicate that the Justice Department has taken the Second Circuit's authorization of its detention practices to heart, and it has continued its secretive and coercive material witness incarcerations.[328]

Conclusion

In *In re Material Witness Warrant*, Chief Judge Mukasey strongly hinted at a result that should have satisfied both parties before the Second Circuit: Rule 15 together with section 3144 might be malleable enough to require a material witness' deposition in lieu of bail or continued incarceration.[329] His suggestion accommodated the interests of all parties. It allowed the government to obtain grand jury testimony, but minimized the intrusion on the material witness' liberty interests by affording them their freedom via bail or a deposition. It is also important to emphasize that were the government required to depose grand jury witnesses who cannot be released on bail, it would not be without weapons to deal with suspected "bad actors" for whom it has no probable cause to detain on a long-term basis. For example, if a material witness has been involved in as-yet-undetected criminal wrongdoing, that information is just as likely to be developed in a prompt, postdetention deposition. If Awadallah did in fact perjure himself before the grand jury as the government alleges, he likely would have testified to the same effect in a deposition.

The Second Circuit, in principle, adopted Chief Judge Mukasey's position and found that prompt depositions were available in the way that he had proposed.[330] However, when one considers the Second Circuit's opinion in tandem with the lengthy detentions of Awadallah and Abdallah Higazy,[331] not to mention the Justice Department's report detailing the abusive conditions endured by September 11 detainees,[332] the court effectively read the deposition alternative out of section 3144. Without providing guidelines to educate the government about the conditions under which depositions are proper for grand jury material witnesses, or when their release on bail would cause a "failure of justice," the Second Circuit gave the government license to detain material witnesses for lengthy periods of time, in highly coercive circumstances, without probable cause of having committed a crime.

It is quite possible that the Second Circuit was, in fact, concerned that Awadallah's testimony would not be adequately captured in a deposition, or that his release would cause a "failure of justice" as that term is used in section 3144. The attacks on the World Trade Center and the Pentagon were still very fresh in Americans' minds when Awadallah was first arrested as a material witness to those attacks. Perhaps the need to discover the person or persons responsible for these unprecedented attacks on American soil or the need to interrupt other imminent attacks might at least be an arguable basis for justifying Awadallah's continued detention. Indeed, it may be plausibly argued that the days and weeks following September 11 were extraordinary times that may have required exceptional and extraordinary means to preserve our country's safety. However, the Second Circuit nowhere limited its ruling in this way. Moreover, while stating in dictum that "it would be improper for the government to use § 3144 for . . . the detention of persons suspected of criminal activity for which probable cause has not yet been established,"[333] the appellate court astonishingly failed to distinguish Awadallah's detention from that very same circumstance—using section 3144 to arrest without probable cause.

As a practical matter, this may not be the end of Awadallah's litigation. As of this writing in early January 2004, one could foresee, for example, Awadallah petitioning the U.S. Supreme Court for a writ of certiorari. Because the government is continuing its practice of coercively detaining grand jury material witnesses for lengthy amounts of time, those who have been denied bail or deposition in lieu of detention may be able to challenge detentions occurring in other federal circuits. Therefore, a circuit split on this issue might be created, attracting the attention of the U.S. Supreme Court, if it does not ultimately consider *Awadallah* itself.

However, if the bewildering nature of the *Bacon*, *Awadallah*, and *In re Material Witness Warrant* litigation suggests anything, it is that section 3144 as presently written is highly confusing and ambiguous. Resolving lengthy federal material witness detentions also calls into play complicated constitutional analysis. The far better approach would be to strive for immediate congressional clarification of the federal material witness statute.

To avoid further judicial wrangling, Congress should promptly revisit section 3144 and clearly rewrite it in a way that accommodates the government's need to secure grand jury testimony, while avoiding what amounts to unjustifiable and coercive detentions of material witnesses. It should provide that: (1) "criminal proceeding" includes grand jury proceedings; and (2) except in highly exigent circumstances, the deposition alternative is available for federal material witnesses who are not eligible for, or cannot meet, conditions of bail.

It cannot be under civilized principles of constitutional jurisprudence that the government can hold a material witness, as it did Awadallah, in prison without probable cause under highly coercive circumstances for an indefinite period of time (or, under the most generous count to the government, twenty days in the case of Awadallah). The constitutional rule announced by the Second Circuit in Awadallah amounts to nothing less than sanctioning the practice of holding detainees in highly coercive circumstances to obtain unreliable, incriminating testimony in the absence of probable cause. A halt must be put to this punitive, suspect, and wholly unnecessary practice.

NOTES

1. CBS News, *Ashcroft Evaluates the War on Terror* (Feb. 13, 2003), *at* www.cbsnews.com/stories/2003/02/13/attack/printable540422.shtml (last visited Oct. 13, 2003).

2. *See, e.g.,* Karen Branch-Brioso, *Fight Over Rights Rages On*, St. Louis Post-Dispatch, Sept. 8, 2002, at B1 (discussing various tactics the Justice Department has used in "War on Terror").

3. *See. e.g., The War on Our Freedoms: Civil Liberties in an Age of Terrorism* (Richard C. Leone and Greg Angrig, Jr. eds., 2003)

4. *See* American Bar Association, Recommendation on Military Commissions (Jan. 2002), *available at* www.abanet.org/leadership/military.pdf (last visited Oct. 13, 2003); American Bar Association, Recommendations on the Treatment of Enemy Combatants (Feb. 2003), *available at* www.abanet.org/leadership recommendations03/109.pdf (last visited Oct. 13, 2003); American Bar Association, Recommendation on Civilian Defense Counsel (Aug. 2003), *available at* www.abanet.org/media/aug03/ABACivilian-DefenseCounselCorrectedFinalReportRecommendation08031.pdf (last visited Oct. 13, 2003).

5. Hamdi v. Rumsfeld, 316 F.3d 450 (4th Cir. 2003), *cert. granted*, __ U.S.L.W. ____ (U.S. Jan. 9, 2004) (No. 03-6696); Padilla *ex rel.* Newman v. Bush, 233 F. Supp. 2d 564 (S.D.N.Y. 2002), *motion for reconsideration granted and adhered sub nom.* Padilla *ex. rel.* Newman v. Rumsfeld, 243 F. Supp. 2d 42 (S.D.N.Y. 2003), *rev'd in part and aff'd in part*, No. 03-2235, 2003 WL 22965085 (2d Cir. Dec. 18, 2003).

6. Al Odah v. United States, 321 F.3d 1134 (D.C. Cir. 2003), *cert. granted*, 72 U.S.L.W. 3327 (U.S. Nov. 10, 2003) (No. 03-343).

7. Ctr. for Nat'l Sec. Studies v. United States Dep't. of Justice, 331 F.3d 918 (D.C. Cir. 2003), *cert. denied*, __ U.S.L.W. ____ (U.S. Jan. 12, 2004) (No. 03-472).

8. N. Jersey Media Group, Inc. v. Ashcroft, 308 F.3d 198 (3d Cir. 2002), *cert. denied*, 123 S. Ct. 2215 (2003); Detroit Free Press v. Ashcroft, 303 F.3d 681 (6th Cir. 2002).

9. United States v. Moussaoui, 282 F. Supp. 2d 480 (E.D. Va. 2003), *notice of appeal filed* (4th Cir. Oct. 7, 2003) (No. 03-4792), *argued* Dec. 3, 2003.

10. Phil Hirschkorn, *Feds Appeal Ruling on Post-Sept. 11 Tactics*, CNN (May 5, 2002), *at* www.cnn.com/2002/LAW/05/03/material.witnesses (last visited Oct. 13, 2003).

11. Bail Reform Act of 1984 § 102, 18 U.S.C. § 3144 (2003) (amending 18 U.S.C. § 3149).

12. *See, e.g.,* Adam Liptak et al., *After Sept. 11, a Legal Battle on the Limits of Civil Liberty*, N.Y. Times, Aug. 4, 2002, § 1, at 1 (discussing the circumstances surrounding detentions of material witnesses).

13. United States v. Awadallah, 202 F. Supp. 2d 82, 89–96 (S.D.N.Y. 2002) [hereinafter *Awadallah IV*] *rev'd*, 349 F.3d 42 (2d Cir. 2003).

14. United States v. Awadallah, 202 F. Supp. 2d 17, 21 (S.D.N.Y. 2002) [hereinafter *Awadallah II*]; *Awadallah IV*, 202 F. Supp. 2d at 89.

15. *Awadallah IV*, 202 F. Supp. 2d at 88 n.8.

16. *Awadallah II*, 202 F. Supp. 2d at 22; United States v. Awadallah, 173 F. Supp. 2d 186, 188–89 n.7 (S.D.N.Y. 2001) [hereinafter Awadallah I].

17. *Awadallah II*, 202 F. Supp. 2d at 21.

18. *Id.* at 21 n.2.

19. *Awadallah IV*, 202 F. Supp. 2d at 86.

20. *Id.*

21. *Id.*

22. *Id.* at 87.

23. *Id.*

24. *Id.*

25. *Id.* at 87–88.

26. *Id.* at 88.

27. *Id.*

28. *Id* at 89.

29. *Id.*

30. *Id.*

31. *Id.*

32. *Id.*

33. *Id.*

34. *Id.*

35. *Id.* at 89–90.

36. *Id.* at 88.

37. *Id.* at 90.

38. *Id.*

39. *Id.*

40. *Id.* at 88, 90.

41. *Id.* at 90, 92.

42. *Id.* at 90–93.

43. *Id.* (quoting FBI agents).

44. *Id.* at 92–93 (quoting FBI agents).

45. *Id.* at 93.

46. *Id.*

47. *Id.*

48. *Id.*

49. *Id.*

50. *Id.*

51. *Id.*

52. *Id.* at 93–94.

53. *Id.* at 94.

54. *Id.*

55. *Id.* (quoting FBI agents).

56. *Id.*

57. *Id.*

58. *Id.*

59. *Awadallah II*, 202 F. Supp. 2d 17, 23 (S.D.N.Y. 2002).

60. United States v. Awadallah, 202 F. Supp. 2d 55, 60 n.4 (S.D.N.Y. 2002) [hereinafter *Awadallah III*], *rev'd*, 349 F.3d 42 (2d Cir. 2003).

61. *Id.* at 60.

62. *See generally*, U.S. Dep't of Justice Office of the Inspector General, Supplemental Report on September 11 Detainees' Allegations of Abuse at the Metropolitan Detention Center in Brooklyn, New York (2003); U.S. Dep't of Justice Office of the Inspector General, The September 11 Detainees: A Review of the Treatment of Aliens Held on Immigration Charges in Connection with the Investigation of the September 11 Attacks (2003).

63. *Awadallah III*, 202 F. Supp. 2d at 59–60.

64. *Awadallah II*, 202 F. Supp. 2d at 23.

65. *Id.*

66. *Id.*

67. *Id.*

68. *Id.*

69. *Id.*

70. *Id.* at 24.

71. *Id.*

72. *Id.*

73. *Id.*

74. *Id.*

75. *Id.*

76. *Id.*

77. *Id.*

78. *Id.* at 24–25; *see also supra* note 62 (providing reports that detail the abusive conditions in nearby detention facilities).

79. *Id.* at 25.

80. *Id.*

81. *Id.*

82. *Id.*

83. *Awadallah III*, 202 F. Supp. 2d 55, 58 (S.D.N.Y. 2002), *rev'd*, 349 F.3d 42 (2d Cir. 2003).

84. *Id.* at 61.

85. *Id.* at 60.

86. *Id.* at 58.

87. *Awadallah II*, 202 F. Supp. 2d at 35.

88. *Awadallah III*, 202 F. Supp. 2d at 59.

89. *Id.*

90. *Awadallah II*, 202 F. Supp. 2d at 35–36.

91. *Id.*

92. *Id.*

93. *Awadallah I*, 173 F. Supp. 2d 186, 188 (S.D.N.Y. 2001).

94. *Awadallah III*, 202 F. Supp. 2d at 59.

95. Pam Louwagie, *Man Arrested in Minneapolis for Terrorism Investigation Faces Many Possible Outcomes*, Minneapolis Star Tribune, *at* www.startribune.com/stories/462/4300773.html (last visited Jan. 6, 2004).

96. *See* United States v. Al-Marri, 230 F. Supp. 2d 535, 537 (S.D.N.Y. 2002); *In re* Application of the United States for a Material Witness Warrant, 213 F. Supp. 2d 287, 300 (S.D.N.Y. 2002); *see also* Louwagie, *supra* note 95, *at* www.startribune .com/stories/462/4300773.html (last visited Jan. 6, 2004); John Riley, *Held Without Charge: Material Witness Law Puts Detainees in Legal Limbo*, N.Y. Newsday, Sept. 18, 2002, at A6; Rachel L. Swarns, *Oregon Muslims Protest Month-long Detention Without a Charge*, N.Y. Times, Apr. 20, 2003, at A16.

97. 18 U.S.C. § 3144 (2003).

98. *See* United States v. Salerno, 481 U.S. 739, 748–50 (1987); Terry v. Ohio, 392 U.S. 1, 22 (1968); Stacey M. Studnicki, *Material Witness Detention: Justice Served or Denied?*, 40 Wayne L. Rev. 1533, 1559–60 (1994).

99. *See* Hurtado v. United States, 410 U.S. 578, 589–90 (1973) (holding that confinement of material witnesses was not unconstitutional under the Fifth or Thirteenth Amendments); Stein v. New York, 346 U.S. 156, 184 (1953) (stating that one may be detained without bail as a material witness because "[t]he duty to disclose knowledge of crime rests upon all citizens").

100. 18 U.S.C. § 3144.

101. *Id.*

102. *Awadallah III*, 202 F. Supp. 2d 55, 65 (S.D.N.Y. 2002), *rev'd*, 349 F.3d 42 (2d Cir. 2003).

103. *See* Riley, *supra* note 96 (providing examples of material witnesses being held without charge for long periods of time). A grand jury can be in session for eighteen months with the possibility of an extension of up to six months. Fed. R. Crim. P. 6(g).

104. Branzburg v. Hayes, 408 U.S. 665, 687 n.23 (1972).

105. Swarns, *supra* note 96.

106. *See* Padilla *ex rel.* Newman v. Rumsfeld, 243 F. Supp. 2d 42, 46 (S.D.N.Y. 2003) (noting that the government admitted, in a declaration by Defense Intelligence Agency Director Lowell E. Jacoby, that allowing Padilla access to counsel could confound the government's attempt "to bring psychological pressure to bear upon Padilla, and could compromise the government's interrogation techniques"), *aff'd in part and rev'd in part*, No. 03-2235, 2003 WL 22965085 (2d Cir. Dec. 18, 2003); Swarns, *supra* note 96.

107. *In re* Application of the United States for Material Witness Warrant, Material Witness No. 38, 214 F. Supp. 2d 356 (S.D.N.Y. 2002).

108. Jane Fritsch, *Grateful Egyptian Is Freed as U.S. Terror Case Fizzles*, N.Y. Times, Jan. 18, 2002, at A1.

109. *In re* Application of the United States for Material Witness Warrant, Material Witness No. 38, 214 F. Supp. 2d at 358.

110. *Id.*

111. *Id.*

112. *Id.*

113. *Id.*

114. *Id.*

115. *Id.*

116. *Id.*

117. *Id.* at 358–59.

118. *Id.* at 358.

119. Riley, *supra* note 96.

120. *Id.* The FBI agent told Higazy that if he did not change his story, he would never pass the polygraph test, and that the FBI would make his family's life "hell." *Id.; see also In re* Application of the United States for Material Witness Warrant, Material Witness No. 38, 214 F. Supp. 2d at 360 (noting that the polygraph tester had used threats to elicit a confession from Higazy).

121. *In re* Application of the United States for Material Witness Warrant, Material Witness No. 38, 214 F. Supp. 2d at 359.

122. *Id.*

123. *Id.*

124. *Id.*

125. *Id.*

126. *Id.* (Higazy filed a related civil lawsuit for damages against the federal agents and the private security guards. Higazy v. Millennium Hotel and Resorts, 2004 WL 219 7083 (S.D.N.Y. 2004)).

127. *See infra* notes 299–326 and accompanying text.

128. 213 F. Supp. 2d 287 (S.D.N.Y. 2002).

129. *Awadallah I*, 173 F. Supp. 2d 186, 192 (S.D.N.Y. 2001).

130. *Awadallah II*, 202 F. Supp. 2d 17, 55 (S.D.N.Y. 2002).

131. *Awadallah III*, 202 F. Supp. 2d 55, 82 (S.D.N.Y. 2002), *rev'd*, 349 F.3d 42 (2d Cir. 2003).

132. *Id.* at 80 n.30.

133. *Awadallah IV*, 202 F. Supp. 2d 82, 109 (S.D.N.Y. 2002), *rev'd*, 349 F.3d 42.

134. *Id.*

135. *Awadallah*, 349 F.3d at 75.

136. 213 F. Supp. 2d 287 (S.D.N.Y. 2002).

137. *Id.* at 300.

138. Stacey M. Studnicki and John P. Apol, *Witness Detention and Intimidation: The History and Future of Material Witness Law*, 76 St. John's L. Rev. 483, 485 (2002).

139. *Id.* at 487–489; *see also* Laurie L. Levinson, *Detention, Material Witnesses, and the War on Terrorism*, 35 Loy. L. A. L. Rev. 1217, 1222 (2002) (discussing the evolution of material witness detentions).

140. Studnicki, *supra* note 98, at 1542–44.

141. *Id.* at 1543–44.

142. James W. Moore et al., 8B Moore's Federal Practice, ¶ 46.11 (1978). This is not the only policy behind such statutes. Often material witnesses in criminal proceedings face physical danger from the accused, and their detention is for their protection. Studnicki, *supra* note 98, at 1544.

143. Judiciary Act of 1789, ch. 20 § 33, 1 Stat. 91 (1st Cong., I Sess. 1789).

144. Studnicki, *supra* note 98, at 1536–37.

145. The Judiciary Act of August 8, 1846, ch. 98, § 7, 9 Stat. 73 (29th Cong., 1st Sess., 1846).

146. *Id.* In 1925, the Judiciary Act, as amended in 1846, was codified in 28 U.S.C. §§ 657 and 659. In 1946, sections 657 and 659 of the United States Code were incorporated into Federal Rule of Criminal Procedure 46(b). The rule was intended to be a restatement of existing law at the time, namely 18 U.S.C. §§ 657, 659 (1946). Advisory Committee on Rules of Criminal Procedure, Notes to the Rules of Criminal Procedure for the District Courts of the United States (March 1945) at 275. Rule 46(b) originally provided, "If it appears by affidavit that the testimony of a person is material in any criminal proceeding and if it is shown that it may become impracticable to secure his presence by subpoena, the court . . . may require him to give bail for his appearance. . . . If the person fails to give bail the court . . . may commit him to the custody of the marshal." Fed. R. Crim. P. 46(b) (1946). After their incorporation into Rule 46(b), Congress repealed sections 657 and 659 in 1948. Studnicki and Apol, *supra* note 138, at 490. In so doing, Congress destroyed the only explicit authority for courts to arrest and detain material witnesses. *Id.* However, Congress corrected this in 1984 when it passed amendments to the Bail Reform Act. *Id.* at 492.

147. Bail Reform Act of 1966, Pub. L. No. 89-465, 3(a), 80 Stat. 214, 216 (codified as amended in scattered sections of 18 U.S.C.). This Act created 18 U.S.C. § 3149 to govern material witness detentions, which was later repealed and amended by 18 U.S.C. § 3144 (1984).

148. *Federal Bail Reform: Hearings before Subcomm. No. 5 of the House Comm. on the Judiciary*, 89th Cong. 15–16 (1965).

149. 18 U.S.C. § 3149 (1966).

150. Bail Reform Act of 1966 § 3(a), 80 Stat. at 216.

151. Bail Reform Act of 1984, Pub. L. No. 98-473, § 203(a), 98 Stat. 1976, 1984, 18 U.S.C. § 3144 (1984).

152. Studnicki and Apol, *supra* note 138, at 494.

153. S. Rep. No. 98-225, at 28 (1983), *reprinted in* 1984 U.S.C.C.A.N. 3182, 3211.

154. *See id.* ("[T]he committee stresses that whenever possible, the depositions of such witnesses should be obtained so that they may be released from custody.").

155. *See supra* note 99 (listing cases that have challenged the practice but on grounds other than the Fourth Amendment).

156. *See* Studnicki and Apol, *supra* note 138, at 510 (noting the absence of litigation on the issue).

157. *See* Riley, *supra* note 96 (noting that after September 11, the Justice Department began to use section 3144 more frequently in grand jury investigations).

158. 449 F.2d 933 (9th Cir. 1971).

159. *Id.* at 934.

160. *Id.* at 935.

161. *Id.*

162. *Id.*

163. *Id.*

164. *Id.*

165. *Id.*

166. *Id.*

167. *Id.* at 939 (quoting 18 U.S.C. 3771 (repealed 1988)).

168. *Id.* at 940 (quoting Fed. R. Crim. P. 2 (1971)) (alteration in original).

169. *Id.*

170. *Id.* (citing Fed. R. Crim. P. 20 advisory committee's note (renumbered 17), Fed. R. Crim. P., Preliminary Draft 107 (1943)).

171. *Id.*

172. *Id.* at 941.

173. *Id.*

174. *Id.* at 941–42.

175. *Id.* at 943 (emphasis added).

176. *Id.*

177. *Id.* at 944–45.

178. *Awadallah III*, 202 F. Supp. 2d 55, 62 (S.D.N.Y. 2002), *rev'd*, 349 F.3d 42 (2d Cir. 2003).

179. *Id.*

180. *Id.* (citing Castillo v. United States, 530 U.S. 120, 124 (2000)).

181. *Id.* at 76.

182. 18 U.S.C. § 3144 (2003) (emphasis added).

183. *Awadallah III*, 202 F. Supp. 2d at 62.

184. *Id.*

185. *Id.* at 63.

186. *Id.*

187. *Id.*

188. *Id.* (citing Fed. R. Crim. P. 6(e)(2)).

189. *Id.*

190. *Id.*

191. *See id.* at 63–64.

192. *Id.* at 63 (citing 18 U.S.C. § 3142(2002)).

193. 18 U.S.C. § 3142 (emphasis added).

194. *Awadallah III*, 202 F. Supp. 2d at 63–64.

195. 18 U.S.C. § 3142(g)(1)-(4).

196. *Awadallah III*, 202 F. Supp. 2d at 64.

197. *Id.*

198. *See id.* at 64–65.

199. *Id.* at 66. The Bail Reform Act of 1984 is found at 18 U.S.C. §§ 3141-56.

200. *Id.*

201. *Id.* (citing 18 U.S.C. § 3141(a)–(b) (2002)).

202. *Id.* at 66–67.

203. 18 U.S.C. § 3146 (2002).

204. *Awadallah III*, 202 F. Supp. 2d at 67.

205. *Id.*

206. *Id.* at 68.

207. *Id.* at 69 (citing *The Treatment of a Material Witness in Criminal Proceedings: Hearings Before the Subcomm. on Improvements in the Judiciary and the Subcomm. on Constitutional Rights of the S. Comm. on the Judiciary*, 89th Cong. 1-322 (1965) (statement of Peter T. Blake et al.) [hereinafter *Senate Hearings*]). In regard to material witnesses, the report observed, "It is strange that a system of laws such as ours which exalts personal right and individual liberties should even permit the incarceration . . . of one who is not even suspected of having violated those laws." *Senate Hearings*, *supra* at 300.

208. *Awadallah III*, 202 F. Supp. 2d at 69–70.

209. *Id.* at 71.

210. *Id.*

211. *Id.* at 65 (citing Fed. R. Crim. P. 15; Fed. R. Crim. P. 46). Rule 46 addresses release prior to and during trial and specifically references 18 U.S.C. §§ 3142 and 3144. *See* Fed. R. Crim. P. 46.

212. 18 U.S.C. § 3144.

213. *Awadallah III*, 202 F. Supp. 2d at 65.

214. *Id.*

215. *Id.*

216. *Id.*

217. *Id.* at 65–66.

218. *Id.* at 71 (citing 449 F.2d 933 (9th Cir. 1971)).

219. *Id.*

220. *Id.*

221. *Id.* (quoting United States v. Henderson, 961 F.2d 880, 882 (9th Cir. 1992)).

222. *Id.* at 74 (citing Bacon, 449 F.2d at 940).

223. *Id.* (quoting Fed. R. Crim. P. 54) (internal citations omitted).

224. *Id.*

225. *Id.* at 76–77.

226. *Id.* at 77 (citing Tennessee v. Garner, 471 U.S. 1, 8 (1985)).

227. *Id.* (quoting Branzburg v. Hayes, 408 U.S. 665, 701 (1972)).

228. *Id.* at 78.

229. 18 U.S.C. § 3144.

230. *Awadallah III*, 202 F. Supp. 2d at 78.

231. The language of Rule 15(a) was changed in 2002 for "stylistic" purposes only as part of an overall rewording of the Federal Rules of Criminal Procedure "to make them more easily understood and to make style and terminology consistent throughout the rules." Fed. R. Crim. P. 15 (2002) advisory committee's note.

232. *Awadallah III*, 202 F. Supp. 2d at 78.

233. *Id.* at 77.

234. *Id.*

235. *Id.* at 78–79.

236. 392 U.S. 1 (1968).

237. *Awadallah III*, 202 F. Supp. 2d at 78 (quoting *Terry*, 392 U.S. at 20, 22).

238. *Id.* at 79.

239. *Id.* (quoting United States v. Salerno, 481 U.S. 739, 755 (1987)).

240. 213 F. Supp. 2d 287, 300 (S.D.N.Y. 2002).

241. *Id.* at 288.

242. *Id.*

243. *Id.*

244. *Id.*

245. *Id.*

246. *Id.* at 291.

247. *Id.*

248. *Id.*

249. *Id.* at 297.

250. *See id.* at 292–93, 297.

251. *Id.* at 292 (quoting Lorillard v. Pons, 434 U.S. 575, 580 (1978)).

252. *Id.*

253. *Id.* at 290.

254. *Id.* at 293.

255. *Id.* (citing 18 U.S.C. §§ 3321-34 (2000)).

256. *Id.* (emphasis added).

257. *Id.* at 296.

258. *Id.* at 293 (citing Post v. United States, 161 U.S. 583, 585 (1896); Thompson v. United States, 319 F.2d 665 (2d Cir. 1963)).

259. *Id.* at 293.

260. *Id.* at 292.

261. *Id.* at 294.

262. *Id.*

263. *Id.* (citing *In re* De Jesus Berrios, 706 F.2d 355, 358 (1st Cir. 1983); United States v. Oliver, 683 F.2d 224, 231 (7th Cir. 1982); Bacon v. United States, 449 F.2d 933, 943 (9th Cir. 1971)).

264. *Id.*

265. 18 U.S.C. § 3144.

266. *See supra* notes 213–215 and accompanying text.

267. *In re* Material Witness Warrant, 213 F. Supp. 2d at 301–02 (emphasis added) (internal citations omitted).

268. *Id.* at 296 (emphasis added).

269. *Id.* at 302.

270. *Id.*

271. *Id.* at 298.

272. *Id.*

273. *See supra* note 232 and accompanying text (discussing *Awadallah III's* analysis of Rule 15).

274. *In re* Material Witness Warrant, 213 F. Supp. 2d at 298–99.

275. *Id.* (quoting Stein v. New York, 346 U.S. 156 (1953) (internal quotation marks omitted)).

276. *Id.* at 299 (citing Allen v. Nix, 55 F.3d 414, 415 (8th Cir. 1995); United States *ex rel.* Allen v. LaVallee, 411 F.2d 241, 243 (2d Cir. 1969); United States *ex rel.* Glinton v. Denno, 339 F.2d 872 (2d Cir. 1964); Stone v. Holzberger, 807 F. Supp. 1325, 1336–37 (S.D. Ohio 1992), *aff'd*, 23 F.3d 408, (6th Cir. 1994)).

277. *Id.* at 300 (citing Arnsberg v. United States, 757 F.2d 971, 976–77 (9th Cir. 1985); *In re* Grand Jury Subpoena United States, Koecher, 755 F.2d 1022, 1024 n.2 (2d Cir. 1985); *In re* De Jesus Berrios, 706 F.2d 355, 357–58 (1st Cir. 1983); United States v. Oliver, 683 F.2d 224, 231 (7th Cir. 1982); United States v. McVeigh, 940 F. Supp. 1541, 1562 (D. Colo. 1996)).

278. *See* Rachel V. Stevens, United States Department of Justice v. Center for National Security Studies: *Keeping the USA PATRIOT Act in Check One Material Witness at a Time*, 81 N.C. L. Rev. 2157, 2173 n.85 (2003) (noting the conflict between *Awadallah III* and *In re Material Witness Warrant*).

279. *Awadallah III*, 202 F. Supp. 2d 55, 76 (S.D.N.Y. 2002).

280. *In re* Material Witness Warrant, 213 F. Supp. 2d at 300.

281. *Awadallah III*, 202 F. Supp. 2d at 72.

282. *In re* Material Witness Warrant, 213 F. Supp. 2d at 291.

283. *Id.* at 297. Chief Judge Mukasey's reliance on legislative history in this case belies his typical reluctance to use such history as an interpretive tool. *See* Beeson v. Fishkill Corr. Facility, 28 F. Supp. 2d 884, 891 (S.D.N.Y. 1998).

284. *Awadallah III*, 202 F. Supp. 2d at 77.

285. *Id.*

286. *See In re* Material Witness Warrant, 213 F. Supp. 2d at 301–02.

287. *Id.* at 297.

288. *Id.* at 302.

289. *See In re* Material Witness Warrant, 213 F. Supp. 2d at 297.

290. *Id.* at 296.

291. INS v. St. Cyr, 533 U.S. 289, 299–300 (2001) (citations omitted); *see also* Edward J. DeBartolo Corp. v. Fla. Gulf Coast Bldg. & Constr. Trades Council, 485 U.S. 568, 575 (1988) (noting that this canon of construction has been used by the courts for so long it is "beyond debate").

292. United States v. Awadallah, 349 F.3d 42, 55, 60 (2d Cir. 2003).

293. *Id.* at 59.

294. *Id.* at 64.

295. *Id.* at 45, 47–48.

296. *Id.* at 48 (citing *Awadallah III*, 202 F. Supp. 2d 55, 59 n.4 (S.D.N.Y. 2002), *rev'd*, 349 F.3d 42).

297. *Awadallah III*, 202 F. Supp. 2d at 60.

298. *See supra* note 62.

299. *Awadallah*, 349 F.3d at 52–53.

300. *See id.*

301. *Id.* at 53.

302. *Id.*

303. *Id.* at 54–55.

304. *Id.* at 54 (citing S. Rep. No. 98-225, at 28 n.98 (1983), *reprinted in* 1984 U.S.C.C.A.N. 3182, 3211).

305. *Id.* at 54–55.

306. *Awadallah III*, 202 F. Supp. 2d 55, 78 (S.D.N.Y. 2002), *rev'd*, 349 F.3d 42.

307. *Awadallah*, 349 F.3d at 59.

308. *Id.* at 59–60.

309. *Id.*

310. *Id.* at 55.

311. *Id.* (quoting Harris v. United States, 536 U.S. 545, 555 (2002)).

312. *Id.* at 64.

313. *Id.* at 63.

314. S. Rep. No. 98-225, at 28 (1983), *reprinted in* 1984 U.S.C.C.A.N. 3182, 3211.

315. *Id.* (emphasis added).

316. Bail Reform Act of 1966, Pub. L. No. 89-465, § 2, 80 Stat. 214, 214.

317. *Awadallah*, 349 F.3d at 53–55.

318. *Id.* at 56–58 (citing New York v. O'Neill, 359 U.S. 1 (1959); Stein v. New York, 346 U.S. 156 (1953), *overruled in part on other grounds*, Jackson v. Denno, 378 U.S. 368 (1964); Barry v. United States *ex rel.* Cunningham, 279 U.S. 597 (1929); United States *ex rel.* Allen v. La Vallee, 411 F.2d 241 (2d Cir. 1969); United States *ex rel.* Glinton v. Denno, 309 F.2d 543 (2d Cir. 1962) [hereinafter *Glinton I*]; United States *ex rel.* Glinton v. Denno, 339 F.2d 872 (2d Cir. 1964) [hereinafter *Glinton II*]).

319. *See Stein*, 346 U.S. 156 (upholding the voluntariness of a confession obtained during a custodial interrogation); *Barry*, 279 U.S. 597 (finding that a Senate committee has the power to issue a warrant of attachment to compel testimony before the Senate without first issuing a subpoena to testify).

320. *See O'Neill*, 359 U.S. at 6–7.

321. *Awadallah*, 349 F.3d at 57 n.11.

322. Glinton II, 339 F.2d at 874; United States *ex rel.* Allen v. Murphy, 295 F.2d 385, 386 (2d Cir. 1961); Allen, 411 F.2d at 242–43.

323. Awadallah, 349 F.3d at 47–48.

324. Louwagie, *supra* note 95, *at* www.startribune.com/stories/462/4300773.html (last visited Jan. 6, 2004).

325. Allen, 411 F.2d at 244 (citing People v. Perez, 90 N.E.2d 40 (N.Y. 1949)).

326. *Awadallah*, 349 F.3d at 57 n.10.

327. *Id.* at 75.

328. *See* Louwagie, *supra* note 95, *at* www.startribune.com/stories/462/4300773 .html (last visited Jan. 6, 2004).

329. *In re* Material Witness Warrant, 213 F. Supp. 2d 287, 301–02 (S.D.N.Y. 2002).

330. *Awadallah*, 349 F.3d at 59–62.

331. *See supra* notes 107–126 and accompanying text (summarizing the facts of Higazy's detention).

332. *See supra* note 62.

333. *Awadallah*, 349 F.3d at 59.

6

Constitutional Safeguards after 9/11

Louis Fisher

Following the terrorist attacks of 9/11, the Bush administration turned to a number of novel techniques of law enforcement: authorizing the creation of military tribunals, concealing the names of hundreds of detainees, holding individuals under the material witness statute without seeking information from them, designating suspects "enemy combatants" without charging them with a crime or permitting access to an attorney, and closing deportation proceedings to the press and the public.

In an age fraught with terrorist attacks, a call for procedural safeguards may seem an impractical luxury. However, without adhering to due process, constitutional government cannot exist. Justice Frankfurter reminded us that "the history of liberty has largely been the history of observance of procedural safeguards."[1] Justice Robert H. Jackson once remarked that he would rather live under Soviet law enforced by American procedures than under American law enforced by Soviet procedures.[2]

The administration justifies its actions as "emergency" measures needed to confront a national crisis. Thus far, executive power has met with few checks from the other branches. Federal courts have displayed only a slight willingness to monitor procedures (or lack thereof) for fairness and constitutionality. Congress has largely supported administration initiatives, including the USA PATRIOT Act. The resistance that has emerged comes primarily from citizens, private organizations, and the press. Resistance at that level will start to move elected leaders.

ARAB AMERICANS AND MUSLIMS

Immediately after 9/11, President Bush—standing with Mayor Rudy Giuliani and Governor George Pataki—cautioned that "our Nation must be mindful that there are thousands of Arab Americans who live in New York City who love their flag just as much as the three of us do."[3] During a visit to the Islamic Center in Washington, D.C., he credited Muslims in America with making "an incredibly valuable contribution to our country. Muslims are doctors, lawyers, law professors, members of the military, entrepreneurs, shopkeepers, moms and dads. And they need to be treated with respect. In our anger and emotion, our fellow Americans must treat each other with respect."[4] Bush emphasized that the war in Afghanistan was not a war against Islam or against the Arab world.[5]

Congress also moved quickly to voice support for the Muslim and Arab American communities. Three days after 9/11, the House passed a concurrent resolution condemning bigotry and violence against Arab Americans, American Muslims, and Americans from South Asia. Rep. George Gekas (R-Pa.) said that part of the purpose of the resolution was to avoid repeating "the insidious events that took place after Pearl Harbor with respect to the treatment of Japanese-American citizens."[6] Rep. Dave Bonior (D-Mich.) defended "the rights of every American of every heritage and faith to live and worship with safety and confidence and pride."[7] The resolution passed Congress with overwhelming support in both chambers.[8]

The USA PATRIOT Act includes Section 102, which condemns discrimination against Arab and Muslim Americans, stating that these groups "play a vital role in our Nation and are entitled to nothing less than the full rights of every American." The statutory language condemns acts of violence against Arab and Muslim Americans and states that anyone who commits acts of violence against these communities "should be punished by the full extent of the law."

Notwithstanding those expressions of support, clearly the brunt of injustices after 9/11 have fallen on the Arab American and Muslim communities. A few examples will suffice. Dr. Al Bader al-Hamzi, a thirty-four-year-old radiologist from Saudi Arabia, was arrested at his townhouse in San Antonio the day after the September 11 terrorist attacks. He was held for twelve days before he was permitted to answer questions put to him by authorities. On September 24, he was finally released. The government brought no charges against him.[9] Supposedly, suspects are held to obtain information about terrorism, but many of them were detained for weeks and months without ever being interrogated by the Federal Bureau of Intelligence (FBI) or the Immigration and Naturalization Service (INS).

Ali Al-Maqtari, born in Yemen, came to the United States with the hope of becoming a French teacher. Four days after the September 11 attacks, he arrived at Fort Campbell, Kentucky, to drop off his American wife, who was reporting for active duty with the U.S. Army. He was ordered out of his car and detained for two months by the INS in Mason, Tennessee. He appeared before a Senate subcommittee to explain what happened to him.[10]

On September 12, 2001, Hady Hassan Omar was placed in jail because the FBI was convinced he had some connection to al Qaeda. Born in Egypt, he lived in Fort Smith, Arkansas, with his American wife and baby daughter. A deputy from the local sheriff's office asked him to come to the station for a few questions. He was then held in captivity for seventy-three days, some of it in solitary confinement, until he became suicidal. He was released, but legal expenses left the couple broke and he was fired from his job. The government never presented charges against him.[11]

Beginning in December 2002, the Justice Department required men from certain countries (predominantly Muslim) to register with the INS, be fingerprinted and photographed, and respond to questions. Exceptions were made for certain categories, such as permanent residents and men with green cards. Failure to register risked deportation. When the men showed up, hundreds were handcuffed and detained for days because their student or work visas had expired. Some of the men lacked proper papers because their application for permanent residency had been delayed for years in INS proceedings.[12] In many cases, the registrants were denied their right to have counsel present for the questioning.[13] Beyond the harassment of the Arab American and Muslim communities, the policy of registration and detention seems to have little bearing on the war against terrorism. Undocumented terrorists are unlikely to show up at an INS office to be registered.

Slowly, Americans are starting to shed some stereotypes about the Arab and Muslim communities. A large number of Arabs in the United States are not Muslim. They may be Christian, as from Lebanon, or belong to other religions. Muslims need not be Arabs. They can come from South Asia or be homegrown African Americans. Similarly, people from the Middle East are not necessarily Arab. They can be Turks, Iranians, Kurds, or come from other ethnic groups. Neither Islam nor "Arab" are monoliths. The categories contain many complicated subsets.

MILITARY TRIBUNALS

The executive branch claimed exclusive authority to issue President Bush's military order of November 13, 2001, authorizing the creation of military

tribunals to try terrorists. The administration did not touch base with anyone on Capitol Hill (even the Judiciary Committees), nor did it consult with
experts in the judge advocate general's office in the Pentagon. To justify the
Bush order, the administration cited *Ex parte Quirin* (1942) as a solid legal
precedent. In that case, a unanimous Supreme Court upheld the use of a military tribunal for eight Nazi saboteurs. Bush clearly modeled his order on a
1942 proclamation by President Franklin D. Roosevelt creating a tribunal to
try the Germans.[14] However, there is a world of difference between the
1942 precedent and the Bush initiative.

First, the FDR proclamation targeted a subgroup of eight specific individuals. The Bush order covers "any individual who is not a United States citizen" (about eighteen million inside U.S. borders) who gave assistance to the
September 11 terrorists. Any noncitizen, including resident aliens, is at risk of
being detained and tried by a military tribunal, perhaps because they donated
to what they thought was a legitimate charitable organization, which the government later determined to be a front for the al Qaeda. Why did Bush limit
his military order to noncitizens? His legal advisers may have convinced him
that U.S. citizens, under *Ex parte Milligan* (1866), are entitled to be tried in
civil courts when they are open and operating.[15] Imagine how different the
public reaction would have been if Bush had given military tribunals jurisdiction over everyone—citizen or noncitizen—who gave assistance to the terrorists.

Second, compare the treatment of the eight Germans in 1942 with the actions by the Justice Department after 9/11. The Germans were charged with
four crimes, assigned defense counsel, tried in a military tribunal, and went
to the Supreme Court to challenge the jurisdiction of the tribunal. Several individuals arrested after 9/11 have been designated "enemy combatants." As
such, they have not been charged, given access to defense counsel, or tried in
any court, civil or military.

The Court's decision in *Ex parte Quirin* is far from an attractive precedent.
Instead of letting the War Department handle the military trial, subject to procedures spelled out in the statutory Articles of War and the published *Manual
for Courts-Martial*, procedures were made up as the trial went along. The Justices were poorly prepared to hear the case. The briefs were dated the same
day that oral argument began. There was only a cursory district court decision, issued the evening before, and no action yet by the D.C. Circuit.[16] The
Court handed down a short per curiam on July 31, but without any legal reasoning.[17]

Three months later, the Court released a full opinion, calling the German
saboteurs "unlawful combatants" who could legitimately be tried by military
tribunal, even if they were U.S. citizens. While the Justices worked on the full

opinion, six of the eight Germans were executed. Chief Justice Stone had his hands full trying to write the opinion for the Court without judicial unity being marred by dissents or concurrences.[18] Constitutional scholar Edward S. Corwin dismissed the final opinion as "little more than a ceremonious detour to a predetermined end."[19] Justice Frankfurter later said that "the *Quirin* experience was not a happy precedent."[20]

The conduct of the military trial in 1942 so offended Secretary of War Henry L. Stimson that he intervened forcefully three years later, when another tribunal was established to try two more saboteurs who had arrived from Germany. Unlike the military order of July 2, 1942, this time President Roosevelt did not name the members of the tribunal or the counsel for the prosecution and defense. Instead, he empowered the commanding generals, under the supervision of the secretary of war, "to appoint military commissions for the trial of such persons." Moreover, the trial record would not go directly to the president, as it did in 1942. The review would be processed within the judge advocate general's office.[21] Unlike 1942, Attorney General Francis Biddle and Judge Advocate General Myron Cramer did not act as prosecutors. The trial took place not in Washington, D.C., but at Governors Island, New York City.[22]

Bush's military order of November 13, 2001, covers any individual "not a United States citizen" that the president determines there is "reason to believe" (i) "is or was a member of the organization known as al Qaeda," (ii) "has engaged in, aided or abetted, or conspired to commit acts of international terrorism, or acts in preparation therefore, that have caused, threaten to cause, or have as their aim to cause, injury to or adverse effects on the United States, its citizens, national security, foreign policy, or economy," or (iii) has "knowingly harbored one of more individuals described in subparagraphs (i) and (ii)." What process is used to "determine" a terrorist or a terrorist organization? The president merely announces the result and forces the target to mount a defense.

USA PATRIOT ACT

The USA PATRIOT Act, enacted on October 26, 2001, strengthens the power of the administration to deter and punish terrorists. Yet the statute goes far beyond the threat of terrorism by giving the government broad new powers to conduct any criminal investigation. Increasing the power of the executive branch—especially over law enforcement—inevitably places at risk some constitutional rights and liberties. This is especially the case for legislation, such as the Patriot Act, that shot through Congress at great speed without the customary care and deliberation of legislative hearings, committee markups, and floor debate.[23]

The House Judiciary Committee held one hearing on September 24, conducted a markup with amendments offered and agreed to, and issued a lengthy committee report on H.R. 2975.[24] This bill, reflecting bipartisan support, passed the committee by a vote of thirty-six to zero and rejected some of the extreme measures advocated by the administration. However, on the floor, the House acted under a closed rule to prohibit amendments, except an amendment in the nature of a substitute consisting of the text of a new bill, H.R. 3108, that few members had seen. A motion to recommit the bill to House Judiciary and have it report back clearer definitions of surveillance procedures was voted down. The House then accepted the substitute bill that few lawmakers had read, much less studied.

On the Senate side, Senator Feingold remarked that there was not "a single moment of markup or vote in the Judiciary Committee."[25] He prepared three amendments for floor consideration, but each was tabled rather than voted on the merits. Senate Majority Leader Tom Daschle (D-S.D.) opposed all amendments, urging his colleagues to join him in tabling the first Feingold amendment and "every other amendment that is offered."[26] When the House acted on the bill that became the Patriot Act (H.R. 3162), it did so under suspension of the rules, a procedure that prohibits amendments. The final bill adopted a four-year sunset for some of the surveillance procedures.

Many of the provisions of the Patriot Act had been considered in previous years and rejected. For example, Section 219 authorizes nationwide service of search warrants in terrorism investigations. A single judge, having authorized the first warrant, may grant future warrants in other jurisdictions. The warrant is not limited to a particular locality. It applies to any district "in which activities related to the terrorism may have occurred." The purpose is to build expertise and accountability in a single judge rather than having to bring judges in other jurisdictions up-to-speed. Law enforcement gains a benefit, but many defendants lack the funds to hire attorneys in distant states.

Section 206 provides for roving wiretaps under the Foreign Intelligence Surveillance Act (FISA). This provision allows surveillance to follow a person, thus avoiding the need for a separate court order that identifies each telephone company every time the target of investigation changes phones. One of the most controversial provisions appears in Section 218, which changed the FISA requirement that had allowed surveillance only if "the purpose" is to obtain foreign intelligence information. The new language is "a significant purpose." Originally, Congress wanted to maintain separation between wiretaps conducted by the intelligence community and criminal investigations pursued by law enforcement officers. For criminal investigations, a wiretap requires both probable cause that a crime has been committed and an authorizing order from a federal judge. Wiretaps for intelligence are conducted with a lower standard, and the information obtained should be used only for foreign intelligence.

There have been two major challenges to the Patriot Act. On July 22, 2003, the House adopted an amendment to prohibit the use of appropriated funds to seek a delay under Section 213 of the Patriot Act. This section, called "sneak and peek," allows the government to conduct searches without immediately notifying the occupant of a private residence. The section permits a delay in giving notice of the execution of a warrant. The amendment, offered by Rep. C. L. "Butch" Otter (R-Idaho), passed the House by the lopsided vote of 309 to 118. Almost all of the Democrats (195 to 4) voted for it, joined by roughly half (113 to 114) of the Republicans.[27] Responding in part to this House vote, Attorney General John Ashcroft launched a nationwide publicity campaign to defend the Patriot Act.[28]

The other challenge comes from the grassroots. Some municipalities have passed resolutions urging local law enforcement officials and others to refuse requests under the Patriot Act that they believe violate constitutional rights.[29] Three states (Alaska, Hawaii, and Vermont) and 150 local governments have passed resolutions condemning all or part of the statute.[30] One of the provisions that have drawn attention is Section 215, which amends the business records section of FISA. Prior to the Patriot Act, federal authorities could seek a FISA court order for access to hotel, airline, storage locker, or car rental business records. The businesses covered by those orders were bound to silence. Section 215 broadens federal authority so that a FISA order may cover any tangible item, no matter who holds it, and provides that "no person shall disclose to any other person (other than those persons necessary to produce the tangible things under this section) that the Federal Bureau of Investigation has sought or obtained tangible things under this section."[31]

Some librarians, offended that the government might try to examine the requests for books and library materials by members of the public, took the initiative to shred the request slips. Libraries posted warning signs about the business records provision in the Patriot Act.[32] The American Library Association, with 64,000 members, formally denounced the Patriot Act provision and urged Congress to repeal it. Emily Sheketoff, executive director of the ALA's Washington office, regarded the statute as dangerous: "I read murder mysteries—does that make me a murderer? I read spy stories—does that mean I'm a spy? There's no clear link between a person's intellectual pursuits and their actions."[33] As explained in the concluding section of this paper, Attorney General Ashcroft announced in August 2003 that the government has not used Section 215 against libraries.

CLOSING DEPORTATION PROCEEDINGS

After 9/11, the INS began to close deportation proceedings to the press and the public. The government used this period to question a number of noncitizens, primarily young men of Arab or Muslim background. Rabih Haddad, cofounder of a Muslim charity in Illinois, was held for nine months because the government suspected that he had supplied money to terrorist organizations. He was finally able to testify at an open hearing after a federal judge ordered the Justice Department to either give him an open hearing or release him.[34] Several court decisions found that the government's interest in closing these proceedings was not compelling.[35]

The Sixth Circuit held that there is a First Amendment right of access by the press and the public to deportation proceedings. In his ruling, Judge Damon J. Keith explained why the press had to watch executive branch decisions: "Democracies die behind closed doors."[36] Interestingly, Judge Keith put little faith in judicial oversight: "In our democracy, based on checks and balances, neither the Bill of Rights nor the judiciary can second-guess government's choices. The only safeguard on this extraordinary governmental power is the public, deputizing the press as the guardians of their liberty."[37] Associate Attorney General Jay Stephens admitted that the release of past transcripts on the Haddad immigration proceedings "will not cause irreparable harm to the national security or to the safety of the American people."[38]

In a case that reached the Supreme Court—a district court decision in New Jersey that supported open deportation hearings—the Court stayed the decision pending appeal.[39] The Third Circuit later overturned the district court decision, finding that the tradition of open hearings for criminal and civil trials did not apply to the same extent to administrative hearings. Writing for a 2–1 majority, Chief Judge Edward R. Becker agreed that, procedurally, "deportation hearings and civil trials are practically indistinguishable,"[40] and that openness in deportation hearings offers all the salutary functions recognized in civil and criminal trials: educating the public; promoting public perception of fairness; providing an outlet for community concern, hostility, and emotion; serving to check corrupt practices in court; enhancing the performance of all involved; and discouraging perjury. However, he accepted the Justice Department's argument that open deportation hearings could threaten national security by revealing sources and methods, giving terrorist organizations an opportunity to see which patterns of entry work and which ones fail, and providing other facts that might assist terrorist attacks. Although closed deportation hearings would shield that type of information, nothing prevents the detainees or their attorneys from making that information public.

Chief Judge Becker, agreeing with the newspapers that the government's representations were "to some degree speculative," declined to "lightly second-guess" the concerns of Attorney General Ashcroft about national security. In reversing the district court, Becker said that he was "keenly aware of the dangers presented by deference to the executive branch when constitutional liberties are at stake, especially in times of national crisis, when those liberties are likely in greatest jeopardy."[41]

In a dissent, Judge Anthony J. Scirica noted that deportation hearings have "a consistent history of openness," and that Congress left deportation hearings presumptively open while expressly closing proceedings to exclude aliens. He agreed that judicial deference to the executive branch is appropriate, but not to the extent of "abdicating our responsibilities under the First Amendment."[42] Instead of accepting the INS policy of a blanket closure rule on deportation hearings, Scirica preferred a case-by-case approach to allow immigration judges to weigh the conflicting values between the First Amendment and the government's national security responsibilities. Judge Becker's decision was appealed to the Supreme Court. On May 27, 2003, the Court denied review and refused to hear the case.[43]

CONCEALING IDENTITIES

Another dispute is the government's decision to conceal the identities of hundreds of people arrested after the 9/11 attacks. Over seven hundred individuals were detained on INS charges. Others were held on federal criminal charges, or were detained after a judge issued a material witness warrant to secure their testimony before a grand jury. On August 2, 2002, District Judge Gladys Kessler ordered that most of the names be released within fifteen days.[44] Secret arrests, she said, are "a concept odious to a democratic society."[45] Judge Kessler suspended her order two weeks later to allow the government to appeal her decision to the D.C. Circuit.[46] The Justice Department insisted that disclosing the names of the INS detainees would help al Qaeda determine how the government is conducting its antiterrorist campaign.[47] However, to the extent that cell members are detained, terrorist groups would already be aware of that.

Judge Kessler was reversed by the D.C. Circuit, which held that the names of detainees and their attorneys could be withheld under FOIA's law enforcement exemption.[48] Although FOIA provides for judicial review of all nine exemptions, the D.C. Circuit chose to eliminate, for all practical purposes, the judiciary's role in FOIA cases that raise national security interests. As the majority noted: "We have consistently deferred to executive affidavits predicting harm to the national security, and have found it unwise to undertake searching judicial review."[49] And again: "The court should not second-guess the executive's judgment in this area."[50] Unconvincingly, the majority claims that "in so deferring, we do not abdicate the role of the judiciary."[51]

In a detailed dissent, Judge David Tatel protests the court's "uncritical deference to the government's vague, poorly explained arguments for withholding broad categories of information about the detainees."[52] He accuses the court of neglecting

> another compelling interest at stake in this case: the public's interest in knowing whether the government, in responding to the attacks, is violating the constitutional rights of the hundreds of persons whom it has detained in connection with its terrorism investigation—by, as the plaintiffs allege, detaining them mainly because of their religion or ethnicity, holding them in custody for extended periods without charge, or preventing them from seeking or communicating with legal counsel.[53]

By accepting the government's vague allegations, "and by filling in the gaps of the government's case with its own assumptions about facts absent from the record, this court has converted deference into acquiescence."[54]

MATERIAL WITNESSES AND DETAINEES

Some individuals were held as "material witnesses," a category Congress authorized in 1984 to ensure the testimony of a person that is "material in a criminal proceeding." If it is shown that it "may become impracticable to secure the presence of the person by subpoena," a judicial officer may arrest the person. Release of a material witness "may be delayed for a reasonable period of time."[55] Thus, Congress did not establish a time limit for detention. Although these people are held to provide information for a criminal proceeding, many of them were never called to testify before a grand jury or even give depositions. Nabil Almarabh, a former Boston cab driver from Kuwait, was arrested one week after the 9/11 attacks. As of November 23, 2002, he had been held in custody for 432 days without appearing before a grand jury.[56]

Two federal district judges from New York's Southern District split on the government's authority to detain individuals under the material witness statute. Judge Shira A. Scheindlin compared the statute to the Fourth Amendment, which prohibits unreasonable seizures and requires probable cause for issuing an arrest warrant. She discussed the resentment of eighteenth century Americans to the British general warrants that were used as an unbridled authority to search and seize. To Scheindlin, Congress enacted the statute to carve out "a carefully limited exception to the general rule that an individual's liberty may not be encroached upon unless there is probable cause to believe that he or she has committed a crime."[57] She read the statute to allow a witness to be detained only "until his testimony may be secured by deposition in the pretrial, as opposed to grand jury, context."[58] Thus, federal authorities could not use the statute to detain witnesses for grand jury proceedings because Congress did not grant authority to the government "to imprison an innocent person in order to guarantee that he will testify before a grand jury conducting a criminal investigation."[59]

On the other hand, Judge Michael B. Mukasey held that the material witness statute does apply to grand jury witnesses, and that detaining someone pursuant to a material witness warrant for purposes of grand jury testimony does not violate an individual's Fourth Amendment rights.[60] The duty of citizens to disclose knowledge of a crime means that "one known to be innocent may be detained, in the absence of bail, as a material witness."[61] This ruling would allow the government to hold someone as a material witness for the length of a grand jury (up to eighteen months).

When the meaning of a criminal statute is unclear, as in this case regarding detention during pretrial versus the length of a grand jury, federal judges should opt for an interpretation that is least restrictive on the constitutional rights of liberties. If a more stringent statute is necessary, the burden should be on Congress to write it, subject to judicial review.

As to the nearly seven hundred suspected terrorists captured in Afghanistan and held at a U.S. military base in Guantanamo Bay, a federal judge held that they had no right to bring a case in federal court. Judge Colleen Kollar-Kotelly rejected their lawsuit, which stated that they were held without charges and without access to attorneys or trial dates. Their geographical location, she said, denied them the right to press their interests in U.S. courts. Because writs of habeas corpus "are not available to aliens held outside the sovereign territory of the United States, this court does not have jurisdiction" to hear the case.[62] That decision was upheld by the D.C. Circuit.[63]

These decisions are not persuasive. The United States has an open-ended lease on the facility at Guantanamo Bay. The base is clearly a U.S. facility. It cannot be argued that the executive branch can hold individuals (citizens as well as noncitizens) at Guantanamo Bay, or any other leased facility outside the United States and out of reach of judicial review. To argue that federal courts have no jurisdiction "outside the sovereign territory of the United States" might have some credibility with regard to Afghanistan, but it is a legal fiction for Guantanamo Bay.

A separate effort to represent the interests of detainees in Guantanamo was brought by a coalition of journalists, lawyers, and clergy. They filed suit as "next friend" of the detainees, even though there was nothing in the record to indicate that the detainees supported their petition, or that the coalition even attempted to communicate with the detainees. A federal district court held that the coalition lacked standing to bring the suit.[64] It also ruled that no district court would have jurisdiction over the petition because the detainees are outside the sovereign territory of the United States.[65] On appeal, the Ninth Circuit agreed that the coalition lacked next-friend standing, but ruled that the district court had no jurisdiction to decide whether it or any other federal court could properly entertain the habeas claims.[66]

"ENEMY COMBATANTS"

The Justice Department adopted a variety of procedures for handling terrorist suspects. John Walker Lindh, born in California but captured in Afghanistan among Taliban forces, was tried in civil court. He pled guilty to assisting the Taliban government in Afghanistan. Yasser Esam Hamdi, born in Louisiana and captured in the same Afghan prison rebellion as Lindh, was held initially at Guantanamo Bay but moved later to a brig at the Norfolk Naval Station. As an "enemy combatant," he has not been charged. Zaccarias Moussaoui, a French citizen of Moroccan descent, was arrested in Minnesota as the "twentieth hijacker." He has been charged and is being tried in civil court. Richard E. Reid, the British "shoe bomber," was also tried and convicted in civil court. Jose Padilla, born in New York, was held by the military as a suspect in a plot to detonate a radiological dispersal device—or "dirty bomb"—in the United States. Although arrested by the FBI on May 8, 2002, and incarcerated since that time, he has yet to be charged with a crime either before or after the administration designated him an enemy combatant.

In addition to Hamdi and Padilla, the administration has designated other suspects as "enemy combatants."[67] Whoever fits that category is held but not charged, is denied the right to an attorney, and (according to the Justice Department) federal judges have no right to interfere with executive judgments. A Department of Justice brief filed in the Fourth Circuit argued that courts

> may not second-guess the military's determination that an individual is an enemy combatant and should be detained as such. . . . Going beyond that determination would require the courts to enter an area in which they have no competence, much less institutional expertise, intrude upon the constitutional prerogative of the Commander in Chief (and military authorities acting at his control), and possibly create "a conflict between judicial and military opinion highly comforting to enemies of the United States."[68]

In other briefs, the Justice Department concedes that federal judges may have a review function in determining whether the president has properly designated an individual as an enemy combatant, but the review function "is limited to confirming based on some evidence the existence of a factual basis supporting the determination."[69] The government wants the judiciary to accept as "some evidence" what executive officials submit without any opportunity for an accused enemy combatant, supported by counsel, to challenge the executive statements. The courts cannot conclude that something is legitimate on its face if they hear only one side.

"Enemy combatant" is another term for "unlawful combatant," which the Court used in *Quirin*. Lawful combatants are held as prisoners of war and may not be prosecuted for criminal violations for belligerent acts that do not constitute war crimes. Lawful combatants wear uniforms with a fixed distinctive emblem and conduct their operations in accordance with the laws and customs of war.[70] On November 26, 2002, the general counsel of the Defense Department defined "enemy combatant" as

> an individual who, under the laws and customs of war, may be detained for the duration of an armed conflict. In the current conflict with al Qaeda and the Taliban, for example, the term includes a member, agent, or associate of al Qaeda or the Taliban. In applying this definition, we note our consistency with the observation of the Supreme Court of the United States in *Ex parte Quirin*, 317 U.S. 1 (1942): "Citizens who associate themselves with the military arm of the enemy government, and with its aid, guidance and direction enter this country bent on hostile acts are enemy belligerents within the meaning of the Hague Convention and the law of war."[71]

However, Hamdi did not enter the United States. He was apprehended in Afghanistan.

Both Hamdi and Padilla, as American citizens, are covered by this provision in the U.S. Code: "No citizen shall be imprisoned or otherwise detained by the United States except pursuant to an Act of Congress."[72] In 1981, the Supreme Court interpreted the "plain language" of this provision as "proscribing detention *of any kind* by the United States, absent a congressional grant of authority to detain."[73] The Bush administration, however, argues that it is not limited by this statute because "Article II alone gives the President the power to detain enemies during wartime, regardless of congressional action."[74]

Yasser Esam Hamdi

In the *Hamdi* case, a federal district judge several times rejected the broad arguments put forth by the Justice Department, which relied on an administration

affidavit (the "Mobbs Declaration") as sufficient evidence that Hamdi was legitimately classified as an enemy combatant. The district judge, insisting that
Hamdi had a right of access to the public defender and without the presence of
military personnel, was repeatedly reversed by the Fourth Circuit.[75] In a ruling
of January 8, 2003, again overturning the district court, the Fourth Circuit jug-
gled two values—the judiciary's duty to protect constitutional rights versus the
judiciary's need to defer to military decisions by the president—and came down
squarely in favor of presidential power.

The Fourth Circuit arrived at that conclusion through a strange reading of
separation of powers. It cites an opinion by the Supreme Court in 1991 that
the "ultimate purpose of this separation of powers is to protect the liberty
and security of the governed."[76] Instead of reading this language as an affir-
mation of the checks and balances that prevent an accumulation of power in
a single branch, the Fourth Circuit interprets the Court's sentence as a warning to the federal judiciary not to interfere with powers vested in another
branch: "For the judicial branch to trespass upon the exercise of the warmaking powers would be an infringement of the right to self-determination
and self-governance at a time when the care of the common defense is most
critical." What kind of "self-determination" and "self-governance" exists
when power is concentrated in the executive branch? The reading is bizarre
because whereas the Fourth Circuit acquiesces wholly to the judgment of the
president, the Supreme Court in 1991 expressly intervened to strike down a
statutory procedure adopted by Congress. No philosophy of deference appears in the 1991 decision.

Although the Fourth Circuit paid lip service to independent judicial
scrutiny ("The detention of United States citizens must be subject to judicial
review"[77]), the review here scarcely exists. The Fourth Circuit left little doubt
about its willingness to defer to the president. "The judiciary is not at liberty
to eviscerate detention interests directly derived from the war powers of Articles I and II."[78] With such a frame of reference, judicial review is emptied
of meaning.

Judicial deference or abdication is reflected in the statement by the Fourth
Circuit that "it is undisputed" that Hamdi was captured "in a zone of active
combat in a foreign theater of conflict."[79] *Undisputed?* The court listened
only to the government's side. Hamdi, through his attorney, was given no opportunity to challenge assertions by executive officials.

On July 9, 2003, the full bench of the Fourth Circuit voted 8 to 4 to deny a
petition requesting a rehearing of its January panel ruling.[80] Judges Wilkinson
and Traxler filed opinions supporting the denial, while Judges Luttig and
Motz wrote separate dissenting opinions. The Luttig opinion faulted the panel
for calling Hamdi's seizure "undisputed." Hamdi, he said, "has not been per-

mitted to speak for himself or even through counsel as to those circumstances." However, Judge Luttig tilted toward presidential power by criticizing the panel's refusal "to rest decision on the proffer made by the President of the United States . . . all but eviscerat[ing] the President's Article II power to determine who are and who are not enemies of the United States during times of war."[81] Judge Luttig wanted the full panel to rehear the case and resolve those issues. Unless the judiciary clarified the range of executive power, an "embedded journalist or even the unwitting tourist could be seized and detained in a foreign combat zone," without meaningful judicial review.[82] However, what kind of judicial review is possible if the Court should defer—as Judge Luttig urges—to the president?

Judge Motz regarded the Mobbs Declaration as a pure hearsay statement by "an unelected, otherwise unknown, government 'advisor.'"[83] Mobbs did not claim "*any* personal knowledge of the facts surrounding Hamdi's capture and incarceration."[84] Instead, Mobbs merely reviewed "undisclosed and unenumerated 'relevant records and reports.'"[85] She also notes: "The panel's decision marks the first time in our history that a federal court has approved the elimination of protections afforded a citizen by the Constitution solely on the basis of the executive's designation of that citizen as an enemy combatant, without testing the accuracy of the designation. Neither the Constitution nor controlling precedent sanction this holding."[86]

Newspaper stories explain that, according to Pakistani intelligence stories, Northern Alliance commanders were slated to receive $5,000 for each Taliban prisoner and $20,000 for each al Qaeda fighter.[87] Obviously, Northern Alliance commanders had a clear financial incentive to assert that a captured prisoner, no matter how ambiguous his standing, belonged to al Qaeda.

Jose Padilla

Although the administration designated both Hamdi and Padilla as enemy combatants, their cases are very different. As explained by Judge Wilkinson of the Fourth Circuit, to compare the battlefield capture of Hamdi "to the domestic arrest in *Padilla v. Rumsfeld* is to compare apples and oranges."[88] The FBI arrested Padilla in Chicago on May 8, 2002, on a material witness warrant to secure his testimony before a grand jury in New York City. After President Bush designated him as an enemy combatant, the material witness warrant was withdrawn and the government moved Padilla to a Navy brig in Charleston, South Carolina. He had access to an attorney, Donna Newman in New York City, but not after his removal to Charleston.

If the government's facts on Hamdi are correct, there would be a basis for designating him an "enemy combatant." It is much more a stretch to make

that case for Padilla because the government does not claim that he participated in hostilities in Afghanistan or engaged in any way as a "combatant" on
a battlefield.[89] According to the government, one can be an enemy combatant
without ever fighting on a battlefield: "In a time of war, an enemy combatant
is subject to capture and detention wherever found, whether on a battlefield
or elsewhere abroad or within the United States."[90] A definition that broad
goes far beyond the traditional meaning of "enemy combatant" and brings
within it a multitude of activities that have, in the past, been litigated in civil
court.

On December 4, 2002, a district judge in New York City ruled that Padilla
had a right to consult with counsel under conditions that would minimize the
likelihood that he could use his lawyers as "unwilling intermediaries for the
transmission of information to others."[91] Judge Michael B. Mukasey held that
Padilla had a right to present facts and the most convenient way to do that was
to present them through counsel.[92] Moreover, on the issue of Padilla's status,
Mukasey insisted on evidence from the government to support Bush's finding that Padilla is an enemy combatant.

Mukasey did not grant to Padilla the right of counsel because of the Sixth
Amendment, which applies only to "all criminal prosecutions." With no
charges filed against him, there was no criminal proceeding. Instead, Mukasey
looked to congressional policy on habeas corpus petitions, entitling an applicant to "deny any of the facts set in the return or allege any other material
facts" (28 U.S.C. § 2243). As to the government's concern that Padilla might
somehow use his attorney to communicate to the enemy, Mukasey noted that
such an argument would even prohibit an indicted member of al Qaeda from
consulting with counsel in an Article III proceeding.[93]

When the government asked the court to reconsider its ruling, Judge
Mukasey granted the motion for reconsideration, but again held that Padilla
was entitled to consult with counsel to aid his habeas petition. Judge Mukasey
described the government's new arguments as "permeated with the pinched
legalism one usually encounters from non-lawyers."[94] The government
thought the "some evidence" standard supported the lawfulness of Padilla's
detention, but Judge Mukasey replied that no court of which he was aware has
applied that standard "to a record that consists solely of the government's evidence, to which the government's adversary has not been permitted to respond."[95]

Judge Mukasey also underscored the difference between the Hamdi and
Padilla cases: "Unlike Hamdi, Padilla was detained in this country, and initially by law enforcement officers pursuant to a material witness warrant. He
was not captured on a foreign battlefield by soldiers in combat. The prospect
of courts second-guessing battlefield decisions, which they have resolutely

refused to do, . . . does not loom in this case."[96] The government decided to appeal to the Second Circuit.

Like Hamdi, Padilla was designated an enemy combatant on the basis of a Mobbs Declaration. Padilla's attorneys, Donna Newman and Andrew Patel, say that Mobbs' own footnotes "conceded that the government's 'confidential sources' probably were not 'completely candid,' and that one source subsequently recanted and another was being treated with drugs." As Patel remarked: "Someone who's a confirmed liar and someone else who's on drugs and one of the two has recanted. You really think someone should be locked up for a year in solitary confinement based on *that*?"[97]

THE MOUSSAOUI ORDEAL

On December 11, 2001, a federal grand jury indicted Zacarias Moussaoui for being part of the al Qaeda conspiracy to kill and maim persons and to destroy structures in the United States. Born in France of Moroccan parents, Moussaoui had been detained in August on immigration charges after officials at a Minnesota flight school became suspicious about his reasons for wanting training to fly commercial airliners. Instead of trying him before a military tribunal, which many thought likely, the government chose to bring him before a civil court in Alexandria, Virginia, which has a strong history of imposing the death penalty.[98]

The government's decision to seek the death penalty marked the first of many complications with the Moussaoui case. Capital punishment has been abolished in all fifteen countries of the European Union. For that reason, such countries as France and Germany were unwilling to release key evidence to the United States.[99] That problem was overcome when French and German authorities agreed to hand over documents on the condition that the Justice Department would not use the material to seek or impose the death penalty.[100]

Second, the trial stretched from month to month, in part because of the District Judge Leonie M. Brinkema's decision to let Moussaoui act as his own lawyer. He used the opportunity to promote al Qaeda goals and create a circus atmosphere. Representing oneself in court is almost always ill-advised, even for seasoned attorneys. For Moussaoui, it was especially harmful. Court-appointed attorneys with security clearances could have been given access to evidence and witnesses. Moussaoui would never have such rights. Even so, prosecutors managed to inadvertently place some classified materials in the hands of Moussaoui.[101] Moreover, Judge Brinkema authorized a limited disclosure of classified information to Moussaoui.[102]

The extent of Moussaoui's ability to represent himself crystallized in September 2002 with the capture of Ramzi bin al-Shibh, a young Yemini apprehended in Pakistan. He was accused of being a key planner of the 9/11 attacks and had been identified in Moussaoui's indictment.[103] Now that the Justice Department had decided to try Moussaoui in civil court, he was entitled under the Sixth Amendment to seek witnesses to prove his innocence and to confront witnesses against him. The rights in the Sixth Amendment apply to any "accused" in a criminal proceeding, not just to a U.S. citizen.

Third, exactly what criminal conduct the government leveled against Moussaoui shifted with time. Initially, high-ranking officials in the Bush government, including Vice President Dick Cheney and FBI Director Robert Mueller, described Moussaoui as the "twentieth hijacker." The Justice Department never fully embraced that theory, which became increasingly difficult to defend. Later, Moussaoui learned through court documents that the Justice Department believed he was involved in a "fifth plane." His attorneys sought access to those statements, made in a secret court hearing, and Judge Brinkema agreed that access was appropriate.[104] The Justice Department told Brinkema that it had evidence that Moussaoui was plotting to fly a hijacked plane into the White House in 2001, an attack separate from the 9/11 attacks.[105] Newspaper reports said that the Justice Department, by August 2003, had backed away from the "fifth plane" theory.[106]

Khalid Sheik Mohammed, an al Qaeda operations chief captured in Pakistan, told U.S. interrogators that Moussaoui was not part of the 9/11 attacks, but was in the United States to take part in a second-wave attack. According to press reports, both Mohammed and bin al-Shibh came to distrust Moussaoui and found him unreliable.[107] Moussaoui offered a third explanation, saying he was to take part in another al Qaeda operation outside the United States after the 9/11 attacks.[108]

Fourth, on January 30, 2003, Judge Brinkema ordered the government to allow Moussaoui's lawyers to take a video deposition of bin al-Shibh. The government balked at her order, arguing that any questioning by his attorneys would disrupt ongoing interrogations and jeopardize access to crucial evidence needed by the government in the war against terrorism. Yet the government alleged that bin al-Shibh wired Moussaoui at least $14,000, making both men part of the conspiracy.[109] A defendant like Moussaoui has a right to challenge a government's witness. After Khalid Sheik Mohammed was captured in Pakistan, Moussaoui's attorneys sought access to him and others. In one memo, Judge Brinkema advised the government that when it chose to bring Moussaoui to trial in a civilian court, "it assumed the responsibility of abiding by well-established principles of due process."[110]

When the government appealed Brinkema's order, the Fourth Circuit sent the case back to district court, urging the two sides to find a middle ground that would allow Moussaoui some access to bin al-Shibh.[111] On May 15, Brinkema rejected the government's proposal that would allow the defense access to some of bin al-Shibh's statements, but deny it the right to depose bin al-Shibh and other potential witnesses.[112]

Fifth, although a civil trial is open for public viewing, much of the Moussaoui trial has been conducted in secret. Judge Brinkema's order to give Moussaoui's attorneys access to bin al-Shibh was made in secret, as was the government brief to the Fourth Circuit appealing her ruling, and also a key hearing before the Fourth Circuit on May 6, 2003.[113] Several news organizations went to court to demand access to these secret court documents.[114] Judge Brinkema criticized the "shroud of secrecy" surrounding the Moussaoui case, expressing doubt that the government could prosecute the case in open court.[115] In response to the action by the news organizations and Brinkema's statement, the government agreed to unseal some of the secret documents.[116] Also, the Fourth Circuit ruled that part of a hearing scheduled for June 3 be open to the public.[117]

At the hearing, Assistant Attorney General Michael Chertoff told the court that Moussaoui's rights were trumped by national security interests. Judge William W. Wilkins, Jr., chief judge of the Fourth Circuit, responded: "National security interests cannot override a defendant's right to a fair trial."[118] Chertoff insisted that "[t]his is not a Sixth Amendment case," and that what Moussaoui "wants is to expand the Sixth Amendment."[119] Chertoff denied that the Sixth Amendment could be extended overseas to potential witnesses who are enemy combatants, and that any effort to interrogate bin al-Shibh would "change the course of a military operation."[120]

On June 26, the three-judge panel ducked these constitutional issues by holding that Brinkema's order was not yet subject to appeal because it was not technically a "final decision."[121] The order would not become final, in a legal sense, "unless and until the government refuses to comply and the district court imposes a sanction."[122] The Justice Department had asked the Fourth Circuit to issue a mandamus, reversing the district court's order, but the Fourth Circuit declined to provide such relief.[123]

The government asked the Fourth Circuit to reconsider its ruling, but on July 3 the court refused.[124] Rebuffed, the government asked the entire Fourth Circuit to rehear the case. Divided 7 to 5, the appellate court voted against an en banc rehearing.[125] The next step was now quite predictable: The government defied Brinkema's order to give Moussaoui access to bin al-Shibh. Instead of taking the case immediately to a military tribunal, the Justice Department hoped to return to the Fourth Circuit and secure a favorable ruling this time.[126] In late August, Judge Brinkema granted Moussaoui access to two other al Qaeda operatives: Khalid Sheik Mohammed and Mustafa Ahmed Hawsawi, a Saudi man who reportedly served as paymaster to the 9/11 hijackers and is named in the indictment against Moussaoui.[127] The Justice Department told Judge Brinkema that it would refuse to produce either man for depositions.[128]

By late September, it appeared that the Justice Department would not object if Brinkema accepted a defense motion to dismiss the indictment. That step would allow the government to have a final order it could appeal to the more friendly Fourth Circuit.[129] However, Brinkema had other options. She could strike portions of the indictment dealing with al Qaeda prisoners, presenting an issue the government would find more difficult to win on appeal.[130] Another option, which she selected on October 2, was to prevent prosecutors from seeking the death penalty for Moussaoui because there was insufficient evidence linking him to 9/11, and he was "a remote or minor participant" in al Qaeda's actions against the United States.[131] Judge Brinkema also ruled that it would be fundamentally unfair to require Moussaoui to defend himself against accusations without the opportunity to seek testimony from witnesses held by the government.[132] Under her ruling, Moussaoui could still be prosecuted for participating in a broad al Qaeda conspiracy against the United States, leading perhaps to life in prison.[133] The ruling may persuade the government to allow Moussaoui to depose bin al-Shibh and other government witnesses, or take the case out of civil court and assign it to a military tribunal.

CONCLUSION

The Department of Justice has vast power in deciding to prosecute. That authority expands during times of emergency, whether it is combating communism in the past or terrorism at present. Much depends on the good judgment and integrity of the attorney general in wielding this power and providing effective leadership to U.S. attorneys and FBI investigators.

Under this test, Attorney General Ashcroft has displayed a fervor, certitude, and intolerance of public debate that raises legitimate concerns about how well he appreciates constitutional rights and how willing he is to protect them. During testimony before the Senate Judiciary Committee on December 6, 2001, he warned that criticizing the administration helps the terrorists: "We need honest, reasoned debate, not fear-mongering. To those who pit Americans against immigrants and citizens against non-citizens, to those who scare peace-loving people with phantoms of lost liberty, my message is this: Your tactics only aid terrorists, for they erode our national unity and diminish our resolve. They give ammunition to America's enemies, and pause to America's friends. They encourage people of good will to remain silent in the face of evil."[134]

A day later, the Justice Department announced that Ashcroft did not intend to discourage public debate. What he found unhelpful to the country "are misstatements and the spread of misinformation about the actions of the Justice Department."[135] That explanation is wholly inadequate. The Bush administration is ill-positioned to single out the "misstatements" that aid terrorists. It made a string of misstatements in attempting to justify the war against Iraq.[136]

Ashcroft has shown little patience for criticism even within his own shop. In June 2003, the Justice Department's inspector general, Glenn A. Fine, issued a report critical of the manner in which the department rounded up hundreds of illegal immigrants after 9/11. People with no connection to terrorism languished in jail for months under harsh conditions. In a Brooklyn detention facility, guards slammed detainees against walls and taunted them. The first reaction from the department's spokeswoman, Barbara Comstock, was one of deep denial: "We make no apologies for finding every legal way possible to protect the American public from further terrorist attacks."[137] In a letter attached to the Fine report, Deputy Attorney General Larry Thompson said it was "unfair to criticize the conduct of members of my staff during this period."[138] After this initial show of indignation, the department agreed to change the way it handles immigration detainees.[139] Yet at a Senate hearing later in June, several officials from the Justice Department largely defended the agency's conduct.[140]

In July, when Inspector General Fine released another report focusing on Justice Department violations of the rights of Muslim and Arab immigrants, the department's response was more professional. His report disclosed that in the six-month period ending on June 15, the IG's office had received thirty-four complaints of civil rights and civil liberties violations by department employees. The complaints, which were considered credible, included accusations that Muslim and Arab immigrants in federal detention centers had been beaten. This time, Comstock released a statement that the department "takes its obligations very seriously to protect civil rights and civil liberties, and the small number of credible allegations will be thoroughly investigated."[141]

In August, Attorney General Ashcroft reverted to form by ridiculing critics of the Patriot Act, especially the charge that the Justice Department had used authority in that statute to seek records from libraries. He released a memo stating that the department had not once sought such records.[142] That statement should have been sufficient to set the record straight, but Ashcroft couldn't leave it at that. He had to rub it in. Resorting to sarcasm, he said that the "charges of the hysterics are revealed for what they are: castles in the air built on misrepresentation, supported by unfounded fears, held aloft by hysteria." Those who charged the department with abuse of power "are ghosts unsupported by fact or example."[143] Yet credible reports of abuse of power had already been made by the department's IG office, and the department had acknowledged problems and the need to correct them. Ashcroft's tirade prompted the *Washington Post* to write an editorial entitled "Mr. Ashcroft's Tantrum." The newspaper said that an attorney general "has no business jeering at those who, rightly or wrongly, disagree with his policies or disfavor a particular law." His conduct showed "contempt for those who have questions."[144]

Ashcroft did not fully level on library records. What does it mean to say that the USA PATRIOT Act has yet to be used against libraries? Former Assistant Attorney General Viet Dinh testified before the House Judiciary Committee in May 2003 that libraries had been contacted approximately fifty times during 2002.[145] How do we reconcile the statements by Ashcroft and Dinh? Section 215 of the USA PATRIOT Act requires a court order to gain access to certain business records.[146] Ashcroft is stating that no court orders have been authorized against libraries. That fact doesn't prevent FBI agents from coming into libraries and requesting records under the threat that, without voluntary cooperation by library employees, they may have to seek a court order. It would have been more forthcoming of Ashcroft to divulge what Dinh had already reported to Congress.

The United States has embarked on a long war against terrorism, likely to persist over a period of decades. Even in normal times, the political and legal powers of federal prosecutors are vast and capable of doing great damage to civil liberties. In periods of real or perceived crisis, the risk increases manyfold. What is needed in such times is a federal government that understands that the Constitution cannot be sacrificed in the name of national security, and that procedures exist to protect both the innocent and the guilty. To ensure that executive officials discharge their duties in appropriate fashion, Congress, federal courts, the media, and private citizens must be willing to challenge and check the government. Relying on self-restraint or even good judgment by executive officials is not a reliable option. As Justice Louis Brandeis reminded us: "The greatest dangers to liberty lurk in insidious encroachment by men of zeal, well-meaning but without understanding."[147]

NOTES

1. McNabb v. United States, 318 U.S. 332, 347 (1943).
2. Leonard W. Levy, *The Origins of the Fifth Amendment* ix (1986 ed.).

3. 37 Wkly. Comp. Pres. Doc. 1306 (Sept. 13, 2001).

4. *Id.* at 1327 (Sept. 17, 2001).

5. *Id.* at 1429 (Oct. 6, 2001).

6. 147 Cong. Rec. H5691 (daily ed. Sept. 14, 2001).

7. *Id.* at H5692.

8. *Id.* at H5698 and S9859 (daily ed. Sept. 26, 2001).

9. Elizabeth A. Palmer and Adriel Bettelheim, *War and Civil Liberties: Congress Gropes for a Role,* CQ Wkly. Rep., Dec. 1, 2001, at 2820.

10. *Department of Justice Oversight: Preserving Our Freedoms While Defending against Terrorism, Hearings before the Senate Committee on the Judiciary,* 107th Cong., 1st Sess. 211–17 (2001).

11. Matthew Brzesinski, *Hady Hassan Omar's Detention,* N.Y. Times, Oct. 27, 2002, at Mag. 50–55.

12. John M. Broder and Susan Sachs, *Facing Registry Deadline, Men From Muslim Nations Swamp Immigration Office,* N.Y. Times, Dec. 17, 2002, at A16; Dan Eggen, *2nd Chance to Register Given,* Wash. Post, Jan. 16, 2003, at A2; Michael Powell, *Pakistanis Flee to Canada and Uncertainty,* Wash. Post, Jan. 18, 2003, at A1; Nurith C. Aizenman, *A Register of Immigrants' Fears.* Wash. Post, Jan. 20, 2003, at A1.

13. George Lardner, Jr., *Registration Program Problems Cited,* Wash. Post, Mar. 20, 2003, at A10.

14. Louis Fisher, Nazi Saboteurs on Trial: A Military Tribunal and American Law 50–53, 159–60 (2003).

15. *Ex parte* Milligan, 4 Wall. (71 U.S.) 2 (1866).

16. *Ex parte* Quirin, 47 F.Supp. 431 (D.D.C. 1942).

17. *Ex parte* Quirin, 63 S.Ct. 1–2 (1942). The per curiam is also reproduced in a footnote in *Ex parte* Quirin, 317 U.S. 1, 18–19 (1942).

18. *Ex parte* Quirin, 317 U.S. 1 (1942); Fisher, Nazi Saboteurs on Trial, at 109–21.

19. Edward S. Corwin, Total War and the Constitution 118 (1947).

20. "Memorandum *Re: Rosenberg v. United States,* Nos. 111 and 687, October Term 1952," June 4, 1953, at 8; Papers of Felix Frankfurter, Manuscript Room, Library of Congress, Part I, Reel 70.

21. Military Order, 10 Fed. Reg. 548 (1945).

22. For further details, *see* Fisher, *Nazi Saboteurs on Trial,* at 138–44.

23. *Terrorism Bill's Sparse Paper Trail May Cause Legal Vulnerability,* CQ Wkly. Rept., Oct. 27, 2001, at 2533–35.

24. H. Rept. No. 107-236 (Part 1), 107th Cong., 1st Sess. (2001).

25. 147 Cong. Rec. S10575 (daily ed. Oct. 11, 2001).

26. *Id.* at S10574.

27. 149 Cong. Rec. H7289-93, H7299 (daily ed. July 22, 2003); Jennifer A. Dlouhy, *House Moves to Eliminate Search and Seizure Portion of Anti-Terrorism Law,* CQ Wkly. Rep., July 26, 2003; at 1905, 1932–33 (House Vote 408).

28. Dan Eggen, *Ashcroft Defends Anti-Terrorism Law,* Wash. Post, Aug. 20, 2003, at A10.

29. Evelyn Nieves, *Local Officials Rise up to Defy The Patriot Act,* Wash. Post, Apr. 21, 2003, at A1.

30. Eggen, *Ashcroft Defends Anti-Terrorism Law,* at A10.

31. 115 Stat. 288 (2001).

32. Dean E. Murphy, *Some Librarians Use Shredder to Show Opposition to New F.B.I. Powers,* N.Y. Times, Apr. 9, 2003, at A11.

33. Rene Sanchez, *Librarians Make Some Noise Over Patriot Act,* Wash. Post, Apr. 10, 2003, at A20.

34. Dan Eggen, *Judge Orders Release or Open Hearings*, Wash. Post, Sept. 18, 2002, at A14; *Sept. 11 Detainee Testifies at Public Hearing*, Wash. Post, Oct. 2, 2002, at A6.

35. Detroit Free Press v. Ashcroft, 195 F.Supp.2d 937 (E.D. Mich. 2002); Detroit Free Press v. Ashcroft, 195 F.Supp.2d 948 (E.D. Mich. 2002).

36. Detroit Free Press v. Ashcroft, 303 F.3d 681, 683 (6th Cir. 2002).

37. *Id.*

38. www.usdoj.gov/opa/pr/2002/April/02_ag_238.htm.

39. Ashcroft v. North Jersey Media Group, Inc., 122 S.Ct. 2655 (2002); North Jersey Media Group, Inc. v. Ashcroft, 205 F.Supp.2d 288 (D. N.J. 2002).

40. North Jersey Media Group, Inc. v. Ashcroft, 308 F.3d 198, 215 (3d Cir. 2002).

41. *Id.* at 220.

42. *Id.* at 226.

43. 123 S.Ct. 2215 (2003); North Jersey Media Group v. Ashcroft.

44. Neil A. Lewis, "Judge Orders U.S. to Release Names of 9/11 Detainees," N.Y. Times, Aug. 3, 2002, at A1.

45. Center for Nat. Security v. U.S. Dept. of Justice, 215 F.Supp.2d 94, 96 (D.D.C. 2002) (quoting Morrow v. District of Columbia, 417 F.2d 728, 741–42 (D.C. Cir. 1969)).

46. Center for Nat. Security v. U.S. Dept. of Justice, 217 F.Supp.2d 58 (D.D.C. 2002).

47. Neil A. Lewis, *U.S. Says Revealing Names Would Aid Al Qaeda*, Wash. Post, Nov. 19, 2002, at A18.

48. Center for Nat. Sec. Studies v. Dept. of Justice, 331 F.3d 918 (D.C. Cir. 2003).

49. *Id.* at 927.

50. *Id.* at 930.

51. *Id.* at 932.

52. *Id.* at 937.

53. *Id.* at 937–38.

54. *Id.* at 940.

55. 98 Stat. 1982, § 3144 (1984); 18 U.S.C. § 3144 (2000).

56. Steve Fainaru and Margot Williams, *Material Witness Law Has Many in Limbo*, Wash. Post, Nov. 24, 2002, at A1, A12.

57. United States v. Awadallah, 202 F.Supp.2d 55, 58 (S.D.N.Y. 2002).

58. *Id.*

59. *Id.* at 82.

60. *In re* Application of U.S. for Material Witness Warrant, 213 F.Supp.2d 287 (S.D.N.Y. 2002).

61. *Id.* at 299.

62. Rasul v. Bush, 215 F.Supp.2d 55, 72–73 (D.D.C. 2002). *Editor's note: See generally* chapter 9, "The Terrorist Detention Cases of 2004."

63. Al Odah v. United States, 321 F.3d 1134 (D.C. Cir. 2003).

64. Coalition of Clergy v. Bush, 189 F.Supp.2d 1036 (C.D. Cal. 2002).

65. *Id.* at 1046–50.

66. Coalition of Clergy, Lawyers, and Professors v. Bush, 310 F.3d 1153 (9th Cir. 2002).

67. For example, Ali S. Marri, a citizen of Qatar; *Enemy Combatant Designation Challenged in Court,* Wash. Post, July 10, 2003, at A11.

68. "Brief for Respondents-Appellants," Hamdi v. Rumsfeld, No. 02-6895 (4th Cir.), at 29–30, 31. See Tom Jackman and Dan Eggen, *Combatants' Lack Rights, U.S. Argues,* Wash. Post, June 20, 2002, at A10.

69. "Repondents' Response to, and Motion to Dismiss, the Amended Petition for a Writ of Habeas Corpus," Padilla v. Bush, at 15. *Editor's note: See generally* chapter 9, "The Terrorist Detention Cases of 2004."

70. Hague Convention of October 18, 1907, 36 Stat. 2296.

71. Letter of November 26, 2002, from William J. Haynes II, General Counsel, Department of Defense, to Senator Carl Levin, at 1–2.

72. 18 U.S.C. § 4001(a) (2000).

73. Howe v. Smith, 452 U.S. 473, 479 n.3 (1981) (emphasis in original).

74. Letter of September 23, 2002, from William J. Haynes II, General Counsel, Department of Defense, to Alfred P. Carlton, Jr., president, American Bar Association, at 2.

75. Hamdi v. Rumsfeld, 294 F.3d 598 (4th Cir. 2002); Hamdi v. Rumsfeld, 296 F.3d 278 (4th Cir. 2002).). *Editor's note: See generally* chapter 9, "The Terrorist Detention Cases of 2004."

76. Hamdi v. Rumsfeld, 316 F.3d 450, 463 (4th Cir. 2003), citing Metro. Wash. Airports Auth. v. Citizens for the Abatement of Aircraft Noise, Inc., 501 U.S. 252, 272 (1991).

77. *Id.* at 464.

78. *Id.* at 466.

79. *Id.* at 459.

80. Hamdi v. Rumsfeld, 337 F.3d 335 (4th Cir. 2003).

81. *Id.* at 357.

82. *Id.* at 358.

83. *Id.* at 368.

84. *Id.* at 373 (emphasis in original).

85. *Id.*

86. *Id.* at 369

87. "Petition for Writ of Certiorari," Hamdi v. Rumsfeld, at 9 n.8.

88. Hamdi v. Padilla, 337 F.3d at 344.

89. "Brief of Amici Curiae Experts on the Law of War in Support of Petitioner-Appellee/Cross-Appellant Jose Padilla and Partial Affirmance and Partial Response," Padilla v. Rumsfeld, at 1–16.

90. "Respondents' Response to, and Motion to Dismiss, the Amended Petition for a Writ of Habeas Corpus," Padilla v. Bush, at 23.

91. Padilla ex rel. Newman v. Bush, 233 F.Supp.2d 564, 569 (S.D.N.Y. 2002).

92. *Id.* at 599.

93. *Id.* at 603–04.

94. Padilla ex rel. Newman v. Rumsfeld, 243 F.Supp.2d 42, 47 (S.D.N.Y. 2003).

95. *Id.* at 54.

96. *Id.* at 56.

97. Paula Span, *Enemy Combatant Vanishes Into a "Legal Black Hole,"* Wash. Post, July. 30, 2003, at A8 (emphasis in original).

98. Don Van Natta, Jr. with Benjamin Weiser, *Compromise Settles Debate Over Tribunal,* N.Y. Times, Dec. 12, 2001, at B1.

99. Peter Finn, *Germany Reluctant to Aid Prosecution of Moussaoui,* Wash. Post, June 11, 2002, at A1.

100. Dan Eggen, *U.S. to Get Moussaoui Data From Europe,* Wash. Post, Nov. 28, 2002, at A19.

101. United States v. Moussaoui, March 19, 2003 Order by Judge Brinkema, 2003 WL 18777698 (E.D. Va. 2003).

102. United States v. Moussaoui, May 7, 2003 Order by Judge Brinkema, 2003 WL 21266319 (E.D. Va. 2003).

103. United States v. Moussaoui, Criminal No. 01-455-A, July 2002 Term—at Alexandria, Superseding Indictment (E.D. Va.) (hereinafter "Moussaoui Indictment").

104. United States v. Moussaoui, April 28, 2003 Order by Judge Brinkema, 2003 WL 21266341 (E.D. Va. 2003); Philip Shenon, *Moussaoui Should Get Details In "Fifth Plane" Theory, Judge Says*, N.Y. Times, Apr.29, 2003, at A13.

105. Philip Shenon, *White House Called Target Of Plane Plot,* N.Y. Times, Aug. 9, 2003, at A7.

106. Josh White, *FBI Intercepts Moussaoui's Mail,* Wash. Post, Aug. 9, 2003, at B2.

107. Susan Schmidt and Ellen Nakashima, *Moussaoui Said Not to Be Part of 9/11 Plot,* Wash. Post, Mar. 28, 2003, at A4.

108. Jerry Markon, *Moussaoui Says He Was to Aid Later Attack,* Wash. Post, May 14, 2003, at A2.

109. Moussaoui Indictment, at 17; Susan Schmidt and Dana Priest, "Judge Orders Access to Detainee for Moussaoui's Lawyers," Wash. Post, Feb. 1, 2003, at A9.

110. Josh White, *Memos Reveal Doubt on Proper Court for Moussaoui,* Wash. Post, June 3, 2003, at A8.

111. Jerry Markon, *Court Seeks Deal on Terror Witness Access,* Wash. Post, Apr. 16, 2003, at A12.

112. Jerry Markon, *Judge Rejects Bid to Block Access to Sept. 11 Planner,* Wash. Post, May 16, 2003, at A3.

113. Jerry Markon, *U.S. Files Terror Briefs in Secrecy,* Wash. Post, Mar. 15, 2003, at A6; Jerry Markon, *Moussaoui's Hearing Closed to Public,* Wash. Post, Mar. 25, 2003, at A2.

114. Philip Shenon, *News Groups Want Terror Case Files*, N.Y. Times, Apr. 4, 2003, at B13.

115. United States v. Moussaoui, April 4, 2003 Order by Judge Brinkema, 2003 WL 21266379 (E.D. Va. 2003). *See also* Patricia Davis and Jerry Markon, *U.S. Secrecy Criticized by Moussaoui Judge,* Wash. Post, Apr. 5, 2003, at A9.

116. Philip Shenon, *Government Agrees Some Secret Documents in Terror Case Can Be Unsealed,* N.Y. Times, Apr. 22, 2003, at A12.

117. Philip Shenon, *In Shift, Appeals Court Opens Hearing on a 9/11 Suspect,* N.Y. Times, May 14, 2003, at A15.

118. Jerry Markon, *Appeals Panel Hears Arguments on Deposition Sought by Moussaoui,* Wash. Post, June 4, 2003, at A10.

119. Philip Shenon, *Justice Dept. Warns of Risk To Prosecution and Security,* N.Y. Times, June 4, 2003, at A21.

120. *Id.*

121. United States v. Moussaoui, 333 F.3d 509, 513–14 (4th Cir. 2003).

122. *Id.* at 515.

123. *Id.* at 516–17.

124. Jerry Markon, *Moussaoui Prosecution Is Dealt Setback,* Wash. Post, July 4, 2003, at A8.

125. United States v. Moussaoui, 336 F.3d 279 (4th Cir. 2003).

126. Jerry Markon, *Moussaoui Prosecutors Defy Judge,* Wash. Post, July 15, 2003, at A1; Philip Shenon, *U.S. Will Defy Court's Order in Terror Case,* N.Y. Times, July 15, 2003, at A1.

127. Jerry Markon, *Moussaoui Granted Access to Witnesses,* Wash. Post, August 30, 2003, at A12.

128. Jerry Markon, *U.S. Refuses to Produce Al Qaeda Officials as Witnesses,* Wash. Post, Sept. 11, 2003, at A7.

129. Jerry Markon, *Defense Calls for Dismissal of Sept. 11 Case,* Wash. Post, Sept. 25, 2003, at A15; Philip Shenon, *In Maneuver, U.S. Will Let Terror Charges Drop,* N.Y. Times, Sept. 26, 2003, at A1.

130. Philip Shenon and Neil A. Lewis, *Appeals Strategy Lies Behind Prosecutors' Decision in Terror Case,* N.Y. Times, Sept. 30, 2003, at A21.

131. Moussaoui v. United States, 282 F.Supp.2d 480, 486 (E.D. Va. 2003).

132. *Id.* at 487.

133. Jerry Markon, *Ruling Shakes up Moussaoui Terror Case,* Wash. Post, Oct. 3, 2003, at A1; Philip Shenon, *Judge Rules out a Death Penalty for 9/11 Suspect,* N.Y. Times, Oct. 3, 2003, at A1.

134. *Department of Justice Oversight: Preserving Our Freedoms While Defending against Terrorism,* hearings before the Senate Committee on the Judiciary, 107th Cong., 1st Sess. 313 (2001); N.Y. Times, Dec. 7, 2001, at B6.

135. Dan Eggen, *Ashcroft Aide Says Criticism Wasn't Aimed at Policy Foes,* Wash. Post, Dec. 8, 2001, at A11.

136. Louis Fisher, *Deciding on War against Iraq,* 118 Pol. Sci. Q. 1 (Fall 2003).

137. Eric Lichtblau, *U.S. Report Faults the Roundup of Illegal Immigrants after 9/11,* N.Y. Times, June 3, 2003, at A1.

138. Steve Fainaru, *Report: 9/11 Detainees Abused,* Wash. Post, June 3, 2003, at A1, A8.

139. *Handling of Terror Cases to Change,* Wash. Post, June 15, 2003, at A11.

140. Edward Walsh, *Treatment of Detainees Defended,* Wash. Post, June 26, 2003, at A3; Eric Lichtbau, *Treatment of Detained Immigrants Is Under Investigation,* N.Y. Times, June 26, 2003, at A18.

141. Philip Shenon, *Report on U.S. Antiterrorism Law Alleges Violations of Civil Rights,* N.Y. Times, July 21, 2003, at A1.

142. Dan Eggen, *Ashcroft: Patriot Act Provision Unused,* Wash. Post, Aug. 18, 2003, at A13.

143. Dan Eggen, *Patriot Monitoring Claims Dismissed,* Wash. Post, Aug. 19, 2003, at A2.

144. *Mr. Ashcroft's Tantrum,* Wash. Post, Sept. 20, 2003, at A30.

145. Audrey Hudson, *Librarians Dispute Justice's Claim on Use of Patriot Act,* Wash. Times, Sept. 19, 2003, at A10.

146. 115 Stat. 287 (2001).

147. Olmstead v. United States, 277 U.S. 438, 479 (1928).

THE SEARCH FOR PERSPECTIVE

7

Voting Rights and Other "Anomalies": Protecting and Expanding Civil Liberties in Wartime

Mark A. Graber

"**W**hen a nation is at war," Justice Oliver Wendell Holmes, Jr., famously declared, "many things that might be said in time of peace are such a hindrance to its effort that their utterance will not be endured so long as men fight and that no Court could regard them as protected by any constitutional right."[1] This passage from *Schenck v. United States* is uniformly regarded as stating both an empirical and a normative truth. War, conventional wisdom proclaims, is bad for civil rights and civil liberties. When military tensions escalate, individual freedoms are diminished in the name of national security. Professor Geoffrey R. Stone asserts, "[i]n times of war — or more precisely, in time of national crisis — we respond too harshly in our restriction of civil liberties."[2] Moreover, conventional wisdom continues, war requires the sacrifice of some civil rights and civil liberties in the name of national security. Committed civil libertarians acknowledge, "in times of national emergency, . . . the relative claims of order and security naturally become stronger."[3] They insist only that government during hot and cold wars too often restricts more individual rights than necessary.

American history belies this near universal assertion that civil rights and liberties are invariably restricted during wartime.[4] Repressive policies have often been adopted when the United States is at war or faced with a severe military threat. The litany of such instances, from the Alien and Sedition Acts of 1798 to the present Patriot Act, is well known.[5] Nevertheless, accounts of civil liberties policymaking during hot and cold wars that discuss only governmental decrees limiting individual rights present an incomplete picture of how national security concerns and war aims have influenced fundamental freedoms in the United States. Civil liberties policy varies within and between wars. No particular civil liberty has always been restricted in the United States whenever war has broken out. In no war has every civil liberty been diminished. Frequently, governing officials have expanded certain civil liberties and rights during periods of military tension or conflict. Consider the experience of African Americans during the Civil War, laborers during World War I, Jehovah's Witnesses during World War II, and persons suspected of ordinary crimes during the Cold War.[6] War and periods of crisis throughout American history are best understood as providing occasions for restricting some rights, protecting some rights, and expanding some rights.

The numerous instances in which civil rights and liberties have been protected or expanded during hot and cold wars cast doubt on the broad generalization that national security requires restrictions on individual rights during periods of military tension. Some military tensions may have provided legitimate grounds for curtailing some civil rights and liberties. Still, the frequency with which civil liberties have been protected during wartime raises questions about whether the justifications relied on for limiting civil liberties were sound. The McKinley administration's decision to permit domestic opposition to the Spanish-American War[7] provides reasons for thinking that the Wilson Administration's decision to suppress dissent during World War I was not necessary to achieve any war aim. The decision not to intern German Americans or Italian Americans during World War II belies the national security rationale invoked to justify interning Japanese Americans. The frequent occasions in which protections for particular civil liberties and rights have been expanded during wars further suggest that national security and war goals sometimes generate powerful reasons for supporting new civil liberties and rights. The Emancipation Proclamation was justified as "a fit and necessary war measure" that would deprive the Confederacy of a valuable source of labor.[8] The Roosevelt administration during World War II delayed deportation hearings for union leaders thought to be Communists for fear of inducing strikes that would disrupt the war effort.[9]

This chapter is part of a broader revisionist project on civil rights and civil liberties policy in the United States during hot and cold wars.[10] A previous paper[11] highlights six counterstories, well-documented instances of protective civil rights and civil liberties policies being adopted during wartime. That essay, building on pioneering analysis done by Philip Klinkner and Rogers Smith on racial equality and war,[12] suggests four conditions under which civil liberties and rights are likely to be protected and expanded in wartime. These are:

1. "[A] large-scale war requir[es] extensive economic [or] military mobilization of [the beneficiaries of a rights protective policy] for success."[13]

2. "[T]he nature of America's enemies . . . prompt[s] American leaders to justify such wars and their attendant sacrifices by emphasizing the nation's inclusive, egalitarian, democratic traditions"[14] or, at least, the national commitment to particular civil rights and liberties.

3. The beneficiaries of the civil right or liberty are, for reasons of race, ethnicity, or ideology, identified as loyal Americans, with American allies or countries whose support the United States is seeking, or at least as enemies of America's enemies.

4. Powerful political actors inside and outside of government see the military conflict as an additional reason for advancing preexisting commitments to particular civil liberties and rights. Other crucial government actors can be persuaded or pressured to support those rights or liberties.[15]

Civil rights and liberties are likely to be restricted whenever the beneficiaries of protective policies are ideologically or ethnically identified with America's enemies, or when government officials see the military conflict as an additional reason for advancing preexisting commitments to further limit the right or liberty in question.

This chapter builds on this analysis by taking a more in-depth look at the historical impact of war on voting rights in the United States. Several scholars have noted that war has inspired virtually all major expansions of the franchise in American history,[16] but this finding has not yet been integrated into scholarship on civil liberties in wartime. The first part of this chapter documents the numerous instances in which war was at least partly responsible for official decisions to expand the suffrage or increase access to the ballot, details the various pragmatic and normative connections Americans have made between war and an expanded suffrage, and explains why studies of civil liberties during wartime have been oblivious to such an obvious counterexample to claims that national security inevitably generates restrictive rights policies. The next section briefly demonstrates that this connection between war and increased voting rights is not an anomaly or an exception to the general rule that civil rights and liberties are limited during wartime. Many individual rights have been expanded during wartime, the justifications for those expansions have invoked the same national security or war aims used to justify expanding voting rights in wartime, and these instances when war has inspired protective policies have been ignored in studies of civil liberties during wartime for the same reasons that voting rights have been ignored. Last, this chapter briefly highlights some implications of voting rights policymaking in wartime for understanding and evaluating civil liberties policymaking during the present war against terrorism. Decisions made by the Bush administration to restrict numerous civil liberties in the name of national security, American history indicates, cannot be defended or justified as the inevitable consequence of September 11, 2001. Closer attention to voting rights and civil liberties policymaking in other wars suggests that an administration more favorably disposed toward various civil rights and liberties, most notably the rights of resident aliens, would adopt far more protective policies.

One moral of this story is that specifics matter when discussing rights policies during wartime. One size does not fit all. Whether a particular civil right or liberty is likely to be restricted, protected, or expanded during periods of military tension has historically depended on the particular civil liberty, the particular persons likely to be influenced by a change in rights policies, and the predispositions of the particular governing officials responsible for determining rights policies. The right to vote has a tendency to expand during war; the right to free speech has a tendency to contract. Persons identified as loyal Americans frequently gain rights as a result of war; persons identified with American enemies frequently lose rights as a result of war. Administrations favorably disposed toward a particular right before the war tend to protect that right during and immediately after the war; administrations unfavorably disposed toward a particular right before the war tend to restrict that right during and immediately after the war. The other, related, moral is that politics matters. Throughout history, political leaders have responded differently to fairly similar wartime conditions. Some have seen war as a reason for maintaining and expanding voting rights. Others have turned a deaf ear to pleas by loyal citizens for access to the ballot. African Americans have fought in all major American wars, but not all wars have inspired greater protections for African American voters. African Americans gained suffrage and other rights during the Civil War and World War II, but not during the War of 1812 and World War I. Whether present wartime conditions should inspire Americans to again expand access to the ballot and provide greater protections for other civil liberties is beyond the scope of this chapter. The crucial point is that proponents of restrictive policies cannot use history to justify or excuse their efforts to curtail fundamental freedoms in the name of national security. Civil liberties policymaking during wartime is a consequence of political choice, not historical necessity.

THE RIGHT TO VOTE IN WAR AND PEACE

The history of voting rights in the United States confounds conventional claims that civil rights are invariably restricted during wartime. Americans have consistently expanded voting rights during military conflicts or because of military conflicts. With rare and relatively minor exceptions, efforts to restrict access to the franchise throughout American history have typically taken place and been successful only during long periods of peace. The primary arguments for voting rights help explain the close connection between war and increased access to the ballot. Americans have historically associated the duty to serve country with the right to vote, that association has seemed most salient during and immediate after military conflicts, and those military conflicts rarely generate any distinctive pressures to restrict access to the ballot. Such well-known extensions of the franchise as the Twenty-Sixth Amendment are nevertheless rarely mentioned in studies devoted to civil liberties in wartime. A canon obsessed with judicial review tends to ignore rights-protective decisions made by elected officials. Moreover, scholarship that focuses on how war generates demands for new restrictions on civil liberties intended to last only during hostilities consistently overlooks how war also transforms preexisting controversies over civil liberties in ways that provide opportunities for proponents of protective policies to win victories that endure long after hostilities cease.

The Voting Rights Scorecard

In a magnificent study, Alexander Keyssar concludes that war has been the major factor responsible for expanding access to the ballot in the United States. "[N]early all of the major expansions of the franchise that have occurred in American history," he documents, took place either during or in the wake of wars. The historical record indicates that this was not a coincidence: The demands of both war itself and preparedness for war created powerful pressures to enlarge the right to vote. Armies had to be recruited, often from the so-called lower orders of society, and it was rhetorically as well as practically difficult to compel men to bear arms while denying them the franchise; similarly, conducting a war meant mobilizing popular support, which gave political leverage to any social groups excluded from the polity. While it may seem less exceptional and romantic than the frontier, without a doubt war played a greater role in the evolution of American democracy.[17]

Other scholars agree. Pamela Karlan asserts, "Virtually every major expansion in the right to vote was connected intimately to war."[18]

The constitutional text confirms the close connection between war and the right to vote. The three amendments most responsible for expanding the franchise, the Fifteenth, the Nineteenth, and the Twenty-Sixth, were all passed during or in the immediate wake of wars. All were justified as wartime or war-related measures. Black soldiers during the Civil War earned the franchise through military duty. General Sherman proved prophetic when he declared, "The hand that drops the musket cannot be denied the ballot."[19] Women's patriotic service during World War I was similarly understood as entitling them to suffrage. Woodrow Wilson in 1918 informed Congress that the Nineteenth Amendment was "a war measure."[20] The dominant justification of the Twenty-Sixth Amendment was that persons old enough to fight in Vietnam were old enough to vote. Repeating what had become an American mantra, proponents asserted, "It is surely unjust and discriminating to command men to sacrifice their lives for a decision which they had no part in making."[21]

From the very beginning of the American republic, wartime conditions and military tensions have inspired policies that extended voting rights to the previously disenfranchised. Responding in large part to members of local militias who protested their exclusion from the polls, at least seven states expanded their electorate during the American Revolution.[22] Several of these new state laws permitted persons of color to vote.[23] Even when satisfactory reform did not take place immediately, the Revolutionary War placed proponents of property restrictions in a defensive posture from which they never recovered. "By the end of the revolution," Keyssar declares, "the policy of keeping those common people from the polls had become significantly harder to defend."[24] The War of 1812 further fueled movements for universal white male suffrage as militiamen again protested their exclusion from the ballot.[25] The possibility of military conflict in the antebellum republic promoted suffrage rights even when the United States was not technically at war. The dominant justification of universal male service in Jacksonian America was that any person who had a legal duty to fight for his community also had a legal right to vote in his community. Suffrage should be granted, most Americans during the first half of the nineteenth century concluded, to "every man who pays his shot and bears his lot."[26] Military conflicts with Native Americans, from this perspective, while responsible for horrible deprivations of Native American rights seem also partly responsible for universal white male suffrage.

Later wars were responsible for further increasing the number of persons entitled to vote and easing restrictions that made voting difficult. State governments first provided absentee ballots during the Civil War as part of an effort to ensure that soldiers could vote. Other states waived property qualifications for soldiers and enfranchised aliens serving in the Union army.[27] By the end of World War I, all states granted soldiers rights to cast absentee ballots. Many states extended that privilege to civilians.[28] Soldiers were federally guaranteed an absentee ballot by the Soldier Voting Acts of 1942 and 1944. Those measures also exempted persons in the service from paying any state-mandated poll tax.[29] Georgia abolished the poll tax for all citizens during World War II and numerous states immediately after the war exempted veterans from that levy.[30] These statutes, Philip Klinkner and Rogers Smith observe, were "the first legislative expansion(s) of black voting rights since the 1870s."[31] World War II provided an occasion for the Supreme Court to overrule a prewar decision and declare white-only primaries unconstitutional.[32] "[T]he real reason for the overturn" of the previous decision that sustained the white primary, the *New York Times* reported, "is that the common sacrifices of wartime have turned public opinion and the Court against previously sustained devices to exclude minorities."[33] "The white primary," several commentators concur, "was one of the casualties of World War II."[34] World War II was also responsible for the death of significant suffrage restrictions on naturalized Asian American citizens and Native Americans. A crucial federal court decision striking down a state law noted, "We all know that these New Mexico Indians have responded to the needs of this country in times of war."[35]

The Cold War created new pressures for expanding voting rights, eventually helping to give birth to the Voting Rights Act of 1965. President Truman's civil rights commission concluded that "interference with the right of a qualified citizen to vote locally cannot today remain a local problem." The committee report continued, "An American diplomat cannot forcefully argue for free elections in foreign lands without meeting the challenge that in many sections of America, qualified voters do not have free access to the polls."[36] When proposing new voting rights measures, President Johnson asserted that nothing harmed America's standing in the world more "than the discriminatory denial of any American citizen at home to vote on the basis of race or color."[37] The Cold War may have been partly responsible for numerous federal and state decisions to remove literacy tests, reduce residency restrictions for voting, and eliminate the last vestiges of property qualifications. That "the virtues of democracy were . . . trumpeted from almost every point on the political spectrum" during the 1950s, 1960s, and early 1970s, Keyssar notes, "made it difficult to oppose a broad franchise."[38]

Major restrictions on access to the ballot have not been associated with any major military conflict. Military conflict is associated with the temporary effort to disenfranchise Confederate soldiers and leaders after the Civil War, as well as suffrage restrictions on immigrants passed in the wake of World War I.[39] Other movements to limit access to the ballot have thrived only during peacetime. As revolutionary rhetoric faded during the first half of the nineteenth century, Northern states repealed laws allowing persons of color to vote.[40] As the memory of the Civil War faded, Southern states, with permission from Northern justices, enacted numerous policies that prevented persons of color from exercising their Fifteenth Amendment rights.

"[T]he complete return to peacetime" after Reconstruction, Karlan observes, "began the period of massive black disenfranchisement . . . that kept blacks from the polls until another war, World War II, revived their struggle for suffrage."[41] Peace also provided occasions for restricting the voting rights of many white persons through a combination of literacy tests, disenfranchisement of aliens (who had typically been allowed to vote in Jacksonian America), and complex voting registration laws.[42] The connection between restrictive policies and peace is not fortuitous. "It does not seem coincidental," Keyssar writes of the period between the Civil War and World War I, "that this prolonged period of franchise contraction occurred during a prolonged period of peace." The only war that took place during this period, the Spanish-American War, "was relatively brief" and "did not require mass recruitment."[43] The period between World War I and World War II was similarly a time of "stasis" for voting rights, as literacy requirements, registration laws, and Jim Crow continued shrinking the voting universe while "the dynamics of war were not in play."[44]

War is closely associated with increased protections for voting rights no matter what criteria are used for determining the relationship between war and voting. Analyses limited to reforms adopted while troops were in the field would include the American Revolution, the Civil War, World War II, and the Vietnam War. Congress approved the Nineteenth Amendment before Armistice Day. The American electoral universe has never contracted during an ongoing military conflict. Analyses that include instances when Americans have been inspired to expand voting rights as an immediate reward for wartime service would discuss the Fifteenth Amendment and state decisions to ratify the Nineteenth Amendment. The former was partly a consequence of Republican partisan needs, but was made possible by the crucial role African American troops played in the final years of the Civil War. As one commentator at that time noted, "Party expediency and exact justice coincide for once."[45] The Spanish-American War is the only military conflict in American history that did not inspire an overall increase in access to the ballot.[46] Thus, even if the Cold War is excluded from the analysis for involving, at most, a threat of military conflict, war and voting rights are closely associated. On no reasonable view of the evidence can the history of voting rights in the United States be said to support the conventional claim that war is bad for civil rights and liberties.

This close connection between war and increased voting rights is not distinctive to the United States. Military conflict is associated with an expanded suffrage throughout the world. "The enfranchisement of soldiers," Keyssar writes, "was an issue in Britain in World War I; and the dynamics of wartime mobilization contributed to the expansion of the suffrage in Belgium, parts of

Canada, and Italy. . . . The cause of women's suffrage . . . was promoted by both world wars."[47]

War similarly expanded the suffrage in France, Norway, and Germany.[48] As has been the case in the United States, democracies or proto-democracies rarely restrict voting rights during or immediately after a military conflict. The right to vote has a global immunity to the ills that frequently afflict other civil liberties in wartime.

Justifications for Expanding Voting Rights in Wartime

The justifications for expanding voting rights during wartime help explain why, contrary to accepted wisdom, civil rights and liberties associated with voting tend to increase during war and be contracted in peacetime. Most commentators assume that constitutional decision makers during wartime balance civil liberties against national security, with the weight of the balance being placed on national security. This common assertion makes two related assumptions. First, maintaining prewar civil liberties and rights will threaten national security during war. Second, maintaining prewar civil liberties and rights will not have other distinctive wartime benefits that compensate for their increased national security costs. The benefits of protective civil liberties policies, analyses routinely assume, remain the same in war and peace. These assumptions are wrong when applied to the franchise. Proponents of voting rights have persuasively argued that expanding access to the ballot promotes national security and facilitates other war aims. War also increases the salience of the connection between the duty to serve and the right to vote that has historically served as the foundation for voting rights in the United States. Opponents of voting rights rarely claim that new restrictions are necessary because of wartime conditions. They insist that existing restrictions on voting should be maintained despite the pragmatic and ideological appeals of expanding the suffrage in wartime. Not surprisingly, their arguments for maintaining a restricted suffrage or further restricting suffrage have historically seemed most compelling during long periods of peace, when the practical and normative connections between the duty to serve and the right to vote seem less pressing to many Americans.

The most powerful justification for expanding eligibility and access to the franchise throughout American history has been that those who have a duty to fight or serve their country in some fashion should also have the right to vote. Elaine Scarry and others speak of an ongoing "interweaving of voting and arms."[49] Americans during the nineteenth century insisted that "those who bear the burdens of the state should choose those that rule it." "If we are called on to do military duty against the rebel enemies in the field," former slaves asked in January 1865, "why should we be denied the privilege of voting?"[50] These same arguments were repeated during the twentieth century. Dwight Eisenhower bluntly asserted, "If a man is old enough to fight he is old enough to vote."[51]

Voting rights have frequently been defended as rewards for faithful service during a war. War facilitates increased support for voting rights by providing opportunities for persons to demonstrate the loyalty and other capacities deemed necessary to qualify for the suffrage. "Have we that degree of moral courage," a Republican asserted after the Civil War, "which will enable us to recognize the services of those black veterans and do them justice?"[52] Henry Ward Beecher agreed that persons of color had "earned" the franchise through "heroic military service" and "unswerving fidelity to the Union."[53] Service need not consist of bearing arms. World War I "could not have been fought," Woodrow Wilson declared when asking the Senate to send the Nineteenth Amendment to the states, "if it had not been for the services of women."[54]

The ideological justifications for particular wars have been invoked in wartime arguments for expanding the suffrage. Wars fought to secure government by consent or to make the world safe for democracy have provided rhetorical grist for movements dedicated to furthering government by consent or democracy at home.[55] Noting that "President Wilson has declared that 'we are at war because of that which is dearest to our hearts—democracy,'" Anna Howard Shaw in 1918 informed Congress that "to fail to ask for the suffrage amendment at this time would be treason to the fundamental cause for which we, as a nation, have entered the war."[56] World War II similarly privileged arguments for expanding the franchise by "recast[ing] democratization as a matter of compelling national interest and therefore as an appropriate, indeed imperative, concern of the national government."[57]

Military conflict provides more tangible benefits for national security. Prominent Americans have frequently insisted that common citizens would not fight or fight hard unless allowed to vote. Benjamin Franklin at the Constitutional Convention feared that proposed voting restrictions would "depress the virtue and public spirit of our common people, of which they displayed a great deal during the war."[58] More crassly, elected officials are typically aware that soldiers, particularly volunteers, are likely to favor the incumbent administration if given the opportunity to vote. Such knowledge has not only inspired measures expanding the right to vote, but measures facilitating the exercise of that right. Republicans during the Civil War passed state statutes ensuring that soldiers in the field would be able to cast absentee ballots in large part because the Union Army was known to be a Republican stronghold. James McPherson notes that more than three-quarters of the soldiers who voted by absentee ballot during the election of 1864 voted for Lincoln. The Union army vote was crucial in several congressional districts and helped decide a Maryland referendum to abolish slavery.[59]

Arguments for restricting the suffrage or making voting more difficult rarely make specific reference to national security concerns or war aims. Persons opposed to granting the ballot to persons of color, women, or the poor do not charge those groups with disloyalty. Instead, the claim is made that such persons lack some quality necessary for voting in war and in peace. Such arguments require opponents of a restricted suffrage to break the link between the duty to serve and the right to vote or, in the case of persons of color, oppose both the duty to serve and the right to vote. As such, arguments for a restrictive suffrage are particularly vulnerable to wartime pressures for mobilizing disenfranchised persons previously not eligible for military service and increased wartime support for rewarding soldiers and others who are contributing or have contributed to the war effort.

The common arguments for and against voting rights explain why conventional wisdom perversely accounts for the ebbs and flows of voting rights policymaking in the United States. Professors Mark Tushnet and Geoffrey Stone observe that Americans frequently adopt civil rights policies during war that they regret after the shooting stops.[60] Voting rights fit this pattern. Americans made voting rights policies during or in the immediate wake of the Revolutionary War, War of 1812, and Civil War that many elites regretted as those wars became distant memories. What distinguishes voting rights from the policies Tushnet and Stone analyze is that the wartime policies Americans regretted were policies that increased civil liberties and civil rights. Just as the decision to intern Japanese Americans during World War II became a national embarrassment during the postwar years, so many Americans by the turn of the twentieth century came to perceive the Fifteenth Amendment and Reconstruction as an unfortunate overreaction to wartime conditions.[61] Only during prolonged periods of peace, when the value of military service diminishes and mass mobilization seems unnecessary, do proponents of restrictive voting policies occasionally break the link between the duty to fight and the right to vote, or persuade their fellow citizens that many Americans ought not be allowed to either fight or vote.

The extent to which wartime arguments for expanding voting rights are successful has historically depended on both the nature of the particular war and the prewar status of the voting right in question. Wars that require mass mobilization have historically generated greater expansions of voting rights than wars that have not strained existing state capacity. The greater the perceived need for military service from persons previously denied the ballot, the more likely the franchise will be expanded. The Civil War and World War II presented more favorable conditions for increasing access to the ballot than the Mexican War and the Spanish-American War. Proponents of increased voting rights are also more likely to take advantage of wartime opportunities to the extent their fellow citizens are already predisposed to support electoral reforms. Many Americans have not needed war or the threat of war to endorse voting rights. The movement for women's suffrage predated World War I by seventy years. By 1918, any military conflict that required service from some women was likely to provide the last impetus needed to pass the Nineteenth Amendment. Many other Americans have not thought war or the threat of war sufficient to justify voting rights. More than Hitler or World War II proved necessary to convince Southern majorities that persons of color ought to be allowed by law and practice to vote as equals in their jurisdictions. Military service has not proved sufficient to yield voting rights when there was too little support for those rights before the shooting started. Persons of color did not gain voting rights after fighting for the United States during the War of 1812 and World War I.[62] Women were not given the ballot as a reward for their service during the Civil War.[63]

Military tensions and conflicts foster voting rights by several interrelated means. As noted above, many arguments for expanding voting rights are more salient immediately before, during, and immediately after a war. Americans during and in the wake of a war are more likely to perceive connections between the duty to serve and the right to vote, reward those who are serving or served in the war, and support policies that further the democratic values underlying public justifications for the war. War often generates more advocates as well as more arguments for voting rights. Military service has emboldened persons previously denied the ballot to demand voting rights.[64] Finally, war generates more effective advocates for voting rights. Soldiers in the army often develop leadership skills that are later put to use in campaigns for expanding the suffrage. African American war veterans led fights for voting rights during and immediately after the Civil War and World War II.[65]

Through a combination of more compelling arguments and more effective advocates, military tensions and conflicts have greased the path for electoral reform. When political efforts to secure the ballot before the war were on the brink of success, as was the case with the movement for women's suffrage before World War I and the movement for giving eighteen-year-olds the vote before Vietnam, military mobilization has provided the last push necessary for significant electoral reform. When the prewar movement was weaker, war often served as a vehicle for putting expanded voting rights permanently on the political agenda and securing minor reforms. Racial liberals during World War II were immediately able to repeal the poll tax only for veterans, but they planted the seeds for a broader political movement that would eventually abolish the poll tax for all civilians. Even when war produces no immediate reform, the military conflict may place movements for voting rights in a better position to take advantage of postwar opportunities, provided those opportunities occur before the glow of war wears off. Persons of color did not gain the ballot in 1865. Nevertheless, by substantially increasing the number of citizens who supported granting voting rights to persons of color, or at least were not militantly opposed, the Civil War, when combined with the partisan struggles of the late 1860s, gave moderate Republicans sufficient political strength and motivation to extend the franchise to African Americans.

The historical justifications for increasing protections for voting rights during wartime cast significant doubt on bald generalizations that national security is invariably threatened by protective civil liberties policies in wartime. To the extent voting rights influence national security, most Americans have thought the influence positive. Americans have frequently asserted that persons who are allowed to vote are more likely to serve their country and serve their country well in time of war. Elites during the Cold War believed that third world countries were more likely to ally with the United States in the struggle against communism if persons of color had greater access to the ballot. The costs of allowing a few disloyal citizens to vote, given the large number of voters in even the most local election, are miniscule. In short, at least in the case of voting rights, wartime concerns typically justify more protective civil liberties policies than may have been thought appropriate in peacetime.

Voting Rights and Civil Liberties during Wartime

Studies of voting rights and studies of civil liberties policy during wartime exhibit a strange asymmetry. War is very visible when voting rights are discussed. Keyssar details the very close association between war and the voting rights of all Americans.[66] Philip Klinkner and Rogers Smith document the very close association between war and the voting rights of African Americans.[67] Voting rights are nevertheless invisible whenever civil liberties in wartime are discussed. Recent scholarship on wartime civil liberties policymaking rarely alludes to the Fifteenth, Nineteenth, and Twenty-Sixth Amendments, discusses any other wartime measure that expanded access to the ballot, or even cites *The Right to Vote* or *The Unsteady March*. The reason voting rights play little role in commentaries on civil liberties in wartime is that those studies focus on new demands for restrictive policies that arose because the United States was at war, were intended to last only for the duration of the war, and were eventually adjudicated by the Supreme Court of the United States. The crucial decisions expanding the suffrage in wartime occurred after the military situation transformed a preexisting conflict; these decisions were intended to endure after the war and were not reviewed by federal courts.

The most frequently discussed restrictions on civil liberties in wartime all involved policies that were adopted because the United States was at war and were intended to be in force only during the war. While these wartime policies had prewar antecedents, Americans did not debate whether to impose martial law before 1860, whether to restrict antiwar speech before 1917, and whether to intern Japanese Americans before 1940. When hostilities ceased, the restrictive policies were abandoned. Debate over whether persons of color, women, and older teenagers should vote, by comparison, predated the Civil War, World War I, and the Vietnam War. Protective policies adopted during or because of a military conflict were intended to be permanent. Hence, while the Sedition Act of 1918 is routinely classified as a wartime measure, the congressional vote on women's suffrage is routinely classified as the culmination of a lengthy political struggle for voting rights that just happened to take place during World War I.

Such analyses fail to recognize how war transforms existing conflicts over civil liberties. Military conflicts change the course of ongoing political struggles by providing advocates with new arguments, affecting the salience of previous arguments, and changing the balance of power between policy activists. Such events as the congressional decision to send the Nineteenth Amendment to the states and the Supreme Court's decision to declare white primaries unconstitutional were consequences of new opportunities for voting rights advocacy that opened up when the United States went to war. Women's service during World War I dramatically improved the political climate for voting reform. Woodrow Wilson and others did not publicly support the suffrage movement until the example of women serving their country during a crisis period converted them.[68] Their wartime experiences explain why the federal legislature endorsed the Nineteenth Amendment in 1918 and not at some later date, if at all. World War II transformed the political status of Jim Crow. Liberals tolerated white primaries in the South until the example of Hitler and the bravery of African American troops inspired renewed commitments to racial equality in the United States.[69] *Smith v. Allwright*[70] was a wartime decision, even though agitation over white primaries predated the war.

Voting rights are also not part of the wartime civil liberties canon because commentary on civil liberties policy during periods of military tension is almost always commentary on the major civil liberties issues adjudicated by courts during and immediately after the war. Such frequently discussed restrictions on civil liberties as Lincoln's suspension of habeas corpus during the Civil War, restrictions on antiwar advocacy during World War I, and the removal of Japanese Americans from the West Coast during World War II were all resolved into judicial questions and decided by the Supreme Court of the United States.[71] *Smith v. Allwright* and *Oregon v. Mitchell*[72] aside, the Supreme Court of the United States has rarely discussed the merits of important measures expanding suffrage rights. The few state cases[73] are not well known. This near-exclusive concern with adjudication is appropriate when the subject is explicitly understood as judicial protection of civil rights and liberties during wartime. Too often, however, commentators equate civil liberties policy during wartime with judicial decisions on wartime civil liberties policies. Indeed, constitutional commentary in the United States is in general too often confined to commentary on decisions handed down by the Supreme Court of the United States.[74] This misidentification helps explain why instances in which elected officials protect civil liberties play little or no role in discussions of civil liberties policymaking in wartime or, for that matter, any other time.

Elected officials in the United States have been the persons primarily responsible for governmental decisions expanding the suffrage, and their protective decisions have rarely been subject to review by federal or state courts. Justices in the United States have no authority to review official decisions protecting or expanding civil rights and civil liberties, unless the decision protecting one person's rights arguably violates the constitutional rights of other persons or impinges on federalism concerns. Challenges to the validity of a constitutional amendment are not justiciable.[75] These standing and other jurisprudential requirements for constitutional adjudication explain why the vast majority of cases on voting rights decided by state and federal courts were brought by persons making constitutional attacks against official decisions to restrict access to the ballot. Persons who favored property qualifications during the eighteenth century had no judicial remedy when their state eased such restriction during the American Revolution. The Twenty-Sixth Amendment foreclosed judicial challenges to the eighteen-year-old vote. For the same reasons, the other numerous instances when elected officials expanded or protected voting rights in wartime make, at most, cameo appearances in the *Supreme Court Reporter* and are even less likely to be seen in jurocentric studies of civil liberties in wartime.

OTHER "ANOMALIES"

The close connection between war and voting rights is not anomalous or an aberration. War has frequently provided occasions for expanding other civil rights and liberties.[76] Philip Klinkner and Rogers Smith note that Americans have made progress toward racial equality primarily during major military conflicts, when mobilization needs and the rhetoric of democratic equality have inspired Americans to increase the constitutional and legal rights of African Americans.[77] To a lesser degree, war has contributed to gender equality, as mobilization needs inspire some Americans to tear down formal and informal barriers to female participation in the workforce. World War I was good for the rights of labor. World War II witnessed substantial improvements in the rights of Jehovah's Witnesses, and by implication, the first amendment rights of all religious minorities. The Cold War inspired further increases in the rights of African Americans and the procedural rights of criminal suspects.

Wartime arguments for expanding these civil rights and liberties were similar to the wartime arguments used to justify increased protection for voting rights. Proponents of numerous civil liberties have historically maintained that recognizing particular individual rights will further national security. Black troops were promised freedom during the Revolutionary War because their service was thought necessary to defeat the British.[78] President Wilson in 1917 insisted that Congress pass legislation mandating an eight-hour day to prevent labor strife during World War I.[79] Proponents of civil rights have successfully linked protective policies with the justification of a particular war or identified restrictive policies with national enemies. Racial liberalism during World War II was consistently associated with the democratic justifications for the fight against Hitler.[80] Compelled flag salutes were effectively analogized to compelled saluting in Nazi Germany.[81] These arguments for adopting protective policies while the United States was involved in a hot or cold war were not always successful. Analogizing McCarthyism to Soviet practices at best slowed the pace of repression during the 1950s. Still, the overall record indicates that proponents of civil liberties were often successful when, preaching to an audience with some disposition to listen, they made a plausible claim that protecting a civil liberty in wartime would promote national security, reward loyal Americans, and reflect the professed war aims of the United States.

The numerous instances in which protective civil liberties policies were adopted while the United States was at war are rarely discussed by scholarship on civil liberties in wartime for the same reason that scholarship ignores wartime decisions to expand voting rights. War often inspires new demands for restricting civil liberties while troops are in the field, but rarely generates similar calls for temporary increases in liberty and equality. Instead, mass mobilization and justifications for military conflict frequently transform pre-existing public policy debates over civil liberties in ways that foster greater support for providing increased statutory or constitutional protections for certain individual rights that are intended as relatively permanent. Antislavery advocacy was not new in 1861, and no Northerner asserted that slaves should be freed only for the duration of the war. Instead, secession further increased Northern antipathy to Southern institutions and provided an additional, military, justification for official decrees aimed at eradicating slavery forever. The Emancipation Proclamation is a wartime measure even though debate over human bondage preceded the Civil War. World War I fostered the eight-hour day partly because mobilization concerns temporarily altered the balance of power between labor and management, enabling railroad employees to place on the statutory books what they hoped were enduring public policies. As has been the case with voting rights, elected officials have been primarily responsible for protecting and expanding civil liberties and rights during military conflicts. Anti-imperialist advocates freely criticized American involvement in the Philippines at the turn of the twentieth century because the McKinley Administration refused to censor domestic dissent.[82] Communists participated more freely in American political life during World War II than during the Cold War because the Roosevelt Administration limited prosecution of party officials while the United States was allied with the Soviet Union.[83] The Supreme Court has adjudicated disputes over whether antiwar speech should be banned only when government officials punished political dissenters. Official decisions to permit antiwar advocacy are not justiciable, even when based on what the justices might believe is an unduly broad interpretation of the First and Fourteenth Amendments.

LESSONS FOR THE PRESENT

An accurate history of voting rights and other civil liberties during wartime in the United States offers grounds for optimism and despair about the direction of contemporary policy during the war against terrorism. The main reason for optimism is that military conflicts and tensions have frequently provided occasions for protecting civil liberties and civil rights in the United States and abroad. Government officials have adopted policies increasing voting rights, speech rights, religious freedom, equality rights, labor rights, and the rights of criminal suspects when combat seemed imminent, when troops were engaged in the field, and in the immediate wake of a war. The main reason for despair is that the conditions that fostered protective policies in the past are largely absent in the present. So far, the war against terrorism has not required the mass mobilization that has historically created public sympathy for those serving their country and given numerous Americans the chance to demonstrate the various capacities thought necessary to merit particular individual rights. The incumbent Bush administration and Congress are not predisposed to interpret national security needs as justifying greater solicitude for the freedoms laid out in the Bill of Rights, with the possible exception of gun and free exercise rights.[84]

Despair seems particularly warranted in the case of voting rights, the civil liberty most often expanded during wartime. Noting how past military conflicts have facilitated greater access to the ballot, Pamela Karlan suggests that Americans might continue this pattern during the present war against terrorism by repealing laws prohibiting persons convicted of various crimes from voting.[85] These laws, she and others observe, provide the only surviving statutory basis for disenfranchising a substantial number of American adults.[86] The forces that generated an expanded suffrage in the past, however, do not seem capable of yielding an expanded suffrage in the present. No hue and cry is currently being made for the service of persons convicted of crimes in the fight against terrorism. Stories are not being told about persons who previously made criminal mistakes redeeming themselves on the field of battle. The military conflict most analogous to the present war against terrorism is the Spanish-American War. That conflict generated little pressure for mobilization and even less pressure for expanding civil rights and liberties.[87]

Matters may change should the war against terrorism prove as relatively enduring as the Cold War. Just as each new administration that took office during the post–World War II era adjusted the civil liberties policies the previous administration thought mandated by the struggle against Communism, so each new administration that takes office after September 11, 2001, is likely to adjust the civil liberties policies the previous administration thought mandated by the struggle against militant Islam. These adjustments, history suggests, will not only concern the extent to which prewar civil liberties are restricted. Rather, many political leaders will think that providing increased protections for certain civil liberties best secures national goals during the war against terrorism. One such future administration might highlight the sacrifices persons previously convicted of criminal offenses have made in Iraq and Afghanistan as part of a campaign aimed at demonstrating that former felons can become valued citizens. Perhaps the franchise will be granted to former convicts willing to perform certain wartime services. Under the right circumstances, Americans might eventually conclude that overcrowded prisons waste human and other resources better put to use combating terrorism.

Proponents of protective civil liberties policies are most likely to be successful at present if they explain why various freedoms serve national security needs, advance other wartime concerns, or follow from the justification of the war against terrorism. The history of voting rights in the United States highlights how the opposition between national security and civil liberties is often a false one. Protecting civil liberties frequently promotes national security and even more frequently facilitates crucial war aims. Voting rights have been expanded during and immediately after military conflicts when proponents of an expanded suffrage have tightly linked the duty to serve with the right to vote, convinced Americans that voting rights facilitated mobilization or were an appropriate reward for service during the war, and associated an expanded suffrage with the democratic and egalitarian justifications for the war.

Numerous civil liberties are capable of similar wartime defenses. Justice Hugo Black's opinion in the Pentagon papers case provided reasons why the benefits associated with the First Amendment increase during wartime. "[P]aramount among the responsibilities of a free press," he wrote,

> is the duty to prevent any part of the government from deceiving the people and sending them off to distant lands to die of foreign fevers and foreign shot and shell. In my view, far from deserving condemnation for their courageous reporting, the *New York Times*, the *Washington Post*, and other newspapers should be commended for serving the purpose that the Founding Fathers saw so clearly. In revealing the workings of government that led to the Vietnam war, the newspapers nobly did precisely that which the Founders hoped and trusted they would do.[88]

In Black's view, "The guarding of military and diplomatic secrets at the expense of informed representative government provides no real security for our Republic."[89] The more important the policy, the more vital are protections for free speech to ensure official decisions are wisely made and reflect democratic sentiment. Restricting civil liberties may similarly be more costly in war than in peace. Those championing the use of torture during the war against terrorism[90] should be reminded that information so obtained is not reliable and distracts from means for obtaining more reliable evidence,[91] that reliance on false information is likely to be particularly damaging when employed to forestall terrorist attacks, that torture may create sympathy for terrorists among numerous third world citizens, and that torture is inconsistent with the democratic values the United States is championing during the present struggle against terrorism. Restrictive peacetime policies that inhibit wartime mobilization are particularly damaging to national security. A military that desperately needs information on the Middle East can ill afford to fire competent Arabic translators who happen to be gay.[92]

Histories of civil liberties policies during wartime must better highlight how, when the United States has been faced with military threats, elected officials have always responded with inducements and rewards for desired behaviors as well as with prohibitions and penalties for undesired behavior. A mandatory draft and bans on antiwar advocacy are popular means for raising an army that will fight hard, but so are laws that remove restrictions on who can serve in the army and expand the individual rights of those who volunteer. Congress during the War of 1812 chose to respond to antiwar advocacy by offering bounties to persons who convinced others to volunteer for military duty and exempting soldiers from laws imprisoning debtors.[93] As these and other G.I. Bills in American history demonstrate, the United States has consistently relied on carrots as well as sticks to induce wartime service. Civil liberties policy is no exception. While elected officials have frequently attempted to prevent perceived disloyal conduct by restricting certain civil rights, all branches of the national government have sought to induce and reward desirable conduct by expanding the voting rights and other freedoms of those willing to participate actively in the war effort.

Crucial Bush administration policies too often rely exclusively on prevention and punishment to the exclusion of inducement and reward. With respect to resident aliens, contemporary policy is "better safe than sorry." The present administration seeks only to forestall and deter undesired behavior. Aliens have been subjected to long terms of detention on the merest suspicion of any affiliation with terrorism. Deportation proceedings have been streamlined. Many aliens have been humiliated by government officials. Few of those responsible have been disciplined.[94] A different approach might emphasize inducements that would encourage resident aliens to engage in such desired behaviors as helping translate vital documents and informing friends in the Middle East that Americans bear no grudge against persons from that part of the world. Such policies might include streamlining naturalization and residency requirements, more liberally extending visas for persons who have reason to fear returning to their home country, and a greater emphasis on treating resident aliens with respect. History cannot determine what combinations of sticks and carrots are appropriate in the present military situation. The story of voting rights and other civil liberties does indicate, however, the existence of numerous policy paths so far not taken.

NOTES

1. Schenck v. United States, 249 U.S. 47, 52 (1919).

2. Geoffrey R. Stone, *Civil Liberties in Wartime,* 28 J. Sup. Ct. Hist. 215, 215 (2003).

3. Alan Brinkley, *A Familiar Story: Lessons from Past Assaults on Freedoms*, in The War on Our Freedoms: Civil Liberties in an Age of Terrorism 23 (Richard C. Leone & Greg Anrig, Jr., eds. 2003). *See* Stephen J. Schulhofer, *No Checks, No Balances: Discarding Bedrock Constitutional Principles*, in The War on Our Freedoms:

Civil Liberties in an Age of Terrorism 74; Richard C. Leone, *The Quiet Republic: The Missing Debate About Civil Liberties After 9/11*, in The War on Our Freedoms: Civil Liberties in an Age of Terrorism 12.

4. For a rare exception, *see* Michael J. Klarman, *Rethinking the History of American Freedom*, 42 Wm. & Mary L. Rev. 265, 273–76 (2000).

5. *See, e.g.,* Stone, *supra* note 2, at 215.

6. Mark A. Graber, *Counterstories: Protecting and Expanding Civil Liberties in Times of War*, in The Constitution in Wartime (Mark Tushnet, ed., 2005) (citing examples where civil rights and liberties were expanded during wartime).

7. Frank Friedel, *Dissent in the Spanish-American War and the Philippine Insurrection*, in Dissent in Three American Wars 85 (1970).

8. Abraham Lincoln, The Collected Works of Abraham Lincoln 29 (vol. 6) (Roy P. Basler, ed., Rutgers Univ. Press, 1953).

9. Francis Biddle, In Brief Authority 300–02 (1962).

10. This chapter and the broader project make no attempt at any specific definition of hot or cold wars or periods of military conflict or tension. Rather, the usual suspects are hauled out. No conclusion would be influenced by including or excluding what might be marginal cases.

11. *See* Graber, *supra* note 6.

12. Philip A. Klinkner and Rogers M. Smith, *The Unsteady March: The Rise and Decline of Racial Equality in America* (1999).

13. *Id.* at 3.

14. *Id.*

15. Klinkner and Smith emphasize "domestic political protest movements willing and able to bring pressure upon national leaders." *Id.* For reasons discussed below, the predispositions of national leaders have historically had as great an influence on civil rights and civil liberties policy in wartime.

16. *See* Alexander Keyssar, *The Right to Vote: The Contested History of Democracy in the United States* (2000); Pamela S. Karlan, *Ballots and Bullets: The Exceptional History of the Right to Vote*, 71 Univ. Cin. L. Rev. 1345 (2003).

17. Keyssar, *supra* note 16, at xxi, 318.

18. Karlan, *supra* note 16, at 1346. *See* Klarman, *supra* note 4, at 273–76; Elaine Scarry, *War and the Social Contract: Nuclear Policy, Distribution, and the Right to Bear Arms*, 139 Univ. Pa. L. Rev. 1257, 1304–309 (1991).

19. Keyssar, *supra* note 16, at 88, 93–104. *See* Karlan, *supra* note 16, at 1348–349; Klinkner & Smith, *supra* note 12, at 66.

20. Keyssar, *supra* note 16, at 215–18. *See* Karlan, *supra* note 16, at 1352–53.

21. *Id.* at 1358–59 (quoting R. Spencer Oliver). *See* Keyssar, *supra* note 16, at 278–81.

22. *See* Karlan, *supra* note 16, at 1346–47.

23. Klinkner & Smith, *supra* note 12, at 20–21; Keyssar, *supra* note 16, at 12.

24. Keyssar, *supra* note 16, at 25.

25. *Id.* at 35.

26. *Id.* at 14. *See* Karlan, *supra* note 16, at 1347–48.

27. Karlan, *supra* note 16, at 1350–351; Keyssar, *supra* note 16, at 104.

28. Keyssar, *supra* note 16, at 130–31.

29. 78 Pub. L. No. 277, 58 Stat. 136 (1944). *See* Karlan, *supra* note 16, at 1354–55.

30. Keyssar, *supra* note 16, at 247.

31. Klinkner & Smith, *supra* note 12, at 174.

32. *See* Smith v. Allwright, 321 U.S. 649 (1944), *overruling* Grovey v. Townsend, 295 U.S. 45 (1935).

33. Klinkner & Smith, *supra* note 12, at 193. *See* Michael J. Klarman, *Civil Rights Law: Who Made It and How Much Did It Matter,* 83 Geo. L.J. 433, 456 (1994); Karlan, *supra* note 16, at 1355–356; Keyssar, *supra* note 16, at 248.

34. Klinkner & Smith, *supra* note 12, at 193 (quoting Darlene Clark Hine).

35. Keyssar, *supra* note 16, at 250–55.

36. Klinkner & Smith, *supra* note 12, at 214–15.

37. *Id.* at 277–78; Karlan, *supra* note 16, at 1357–358.; Keyssar, *supra* note 16, at 151–52, 156–57, 260, 265, 268. *See also* Mary L. Dudziak, *Cold War Civil Rights: Race and the Image of American Democracy* (2000) (detailing the influence of the Cold War on civil rights).

38. Keyssar, *supra* note 16, at 268.

39. Keyssar, *supra* note 16, at 104, 145–46.

40. Klinkner & Smith, *supra* note 12, at 28–29, 35–36; Keyssar, *supra* note 16, at 54–55.

41. Karlan, *supra* note 16, at 1350. *See* Klinkner & Smith, *supra* note 12, at 93–94, 103–05.

42. Keyssar, *supra* note 16, at 134, 142, 151–59.

43. *Id.* at 169–70.

44. *Id.* at 227–28, 230, 235.

45. Klinkner & Smith, *supra* note 12, at 80 (quoting Congressman William D. Kelley). *See* Keyssar, *supra* note 16, at 93–94.

46. *See* Klinkner & Smith, *supra* note 12, at 99.

47. Keyssar, *supra* note 16, at 319.

48. *Id.* at xxiii.

49. Scarry, *supra* note 18, at 1304; Karlan, *supra* note 18, at 1347.

50. Keyssar, *supra* note 16, at 44, 81–82; *see id.* at 14–15, 36, 59, 91.

51. Karlan, *supra* note 18, at 1359.

52. Klinkner & Smith, *supra* note 12, at 66 (quoting Governor William Stone of Iowa).

53. Keyssar, *supra* note 16, at 89.

54. *Id.* at 216.

55. *See* Karlan, *supra* note 16, at 1353.

56. Keyssar, *supra* note 16, at 211.

57. *Id.* at 245.

58. *Id.* at 15; *see also id.* at 37–38.

59. *See* James M. McPherson, *Battle Cry of Freedom: The Civil War Era* (1988).

60. Stone, *supra* note 2, at 215; Mark Tushnet, *Defending* Korematsu? *Reflections on Civil Liberties During Wartime,* 2003 Wis. L. Rev. 273 (2003).

61. *See* Klinkner & Smith, *supra* note 12, at 72–73 (quoting Charles Francis Adams).

62. *See id.* at 30–31, 111–12.

63. Keyssar, *supra* note 16, at 177.

64. *See id.* at 16.70.

65. *Id.* at 250.

66. *See generally id.*

67. *See generally* Klinkner & Smith, *supra* note 12.

68. Keyssar, *supra* note 16, at 213.

69. Klinkner & Smith, *supra* note 12, at 161–201.

70. 321 U.S. 649 (1944).

71. *See* Ex parte Milligan, 71 U.S. (1 Wall.) 2 (1866); *Schenck,* 249 U.S. 47; Korematsu v. United States, 323 U.S. 214 (1944).

72. Oregon v. Mitchell, 400 U.S. 112 (1970).

73. *See, e.g.,* State ex rel. Chandler v. Main, 16 Wis. 398, 423 (Wis. 1863) (sustaining laws providing soldiers with absentee ballots).

74. *See* Paul Brest, Sanford Levinson, J.M. Balkin, and Akhil Reed Amar, Processes of Constitutional Decisionmaking: Cases and Materials xxix (4th ed. 2000).

75. *See* Leser v. Garnett, 258 U.S. 130 (1922); Fairchild v. Hughes, 258 U.S. 126 (1922). *But cf.* Arthur W. Machen, Jr., *Is the Fifteenth Amendment Void?,* 23 Harv L. Rev. 169 (1910) (infamously claiming that the justices should have declared the Fifteenth Amendment unconstitutional).

76. For a more detailed account of the claims made in this paragraph, *see generally* Graber, *supra* note 6.

77. *See* Klinkner & Smith, *supra* note 12.

78. *Id.* at 21.

79. Woodrow Wilson, *The Public Papers of Woodrow Wilson* 414 (vol. 41) (Arthur Link ed., 1982) (1966).

80. Klinkner & Smith, *supra* note 12, at 167–68.

81. Shawn Francis Peters, *Judging Jehovah's Witnesses: Religious Persecution and the Dawn of the Rights Revolution* 96–98 (2000).

82. *See* Friedel, *supra* note 7 and accompanying text.

83. William M. Wiecek, *The Legal Foundations of Domestic AntiCommunism: The Background of* Dennis v. United States, 2001 Sup. Ct. Rev. 375, 403 (2001).

84. *See* Lynn Neary, *Nation's Gun Laws and Their Many Loopholes Remain Unchanged Though the Bush Administration Has Changed Many Laws to Help Its War on Terrorism,* (NPR *All Things Considered* radio broadcast, Nov. 15, 2002); Schulhofer, *supra* note 3, at 75; Leone, *supra* note 3, at 12.

85. Karlan, *supra* note 16, at 1346, 1362–72.

86. Alec C. Ewald, *"Civil Death": The Ideological Paradox of Criminal Disenfranchisement Law in the United States,* 2002 Wis. L. Rev. 1045, 1045–46 (2002); Karlan, *supra* note 16, at 1364.

87. Klinkner & Smith, *supra* note 12, at 99–103.

88. New York Times Co. v. United States, 403 U.S. 713, 717 (1971) (Black, J., concurring).

89. *Id.* at 719.

90. *See generally* Alan Dershowitz, *Why Terrorism Works: Understanding the Threat, Responding to the Challenge* (2002).

91. Chanterelle Sung, *Torturing the Ticking Bomb Terrorist: An Analysis of Judicially Sanctioned Torture in the Context of Terrorism,* 23 B.C. Third World L.J. 193, 210 (2003).

92. *See* Anne Hull, *How "Don't Tell" Translates: The Military Needs Linguists, But It Doesn't Want This One,* Wash. Post, Dec. 3, 2003, at A1.

93. Donald R. Hickey, *The War of 1812: A Forgotten Conflict* 111–12, 164, 243 (1989).

94. *See generally* Roberto Suro, *Who Are "We" Now: The Collateral Damage to Immigration,* in *The War on Our Freedoms: Civil Liberties in an Age of Terrorism* (2003).

8

Emergencies and the Idea of Constitutionalism

Mark V. Tushnet

How should war be incorporated into American constitutionalism? I believe that there are three basic positions. The first is that the Constitution's *general* standards should be applied in wartime. But the fact that the nation is engaged in war might be relevant to determining whether those standards are satisfied.[1] So, for example, race-based classifications are subject to strict scrutiny and can survive constitutional challenge only if they are narrowly tailored to advance compelling government interests. Suppose a government adopted a race-based classification in wartime and defended it on the ground that the classification advanced an interest in winning the war. That interest is clearly more "compelling" than other interests sometimes offered in defense of race-based classifications, and—on at least some understandings of the relevant tests—the more compelling an interest is, the less narrowly tailored the classification must be. A race-based classification that would be unconstitutional during peacetime might be constitutional during wartime—not because the constitutional standards differ, but because their rational application leads to different results.

The second position is that the constitutional rules applicable during wartime are categorically different from those applicable during peacetime.[2] Perhaps a race-based classification employed during wartime need satisfy only rational basis review, for example. We can describe this view as acknowledging that the Constitution applies during wartime, but as contending as well that the Constitution is bifurcated into one set of provisions applicable during wartime and another applicable during peacetime.

The differences between the first and the second positions may well be rather small. The first position requires decision makers to think that war is

177

relevant to the application of universal standards, while the second allows them to think that war triggers the application of a distinctive set of standards. But nothing in the conceptual scheme rules out the possibility that, with respect to any particular constitutional problem, the substantive standard to be applied under the second approach will lead to the same outcome that application of the universal standard, taking war into account, would lead to under the first approach.

The third approach is different. It treats war as presenting the possibility of justifying a widespread suspension of legality. This approach is most closely associated with the legal theorist Carl Schmitt, whose work, discredited for a generation because of the role it played in rationalizing the Nazi regime, has attracted a great deal of recent attention.

This chapter outlines the three approaches and concludes by arguing that U.S. constitutionalists should take the third one seriously, so as to avoid providing law-based justifications for actions that, while perhaps understandable in pragmatic and perhaps even in nonpragmatic moral terms, undermine the values expressed in the rule-of-law tradition.

THE FIRST TWO APPROACHES

Emergency as the Occasion for Applying Ordinary Constitutional Standards, and Emergency as the Occasion for Applying Categorically Different Standards

Addressing Congress in December 1862, Abraham Lincoln said, "The dogmas of the quiet past are inadequate for the stormy present. The occasion is piled high with difficulty, and we must rise to the occasion. As our case is new, so we must think anew, and act anew. We must disenthrall ourselves, and then we shall save our country."[3] Lincoln elegantly put what has become a standard point about legal and constitutional analysis: Circumstances alter cases. That is, the constitutional doctrines developed in connection with commercial advertising or even political speech in ordinary times may not be appropriate in other circumstances.

The Case For

Writing in the context of an economic rather than a military crisis, Justice Harlan Fiske Stone argued that constitutional law did not need to be displaced, but only properly interpreted, to deal effectively with the crisis. As he put it, "Emergency does not create power, [but] emergency may furnish the occasion for the exercise of power."[4] And, just as emergency may create the occasion for the exercise of power, emergency may provide a justification for actions that would, absent the emergency, be unjustified intrusions on civil liberties. As Justice Holmes put it, "When a nation is at war many things that might be said in time of peace are such a hindrance to its effort that their utterance will not be endured so long as men fight and that no court could regard them as protected by any constitutional right."[5] Holmes might be read as expressing a resigned acceptance of the inevitable. But, because Holmes was himself a member of a court that was at the very moment deciding whether the speech in question was constitutionally protected, it is better to read him as asserting that what counts as a violation of free expression in peacetime is just different from what might count as a violation of free speech in wartime.

According to the first approach, this must be right. Its proponents believe that, at the most abstract level, a nation's commitment to principles of free expression persists undiminished no matter what the circumstances. The question is whether the scope of the particular civil liberty at issue is properly defined with reference to wartime conditions.

Here we can distinguish between two general approaches to the definition of constitutional rights, a balancing approach and a categorical approach. Plainly, wartime conditions are relevant when constitutional rights are defined by balancing competing interests. Balancing approaches, though, raise in acute form the concern that wartime will distort the law. Judges, no less than other government officials, are susceptible to the pressures of events. Justice Robert Jackson made some astute observations about the war power that also apply to the definition of constitutional rights with reference to wartime conditions: "[T]his vague, undefined and indefinable 'war power' . . . is usually invoked in haste and excitement when calm legislative consideration of constitutional limitation is difficult. It is executed in a time of patriotic fervor that makes moderation unpopular. And, worst of all, it is interpreted by judges under the influence of the same passions and pressures."[6] Judges, one might fear, will undervalue some and overvalue other elements in the balance, and so define constitutional rights in a way that, on reflection, should be troubling.

Categorical approaches are designed to offset this tendency by screening out of consideration the features of the circumstances that are likely to induce misjudgment. And, under some conditions, they may succeed in doing so, when the categorical rules address decision makers who might not appreciate the importance of considerations that the decision makers might think peripheral to their more central tasks. Consider, for example, a categorical rule against torture by police officers. Judges might think that in the abstract they can imagine situations in which torture might be a valuable investigative technique. Judges might think that they must communicate rules effectively to police officers. They might also think that any verbal formulation of the (limited) circumstances in which torture might be acceptable is too likely to be misinterpreted in ways that would lead the officers to engage in torture more often than they should. The judges could then conclude that they should announce a categorical rule against torture despite their awareness that such a rule does not correspond to their own sense of what is acceptable.

Categorical approaches make most sense, then, when the judges are designing rules for others to follow. Unfortunately, they do so in the form of precedents—that is, in the form of rules that they themselves are to follow. It takes a mindset that is, I think, quite difficult to achieve for a person to rule out of consideration for himself or herself in the future something that the person today thinks plainly relevant to the decision.[7] The difficulty in the context of defining constitutional rights in wartime is obvious. The circumstances of war are something like an elephant in the living room. Judges might agree that a categorical rule is desirable, but say that the rules simply differ in wartime. That is, they would take the category *war* as relevant to defining the applicable rule, and screen out *other* considerations. Alternatively, the judges might *try* to screen out the wartime circumstances in their formulation of the rule. But, try as they might, judges are quite unlikely to be able to ignore the elephant's presence. True, they might not explicitly mention the elephant in defining the categorical rule they invoke, but one can rightly be skeptical about any claim that the elephant played no part as they thought about what the rule should be.

What this means, though, is that one will be hard-pressed to say, in anything but an advocate's voice, that civil liberties are violated in wartime. Judges will test government actions against the Constitution. They may often find that the actions do not violate the Constitution, either because the judges place the wartime circumstances in the balance as they define constitutional rights or because they formulate categorical rules that take the fact of war as relevant to triggering one or another rule. It is not, then, that law is silent in wartime. Rather, it is that sometimes it speaks in tones that advocates of particular positions do not like. But, after all, how is that different from any other time?

The Case Against

Suppose we took the original Constitution as the sole guide for determining whether the exercise of emergency powers is permitted. *Blasidell*—the case saying that emergency does not create power—itself illustrates the primary difficulty with this course. The case involved a state law suspending the obligation of debtors to pay their debts during a period of national economic distress. In writing the ban, the Constitution's drafters had in mind Rhode Island statutes suspending the obligation of debtors to repay their debts during a period of local (and, to a degree, national) economic distress. As the dissenters in *Blaisdell* pointed out, this was precisely the kind of law that the constitutional ban on state laws impairing the obligation of contracts was directed at. Or, as Lino Graglia puts it, in *Blaisdell* "the Court missed its best, if not its only, chance to hold unconstitutional a law that really was."[8]

The general point is clear. Constitution drafters anticipate some emergencies, but they fail to anticipate all the ones future decision makers will believe they must deal with. Facing a constitution that seems either to fail to authorize or, worse, even to prohibit actions policy makers deem necessary to respond to the perceived emergency, decision makers, including courts, will feel pressure to "interpret" the constitution to allow the actions.

Perhaps there is nothing wrong with this sort of creative interpretation. After all, as John Marshall said in one of his great opinions, "we must never forget that it is *a constitution* we are expounding," one that is "to be adapted to the various *crises* of human affairs."[9] One might worry, though. What is one to make of a decision upholding a policy because it was a permissible response to crisis? I think there are two possibilities. The Whiggish one is that the exaggerated perception of crisis will discredit the decision as a precedent. The other, more worrisome, is that later policy makers, including courts, will say, "Well, the action taken then didn't violate the constitution even though there wasn't such a severe threat to social order, so the action under consideration today certainly won't violate the constitution because we face a more severe threat, and the courts upheld the earlier policy in the face of a less substantial one."[10]

The worrisome possibility deals with the *consequences* of treating the action in question as lawful. Courts may well succumb to the understandable pressure to rationalize the inevitable with the Constitution; judges as members of the governing elites will feel the need for emergency powers that other members of those elites do (although perhaps fewer judges than executive officials will feel that need, or perhaps judges will feel the need to a lesser extent); and judges as judges will feel some need to make what seems necessary be lawful as well. But, in explaining why the current circumstances fit within constitutional provisions designed for other circumstances, judges may make the exceptional the normal. As David Dyzenhaus has put the point in a related context, "one cannot, as Carl Schmitt rightly argued, confine the exception. If it is introduced into legal order and treated as such, it will spread."[11] The temporary will be made permanent, threatening civil liberties well beyond the period of the emergency.[12]

Posner and Vermeule properly question this consequentialist challenge to the rationalization of emergency powers.[13] The consequentialist challenge rests on two assumptions. The first, which they concede might be correct, is that conditions change after the emergency has passed. The second, which they question, is that judges will be unable to distinguish between the earlier circumstances, which justified the suspension of legality, and the present ones, which do not. Posner and Vermeule note that proponents of the consequentialist fear do not identify the psychological mechanism by which a precedent is extended beyond the point to which its reason extends.

Yet, the consequentialist concern might be different. Posner and Vermeule's response follows the typical consequentialist in assuming that emergencies end, and question the consequentialist's fear that action taken during an emergency will become a precedent for actions taken during normal times. But, perhaps the consequentialist's concern is that the (purported) emergency will never end.

Early statements by the Bush administration about the war on terrorism were to the effect that the war was one of indefinite duration. And, indeed, it is worth noting that statements about the existence of a war on terrorism go back quite a long way. President Ronald Reagan's first inaugural address, delivered as the Iranian hostage crisis was ending, said that the United States would use "the will and courage of free men and women" as a "weapon" against "those who practice terrorism and prey upon their neighbors."[14] The 1996 revision of the federal habeas corpus statute goes by the acronym AEDPA—the last letters stand for "Effective Death Penalty Act," while the first stands for "Anti-terrorism."

The already long duration of the "War on Terrorism" suggests that we ought not think of it as a war in the sense that World War II was a war. It is, perhaps, more like a condition than a war—more like the war on cancer, the war on poverty, or, most pertinently, the war on crime. Designing appropriate rules to apply in wartime, when the war is understood to be time-limited, is one thing. Doing so for a more-or-less permanent condition is quite another. Or rather— it is the ordinary job of constitutional interpretation.

In this connection, it might be worth noting the possibility that the most relevant retrospective evaluation of current policies might be predicated on the judgment that those policies rested on the proposition that the United States was engaged in a war on terrorism, whereas in retrospect it will seem that in fact the United States was experiencing a condition of terrorism. Judge Michael Mukasey's discussion of the possibility that indefinite detention of a U.S. citizen as an enemy combatant might become "moot" may perhaps be understood as the judge's recognition of the possibility that what is today perceived as a war will later become perceived as a condition, although there are other reasons one might have for thinking that a detention justified today might become unjustified in light of later events.[15]

To the extent that the war on terrorism is a condition rather than a more traditional war, it seems clear that the proper response for legal analysis is to think through what the more-or-less permanent balance between liberty and security should be. Put another way, war-as-condition is a *normal* state of affairs, not an emergency in which extraordinary measures might be appropriate. And, the normal constitutional rules ought to apply in normal conditions—although, again, what the normal rules are might take into account the conditions the nation is experiencing.

EMERGENCY AS THE OCCASION FOR EXTRALEGAL DECISIONS

The case for treating emergency as the occasion for the suspension of legality rests on a set of judgments.[16] First, that suspension of legality is (almost) inevitable. Second, that attempting to identify—in law—the circumstances under which legality can be suspended is futile. And, third, that attempting to do so also is pernicious because it undermines the important values captured in the rule-of-law tradition.

Why is suspension of legality almost inevitable? Constitution designers cannot anticipate all the forms of emergency that will arise and elicit interest among governing elites in expansive exercises of power, perhaps going beyond the limits placed on power by the constitution designers. In referring to interest among governing elites in exercising this sort of power, I do not mean to suggest that the elites will be unified either on the appropriateness of exercising emergency powers in any particular situation, or on the choice of policies to pursue in that situation. What matters for me is that some significant members of the governing elites will press for the adoption of expansive powers in the face of a constitution that appears both to fail to anticipate the situation these members of the elite say the nation faces, and to constrain the adoption of policies in response to the perceived emergency.

At best, constitution designers will use the crises they have experienced to develop some general criteria to identify crises, but even such modeling will inevitably fall short. What, if anything, can constitutional law contribute to thinking about the role of law in emergencies?

We could follow the first or second approaches discussed earlier, leaving the regulation of emergency powers to the initial constitution. Or, we could place legal restraints—in the Constitution—on triggering emergency powers and on the powers that can be used in emergencies. And, finally, we could acknowledge that executive officials will exercise extra-constitutional emergency powers. I use the term "*extra*-constitutional" to introduce a third term, distinct from *legal* or *illegal*. Extra-constitutional powers are neither legal—a person exercising them is not *by definition* immune from sanction pursuant to law—nor illegal— a well-functioning legal system does not require the invocation of sanctions (public or private) against a person exercising them. Rather, extra-constitutional powers are "reviewed"—and disciplined—not by law but by a mobilized citizenry. Having dealt with the first course already, I take up the others here.

Constraining Emergency Powers by Constitutionalizing Them

Constitution writers can acknowledge the fact that emergencies will arise by attempting to anticipate them and regulate the responses emergencies elicit. The U.S. Constitution, for example, contains a provision on emergencies: "The Privilege of the Writ of Habeas Corpus shall not be suspended, unless when in Cases of Rebellion or Invasion the public Safety shall require it."[17] This identifies the *occasions* on which the protection afforded by the writ of habeas corpus can be suspended—rebellion or invasion—and provides a *criterion* for determining when the writ can be suspended—public safety.[18] And, at least according to the conventional interpretation, the Suspension Clause defines a *procedure* by which emergency power is to be invoked: by congressional action. (Committing the decision to suspend the writ to Congress seems to deal with the problem of aggressive assertions of executive authority in emergencies. But, the commitment may be illusory. Perhaps the Constitution can be read, as Lincoln thought it could, to authorize the president to suspend the writ as long as he seeks congressional approval as speedily as possible thereafter. Even more, presidents will almost always be able to identify some statute that, they will say, authorizes them to suspend the writ. A court might eventually find that the president's interpretation of the statutes is erroneous, but in the meantime the writ will have been effectively suspended by action of the president alone.)

The Suspension Clause provides an example as well of some problems associated with seeking to constrain emergency powers by addressing them in a constitution. The primary difficulty is the fundamental one, that constitution writers cannot anticipate all the occasions on which governing elites will think that it is good policy to invoke emergency powers, nor can they specify in detail all the criteria regulating such invocations. For example, was the attack on the World Trade Center towers an "invasion" within the meaning of the Suspension Clause? If so, is the *threat* of an invasion, in the form of some similar attack, ground for suspending the writ?

The fact that emergencies arise with unanticipated characteristics means that such emergencies will place pressure on whatever constitutional provisions there are. If the attack on the World Trade Center towers was not exactly an invasion of the sort the framers had in mind, still, governing elites may think, it is enough like such an invasion to mean that the Constitution permits suspension of the writ. And, if that attack is enough like a (true) invasion, so the threat of another attack might be enough like a (true) invasion. If the threat of another attack similar to the ones of September 11 counts as an invasion, why would not the threat of an attack from Iraq?

The general point is obvious: Constitutional provisions that purport to regulate the invocation of emergency powers will be subject to pressure on precisely those occasions when the provisions seem not to address the situation facing policy makers, which are also precisely the occasions when restrictions on the invocation of emergency powers would seem most important. Including emergency powers provisions in a constitution might well be futile because those powers will be exercised no matter what the constitution says.

One might think, as Oren Gross does, that we can avoid these difficulties by imposing only procedural obligations on officials who suspend legality. They must, Gross says, "openly and publicly acknowledge the nature of their actions."[19] They are then subject to retrospective evaluation, criticism, and perhaps sanction. Yet, Gross's approach cannot avoid *some* substantive elements because those elements serve as the triggers for invocation of his approach. Consider the official who says (to himself or herself, of course), "The nature of the present emergency is such that an open and public acknowledgment that I am departing from legality would undermine the effectiveness of the action that must be taken." Gross's approach simultaneously licenses the official to do so and—by definition, not by the social reaction he anticipates—condemns the official for doing so.

Louis Michael Seidman has forcefully made the general point here. One cannot use law to determine when legality should be suspended.[20] Suppose we think that suspension of legality is dangerous and ought not be done except when circumstances most urgently require it. We list the circumstances that, in our present judgment, would justify the suspension of legality, and the procedures to be used to determine when those circumstances exist (or, in Gross's approach, simply specify procedures that must be used whenever an official seeks to suspend legality). Along comes an emergency. Perhaps it has characteristics that can, with a lawyer's ingenuity, be found on the list. All well and good. But, suppose the emergency is new, that the specified procedures are ill-suited to determining whether *this* is an emergency, or that the official believes that invoking the procedures will vitiate the action being taken. In all these cases, the government can contend, the emergency is so pressing that it requires suspension of the legality expressed in the list of criteria for determining whether legality should be suspended, and the procedures for doing so.

There is, I think, no response to this argument available to those who believe that suspension of legality is sometimes defensible.

But, there is a further point. Governments operating after the invocation of emergency powers provisions are sometimes called *regimes of exception*.[21] That term properly recalls the proposition stated by Carl Schmitt, that the person who has the power to invoke the exception is the true sovereign in a nation.[22] Further, Schmitt argued that the (liberal) rule of law could not— either conceptually or practically—limit a nation's response to perceived emergencies. Schmitt initially distinguished between an absolute form of emergency rule, in which the invocation and use of emergency powers was completely unconstrained, and a rule-of-law form, in which the law identified the occasions for invoking emergency power, the criteria for doing so, and the precise types of action that emergency power justifies.[23] A year later, Schmitt rejected this distinction, arguing that only the first form of emergency power is available because emergencies are situations in which a nation's very existence is perceived to be at stake, and the rule of law cannot constrain a nation's efforts to survive. This third approach, Schmitt understood, cannot be cabined by legality itself. Officials may suspend legality whenever they think it appropriate, that power being inherent in offices they hold. The public's recourse lies in the future, not in controls imposed in the short run.

It is important to emphasize the breadth of the foregoing argument. As Schmitt understood, the invocation of emergency powers is continuous with, not distinct from, quotidian politics, which are *always* open to the arguments for suspension of legality I have outlined. It would be pretty if it were otherwise, but the possibility that ordinary politics can be transformed into the suspension of legality needs to be acknowledged, if only so we can understand what politics is.

As I have emphasized, regimes of exception *will* arise; the only real question is how to locate them in relation to the nation's constitution. Or, put another way, was Schmitt right the first time (in holding out the possibility of a constrained system of emergency powers), or the second (in insisting that only the absolute form of emergency rule was possible)? Consider one aspect of emergency powers under Schmitt's first view. Constitutional provisions dealing with emergency powers place regimes of exception *within* the constitutional order. Constitutional provisions dealing with emergency powers provide a language of justification for the invocation of emergency powers, even though the precise language used in the Constitution may be inapt for the occasions on which emergency powers are invoked. The provisions provide executive officials with a fig leaf of legal justification for expansive use of sheer power. What appears to be emergency power limited by the rule of law is actually unlimited emergency power. As a matter of social self-understanding, it is better to see the thing as it is, not as one might wish it to be. Doing so *might* make it possible to arrive at more accurate retrospective evaluations. But, no matter what, we are better off understanding how our constitutional system works—in emergencies and, according to Schmitt, therefore in normal times as well—than we are in misunderstanding it.

Emergency Powers outside the Constitution

David Dyzenhaus argues that judges can domesticate emergency powers by subjecting their exercise to the ordinary requirements of the rule of law. Other authors—taking the position Schmitt initially did—argue that well-designed emergency powers provisions can avoid the difficulties that have arisen with existing ones. The second option is, as Seidman has shown, not really available. And, the first may overestimate the ability of judges to resist the pressures that lead other public officials to suspend legality.

Dyzenhaus hints at another path. Decision makers might treat emergency powers as extraconstitutional, an understandable departure from norms of legality. Justice Robert Jackson's opinion in *Korematsu* suggests how courts could conceptualize emergency powers in this way. Jackson wrote,

> [I]f we cannot confine military expedients by the Constitution, neither would I distort the Constitution to approve all that the military may deem expedient. . . . [A] judicial construction of the due process clause that will sustain this order is a far more subtle blow to liberty than the promulgation of the order itself. . . . [O]nce a judicial opinion rationalizes such an order to show that it conforms to the Constitution or rather rationalizes the Constitution to show that the Constitution sanctions such an order, the Court for all time has validated . . . [a] principle [that] lies about like a loaded weapon ready for the hand of any authority that can bring forward a plausible claim of an urgent need. . . . The chief restraint upon those who command the physical forces of the country, in the future as in the past, must be their responsibility to the political judgments of their contemporaries and to the moral judgments of history.[24]

Jackson does not quite make the point I extract from his opinion, which is that it is better to have emergency powers exercised in an extraconstitutional way, so that everyone understands that the actions are extraordinary, than to have the actions rationalized away as consistent with the Constitution and thereby normalized. One might call this a claim that the actions have an extraconstitutional validity, one that the *courts* can neither endorse nor condemn, but that is consistent with the persistence of the constitutional regime—which is sustained by the vigilance of the public acting, as was put in the era of the American Revolution, "out of doors."[25]

Why, then, worry about whether emergency powers are rationalized within the law, or treated as extraconstitutional? If emergency powers are extraconstitutional, decision makers can then understand that they should regret that they find themselves compelled to invoke emergency powers. (That is why I describe the invocation of emergency powers as an understandable departure from legality rather than a justified one. A justified departure from legality would not be regrettable.) Once the emergency has passed, they should not only revert to the norms of legality that were suspended during the emergency, but should do what they can to make reparation for the actions they took.[26] Here, too, Lincoln should be our guide, for among his observations in his second inaugural address, delivered in anticipation of a successful conclusion of the Civil War, was the injunction that we "strive on . . . to bind up the nation's wounds."[27]

Again, it is important to note that, according to this analysis, decision makers must be aware that they are acting extraconstitutionally in an emergency. They can be brought to that awareness by, among other things, the repeated assertions of civil liberties alarmists that the officials are acting, not extraconstitutionally, but *illegally*.

Posner and Vermeule treat this problem as a simple variant of the more common problem of finding a conflict between the requirements of law and those of morality.[28] Officials can, they say, always choose to act morally, in disregard of the law, and then hope to persuade others that their actions were justified. The problem of the justified suspension of legality is related to, but not the same as, the one Posner and Vermeule describe.

The differences are these. First, in the ordinary case, the official says, "My obligations under the law direct me to do X, but my moral duties require that I do Y." In the case of suspension of legality, the official says, "The law gives me the power that I have, but in exercising that power morality requires that I disregard the law—all the law, including the law that enables me to deploy the power at hand." The circularity is apparent. It arises from the use of a position created by law to suspend the law. In the ordinary case, the official has the option of resigning his or her position to avoid acting immorally. In the case of the suspension of legality, that option is unavailable.

Second, and probably more important, the ordinary case involves a discrete, limited-issue departure from legality in the service of morality. The official who acts morally but illegally can take some comfort in the fact that his or her actions do not pose a threat to the ideal of the rule of law. Certainly, there will be occasional conflicts between morality and law in a well-functioning rule-of-law system, but the overlap between law and morality in such a system is likely to be so large that an official who disregards the law to act morally will not cast doubt on the continuing value of the rule-of-law system itself. In contrast, the entire point of suspending legality in emergencies is to displace the rule of law. Perhaps this means only that the stakes are much higher when legality is suspended, but I think the difference in degree justifies distinctive analytic treatment.

CONCLUSION

The problem of taking action in emergency situations raises deep questions of constitutional theory—questions that are not well-addressed by treating emergencies either as occasions for the deployment of ordinary constitutional law or as occasions for the deployment of a special kind of constitutional law adapted to emergencies, the course recommended by those who are complacent about the relation between war and constitutionalism. I have argued that we can get a better handle on thinking about constitutional law during emergencies by treating emergencies as occasions for the extraconstitutional suspension of legality. The career of Schmitt's ideas suggests the dangers of such a course. (I use this formulation because Schmitt denied that he personally supported the Nazi regime, although it seems clear that Nazi legal theorists found Schmitt's ideas congenial.) Yet, his arguments seem to me to get at something important about the real-world behavior of legal elites. Perhaps the best we can hope for is the development of a more satisfactory structure of analysis to help us think about what policy makers should do, and then worry about what that means for political theory—and for our nation.

NOTES

An earlier version of this essay chapter appeared as part of Mark Tushnet, *Defending Korematsu?: Reflections on Civil Liberties in Wartime*, 2003 Wis. L. Rev. 273, and another version will appear in *War and the Constitution* (Mark Tushnet ed., 2004).

1. Eric Posner and Adrian Vermeule, *Accommodating Emergencies*, 56 Stan. L. Rev. 605 (2003), describe this as the *strict enforcement* approach to constitutional law during wartime.
2. Posner and Vermeule, *passim*, describe this as the *accommodationist* approach.
3. Abraham Lincoln, Annual Message to Congress, Dec. 1, 1862 (available at www.bartleby.com/66/21/36221.html, visited Dec. 31, 2003).
4. Home Building & Loan Ass'n v. Blaisdell, 290 U.S. 398, 426 (1934).
5. Schenck v. United States, 249 U.S. 47, 52 (1919).

6. Woods v. Cloyd W. Miller Co., 333 U.S. 138, 146 (1948) (Jackson, J., concurring).

7. *See* Posner and Vermeule, *supra* note 2 at 638–39 (describing the "psychological unrealism" of this approach).

8. Lino A. Graglia, *Constitutional Law: A Ruse for Government by an Intellectual Elite*, 14 Ga. St. L. Rev. 767, 772 (1998).

9. McCulloch v. Maryland, 17 U.S. (4 Wheat.) 316, 407, 415 (1819).

10. Oren Gross distinguishes three types of "separation," of which the temporal one I use here is one. (The others involve separations of space and between the true domestic community and mere temporary residents.) He argues, I believe correctly, that the analytic points are the same for all three types. Oren Gross, *Chaos and Rules: Should Responses to Violent Crises Always Be Constitutional?*, 112 Yale L. J. 1011, 1073–96 (2003).

11. David Dyzenhaus, *Humpty Dumpty Rules or the Rule of Law: Legal Theory and the Adjudication of National Security*, Austr. J. Leg. Phil. I (2003).

12. *See* David Dyzenhaus, "The Permanence of the Temporary: Can Emergency Powers Be Normalized?" 21, in *The Security of Freedom: Essays on Canada's Anti-Terrorism Bill* (Ronald J. Daniels, Patrick Macklem, and Kent Roach eds., 2001). Dyzenhaus notes that the title of his chapter comes from a work written by two South Africans dealing with emergency powers under apartheid. *Id.* at 23.

13. Posner and Vermeule, *supra* note 2 at 614–18.

14. Available at www.bartleby.com/124/pres61.html (visited Dec. 31, 2003).

15. Padilla v. Bush, 233 F. Supp. 2d 564 (S.D. N.Y. 2002).

16. Gross, *supra* note 11, refers to the subject of this section as the Extra-Legal Measures Model.

17. U.S. Const., art. I, § 9, cl. 2.

18. Other constitutions provide a more extensive list of occasions and criteria, and identify substantive constitutional protections that can be suspended during periods of emergency. These provisions are sometimes described as following a "reference model" for emergency powers. *See, e.g.,* Joan Fitzpatrick, *Human Rights in Crisis: The International System for Protecting Rights During States of Emergency* 21 (1994) (drawing the term from a report by Nicole Questiaux to the United Nations Sub-Commission on the Prevention of Discrimination and Protection of Minorities).

19. Gross, *supra* note 11 at 1023.

20. Louis Michael Seidman, *The Secret Life of the Political Question Doctrine*, John Marshall L. Rev. (forthcoming 2004).

21. *See, e.g.*, Brian Loveman, *The Constitution of Tyranny: Regimes of Exception in Spanish America* (1993).

22. Carl Schmitt, Political Theology 1 (George Schwab trans., 1988).

23. For a discussion, see Gross, *The Normless and Exceptionless Exception: Carl Schmitt's Theory of Emergency Powers and the "Norm-Exception" Dichotomy*, 21 Cardozo L. Rev. 1825 (2000).

24. 323 U.S. at 245–46 (Jackson, J., dissenting).

25. I am indebted to Wayne Moore, in a personal communication, for this term. Moore suggests as well that the first two approaches I described could be called "constitutional legality" and "extra-legal constitutional validity."

26. The Civil Liberties Act of 1988, 50 U.S.C. 1989a *et seq.*, can then be understood as an expression of the view developed here.

27. Second inaugural address, in *Abraham Lincoln: Speeches and Writings 1859–1865*, at 697 (D. Fehrenbacher ed. 1989).

28. Posner and Vermeule, *supra* note 2 at 606 n. 1.

9

The Terrorism Detention Cases of 2004

Edited by Thomas E. Baker

The Supreme Court handed down three important decisions on June 28, 2004, having to do with the government's detention of prisoners captured in the War on Terrorism that the United States has been waging since the horrific attack on this country that occurred on September 11, 2001.

- *Rasul v. Bush* involved non-Afghan nationals (Australians and Kuwaitis) who were captured during the American invasion of Afghanistan and transported to the American naval base at Guantanamo Bay, Cuba.
- *Hamdi v. Rumsfeld* involved an American citizen captured in Afghanistan who allegedly was fighting against American troops in support of al Qaeda and the Taliban regime.
- *Rumsfeld v. Padilla* involved an American citizen arrested on a flight from Pakistan to Chicago and held incommunicado in military custody—without ever being charged—because the government suspected him of planning acts of terror such as exploding a so-called dirty bomb, a device that would explode and contaminate a wide area with nuclear radiation.[1]

In *Rumsfeld v. Padilla*, the Supreme Court divided 5 to 4. In a bloodless, lawyerlike opinion written by Chief Justice Rehnquist, and joined by Justices O'Connor, Scalia, Kennedy, and Thomas, the majority interpreted the relevant rules of procedure and jurisdictional statutes to conclude that Padilla had followed the wrong procedures: He had sued the Secretary of Defense in the U.S. District Court for the Southern District of New York, where previously he had been held and questioned, but he should have sued the commander of the naval brig in Charleston, South Carolina, where he had been moved and was currently being detained. That was the proper venue and respondent for his petition for a writ of habeas corpus. Justice Kennedy, joined by Justice O'Connor, separately concurred along those same lines to conclude that Padilla would have to refile and start all over again.

Justice Stevens filed a strident dissent, joined by Justices Souter, Ginsburg, and Breyer, that rejected the assumptions and the conclusions of the majority in all their particulars. He began:

> The petition for a writ of *habeas corpus* filed in this case raises questions of profound importance to the Nation. The arguments set forth by the Court do not justify avoidance of our duty to answer those questions. It is quite wrong to characterize the proceeding as a "simple challenge to physical custody" that should be resolved by slavish application of a "bright-line rule" designed to prevent "rampant forum shopping" by litigious prison inmates. As the Court's opinion itself demonstrates, that rule is riddled with exceptions fashioned to protect the high office of the Great Writ. This is an exceptional case that we clearly have jurisdiction to decide.[2]

After elaborately detailing the dissenters' legal disagreements with the majority's interpretations of the rules of procedure, statutes, and prior cases, Justice Stevens sounded the general alarm for civil rights and civil liberties in times of war. His words resonate with these three cases and they certainly will resonate in the cases to come during the ongoing War on Terrorism, which has no end in sight:

> Whether respondent is entitled to immediate release is a question that reasonable jurists may answer in different ways. There is, however, only one possible answer to the question whether he is entitled to a hearing on the justification for his detention.
>
> At stake in this case is nothing less than the essence of a free society. Even more important than the method of selecting the people's rulers and their successors is the character of the constraints imposed on the Executive by the rule of law. Unconstrained Executive detention for the purpose of investigating and preventing subversive activity is the hallmark of the Star Chamber. Access to counsel for the purpose of protecting the citizen from official mistakes and mistreatment is the hallmark of due process.
>
> Executive detention of subversive citizens, like detention of enemy soldiers to keep them off the battlefield, may sometimes be justified to prevent persons from launching or becoming missiles of destruction. It may not, however, be justified by the naked interest in using unlawful procedures to extract information. *Incommunicado* detention for months on end is such a procedure. Whether the information so procured is more or less reliable than that acquired by more extreme forms of torture is of no consequence. For if this Nation is to remain

true to the ideals symbolized by its flag, it must not wield the tools of tyrants even to resist an assault by the forces of tyranny.[3]

What follows are redacted versions of the various opinions in the other two of the Terrorist Detention Cases of 2004: *Rasul v. Bush* and *Hamdi v. Rumsfeld*. These excerpts are intended for the educational purposes of this book and not for legal research purposes: The original full versions cover more than one hundred pages in the *U.S. Reports*. Most of the citations and the extraneous legalisms have been omitted; the opinions have been edited to make them accessible and understandable to a wider readership *sans* indicator ellipses and proofreader's brackets that add nothing of meaning and get in the way of the reader. Thus, here is how the justices on our High Court have responded in the name of the Constitution—in their own words. These opinions oblige every American to contemplate the nature of the War on Terrorism, civil rights and civil liberties of citizens and noncitizens, the great writ of *habeas corpus*, the warmaking power of the executive, the power and responsibility of Congress, and the proper role of the Supreme Court. The stakes could not be higher for our country and for its citizens: Our way of life and our system of constitutional self-government lie in the balance.

Shafiq Rasul, et al., Petitioners,

v.

George W. Bush, President of the United States, et al.
Fawzi Khalid Abdullah Fahad Al Odah, et al., Petitioners,

v.

United States, et al.
Nos. 03-334, 03-343
Argued April 20, 2004
Decided June 28, 2004
542 U.S. _ _, 124 S.Ct. 2686, 159 L.Ed.2d 548 (2004)

Justice Stevens delivered the opinion of the Court:

These two cases present the narrow but important question whether United States courts lack jurisdiction to consider challenges to the legality of the detention of foreign nationals captured abroad in connection with hostilities and incarcerated at the Guantanamo Bay Naval Base, Cuba.

On September 11, 2001, agents of the al Qaeda terrorist network hijacked four commercial airliners and used them as missiles to attack American targets. While one of the four attacks was foiled by the heroism of the plane's passengers, the other three killed approximately 3,000 innocent civilians, destroyed hundreds of millions of dollars of property, and severely damaged the

U.S. economy. In response to the attacks, Congress passed a joint resolution authorizing the President to use "all necessary and appropriate force against those nations, organizations, or persons he determines planned, authorized, committed, or aided the terrorist attacks . . . or harbored such organizations or persons." Acting pursuant to that authorization, the President sent U.S. Armed Forces into Afghanistan to wage a military campaign against al Qaeda and the Taliban regime that had supported it.

Petitioners in these cases are 2 Australian citizens and 12 Kuwaiti citizens who were captured abroad during hostilities between the United States and the Taliban. Since early 2002, the U.S. military has held them—along with, according to the Government's estimate, approximately 640 other non-Americans captured abroad—at the Naval Base at Guantanamo Bay. The United States occupies the Base, which comprises 45 square miles of land and water along the southeast coast of Cuba, pursuant to a 1903 Lease Agreement executed with the newly independent Republic of Cuba in the aftermath of the Spanish-American War. Under the Agreement, "the United States recognizes the continuance of the ultimate sovereignty of the Republic of Cuba over the [leased areas]," while "the Republic of Cuba consents that during the period of the occupation by the United States . . . the United States shall exercise complete jurisdiction and control over and within said areas." In 1934, the parties entered into a treaty providing that, absent an agreement to modify or abrogate the lease, the lease would remain in effect "[s]o long as the United States of America shall not abandon the . . . naval station of Guantanamo."

In 2002, petitioners, through relatives acting as their next friends, filed various actions in the U.S. District Court for the District of Columbia challenging the legality of their detention at the Base. All alleged that none of the petitioners has ever been a combatant against the United States or has ever engaged in any terrorist acts. They also alleged that none has been charged with any wrongdoing, permitted to consult with counsel, or provided access to the courts or any other tribunal.

Congress has granted federal district courts, "within their respective jurisdictions," the authority to hear applications for *habeas corpus* by any person who claims to be held "in custody in violation of the Constitution or laws or treaties of the United States." 28 U.S.C. §§ 2241(a), (c)(3). The statute traces its ancestry to the first grant of federal court jurisdiction. *Habeas corpus* is, however, "a writ antecedent to statute, . . . throwing its root deep into the genius of our common law." The writ appeared in English law several centuries ago, became "an integral part of our common-law heritage" by the time the Colonies achieved independence, and received explicit recognition in the Constitution, which forbids suspension of "[t]he Privilege of the Writ of

Habeas Corpus . . . unless when in Cases of Rebellion or Invasion the public Safety may require it," Art. I, § 9, cl. 2.

As it has evolved over the past two centuries, the *habeas* statute clearly has expanded *habeas corpus* "beyond the limits that obtained during the 17th and 18th centuries." But "at its historical core, the writ of *habeas corpus* has served as a means of reviewing the legality of Executive detention, and it is in that context that its protections have been strongest." As Justice Jackson wrote in an opinion respecting the availability of *habeas corpus* to aliens held in U.S. custody: "Executive imprisonment has been considered oppressive and lawless since John, at Runnymede, pledged that no free man should be imprisoned, dispossessed, outlawed, or exiled save by the judgment of his peers or by the law of the land. The judges of England developed the writ of *habeas corpus* largely to preserve these immunities from executive restraint."

Consistent with the historic purpose of the writ, this Court has recognized the federal courts' power to review applications for *habeas* relief in a wide variety of cases involving Executive detention, in wartime as well as in times of peace. The Court has, for example, entertained the *habeas* petitions of an American citizen who plotted an attack on military installations during the Civil War, *Ex parte Milligan* (1866), and of admitted enemy aliens convicted of war crimes during a declared war and held in the United States, *Ex parte Quirin* (1942), and its insular possessions, *In re Yamashita* (1946).

The question now before us is whether the *habeas* statute confers a right to judicial review of the legality of Executive detention of aliens in a territory over which the United States exercises plenary and exclusive jurisdiction, but not "ultimate sovereignty."

Respondents' primary submission is that the answer to the jurisdictional question is controlled by our decision in *Johnson v. Eisentrager* (1950). In that case, we held that a Federal District Court lacked authority to issue a writ of *habeas corpus* to 21 German citizens who had been captured by U.S. forces in China, tried and convicted of war crimes by an American military commission headquartered in Nanking, and incarcerated in the Landsberg Prison in occupied Germany. This Court summarized the six critical facts in the case:

> We are here confronted with a decision whose basic premise is that these prisoners are entitled, as a constitutional right, to sue in some court of the United States for a writ of *habeas corpus*. To support that assumption we must hold that a prisoner of our military authorities is constitutionally entitled to the writ, even though he (a) is an enemy alien; (b) has never been or resided in the United States; (c) was captured outside of our territory and there held in military custody as a prisoner of war; (d) was tried and convicted by a Military Commission

sitting outside the United States; (e) for offenses against laws of war committed
outside the United States; (f) and is at all times imprisoned outside the United
States.

On this set of facts, the Court concluded, "no right to the writ of *habeas corpus* appears."

Petitioners in these cases differ from the *Eisentrager* detainees in important
respects: They are not nationals of countries at war with the United States,
and they deny that they have engaged in or plotted acts of aggression against
the United States; they have never been afforded access to any tribunal, much
less charged with and convicted of wrongdoing; and for more than two years
they have been imprisoned in territory over which the United States exercises
exclusive jurisdiction and control.

Not only are petitioners differently situated from the *Eisentrager* detainees,
but the Court in *Eisentrager* made quite clear that all six of the facts critical
to its disposition were relevant only to the question of the prisoners' constitutional entitlement to *habeas corpus*. The Court had far less to say on the
question of the petitioners' statutory entitlement to *habeas* review. Its only
statement on the subject was a passing reference to the absence of statutory
authorization: "Nothing in the text of the Constitution extends such a right,
nor does anything in our statutes."

Because subsequent decisions of this Court have filled the statutory gap
that had occasioned *Eisentrager*'s resort to "fundamentals," persons detained
outside the territorial jurisdiction of any federal district court no longer need
rely on the Constitution as the source of their right to federal *habeas* review.
In *Braden v. 30th Judicial Circuit Court of Ky.* (1973), this Court held that the
prisoner's presence within the territorial jurisdiction of the district court is not
"an invariable prerequisite" to the exercise of district court jurisdiction under
the federal *habeas* statute. Rather, because "the writ of *habeas corpus* does
not act upon the prisoner who seeks relief, but upon the person who holds him
in what is alleged to be unlawful custody," a district court acts "within [its]
respective jurisdiction" within the meaning of § 2241 as long as "the custodian can be reached by service of process." Because *Braden* overruled the
statutory predicate to *Eisentrager*'s holding, *Eisentrager* plainly does not preclude the exercise of § 2241 jurisdiction over petitioners' claims.

Respondents contend that we can discern a limit on § 2241 through application of the "longstanding principle of American law" that congressional legislation is presumed not to have extraterritorial application unless such intent is
clearly manifested. Whatever traction the presumption against extraterritoriality
might have in other contexts, it certainly has no application to the operation of
the *habeas* statute with respect to persons detained within "the territorial juris-

diction" of the United States. By the express terms of its agreements with Cuba, the United States exercises "complete jurisdiction and control" over the Guantanamo Bay Naval Base, and may continue to exercise such control permanently if it so chooses. Respondents themselves concede that the *habeas* statute would create federal-court jurisdiction over the claims of an American citizen held at the base. Considering that the statute draws no distinction between Americans and aliens held in federal custody, there is little reason to think that Congress intended the geographical coverage of the statute to vary depending on the detainee's citizenship. Aliens held at the base, no less than American citizens, are entitled to invoke the federal courts' authority under § 2241.

In the end, the answer to the question presented is clear. Petitioners contend that they are being held in federal custody in violation of the laws of the United States. No party questions the District Court's jurisdiction over petitioners' custodians. Section 2241, by its terms, requires nothing more. We therefore hold that § 2241 confers on the District Court jurisdiction to hear petitioners' *habeas corpus* challenges to the legality of their detention at the Guantanamo Bay Naval Base.

Whether and what further proceedings may become necessary after respondents make their response to the merits of petitioners' claims are matters that we need not address now. What is presently at stake is only whether the federal courts have jurisdiction to determine the legality of the Executive's potentially indefinite detention of individuals who claim to be wholly innocent of wrongdoing. Answering that question in the affirmative, we reverse the judgment of the Court of Appeals and remand for the District Court to consider in the first instance the merits of petitioners' claims.

Justice Kennedy, concurring in the judgment.

The Court is correct, in my view, to conclude that federal courts have jurisdiction to consider challenges to the legality of the detention of foreign nationals held at the Guantanamo Bay Naval Base in Cuba.

Eisentrager considered the scope of the right to petition for a writ of *habeas corpus* against the backdrop of the constitutional command of the separation of powers. The Court concluded the petition could not be entertained. The petition was not within the proper realm of the judicial power. It concerned matters within the exclusive province of the Executive, or the Executive and Congress, to determine.

The Court began by noting the "ascending scale of rights" that courts have recognized for individuals depending on their connection to the United States. Citizenship provides a longstanding basis for jurisdiction, the Court noted, and among aliens physical presence within the United States also "gave the Judiciary power to act." This contrasted with the "essential pattern for seasonable Executive constraint of enemy aliens." The place of the detention was also important to the jurisdictional question, the Court noted. Physical presence in the United States "implied protection," whereas in *Eisentrager* "th[e] prisoners at no relevant time were within any territory over which the United States is sovereign." The Court next noted that the prisoners in *Eisentrager* "were actual enemies" of the United States, proven to be so at trial, and thus could not justify "a limited opening of our courts" to distinguish the "many [aliens] of friendly personal disposition to whom the status of enemy" was unproven. Finally, the Court considered the extent to which jurisdiction would "hamper the war effort and bring aid and comfort to the enemy." Because the prisoners in *Eisentrager* were proven enemy aliens found and detained outside the United States, and because the existence of jurisdiction would have had a clear harmful effect on the Nation's military affairs, the matter was appropriately left to the Executive Branch and there was no jurisdiction for the courts to hear the prisoner's claims.

The decision in *Eisentrager* indicates that there is a realm of political authority over military affairs where the judicial power may not enter. The existence of this realm acknowledges the power of the President as Commander in Chief, and the joint role of the President and the Congress, in the conduct of military affairs. A faithful application of *Eisentrager*, then, requires an initial inquiry into the general circumstances of the detention to determine whether the Court has the authority to entertain the petition and to grant relief after considering all of the facts presented. A necessary corollary of *Eisentrager* is that there are circumstances in which the courts maintain the power and the responsibility to protect persons from unlawful detention even where military affairs are implicated.

The facts here are distinguishable from those in *Eisentrager* in two critical ways, leading to the conclusion that a federal court may entertain the petitions. First, Guantanamo Bay is in every practical respect a United States territory, and it is one far removed from any hostilities. The opinion of the Court well explains the history of its possession by the United States. What matters is the unchallenged and indefinite control that the United States has long exercised over Guantanamo Bay. From a practical perspective, the indefinite lease of Guantanamo Bay has produced a place that belongs to the United States, extending the "implied protection" of the United States to it.

The second critical set of facts is that the detainees at Guantanamo Bay are being held indefinitely, and without benefit of any legal proceeding to determine their status. In *Eisentrager*, the prisoners were tried and convicted by a military commission of violating the laws of war and were sentenced to prison terms. Indefinite detention without trial or other proceeding presents altogether different considerations. It allows friends and foes alike to remain in detention. It suggests a weaker case of military necessity and much greater alignment with the traditional function of *habeas corpus*. Perhaps, where detainees are taken from a zone of hostilities, detention without proceedings or trial would be justified by military necessity for a matter of weeks; but as the period of detention stretches from months to years, the case for continued detention to meet military exigencies becomes weaker.

In light of the status of Guantanamo Bay and the indefinite pretrial detention of the detainees, I would hold that federal-court jurisdiction is permitted in these cases. This approach would avoid creating automatic statutory authority to adjudicate the claims of persons located outside the United States, and remains true to the reasoning of *Eisentrager*. For these reasons, I concur in the judgment of the Court.

Justice Scalia, with whom the Chief Justice and Justice Thomas join, dissenting.

The Court today holds that the *habeas* statute, 28 U.S.C. § 2241, extends to aliens detained by the United States military overseas, outside the sovereign borders of the United States and beyond the territorial jurisdictions of all its courts. This is not only a novel holding; it contradicts a half-century-old precedent on which the military undoubtedly relied, *Johnson v. Eisentrager* (1950). The Court's contention that *Eisentrager* was somehow negated by *Braden v. 30th Judicial Circuit Court of Ky.* (1973)— a decision that dealt with a different issue and did not so much as mention *Eisentrager*—is implausible in the extreme. This is an irresponsible overturning of settled law in a matter of extreme importance to our forces currently in the field. I would leave it to Congress to change § 2241, and dissent from the Court's unprecedented holding.

The petitioners do not argue that the Constitution independently requires jurisdiction here. Accordingly, this case turns on the words of § 2241, a text the Court today largely ignores. Even a cursory reading of the *habeas* statute shows that it presupposes a federal district court with territorial jurisdiction over the detainee. Section 2241(a) states: "Writs of *habeas corpus* may be granted by the Supreme Court, any justice thereof, the district courts and any circuit judge within their respective jurisdictions." It further requires that "[t]he order of a circuit judge shall be entered in the records of the district court of the district wherein the restraint complained of is had." And § 2242 provides that a petition "addressed to the Supreme Court, a justice thereof or a circuit judge . . . shall state the reasons for not making application to the district court of the district in which the applicant is held." No matter to whom the writ is directed, custodian or detainee, the statute could not be clearer that a necessary requirement for issuing the writ is that some federal district court have territorial jurisdiction over the detainee. Here, as the Court allows, the Guantanamo Bay detainees are not located within the territorial jurisdiction of any federal district court. One would think that is the end of this case.

The Court asserts, however, that the decisions of this Court have placed a gloss on the phrase "within their respective jurisdictions" in § 2241 which allows jurisdiction in this case. That is not so. In fact, the only case in point holds just the opposite (and just what the statute plainly says). That case is *Eisentrager*.

Eisentrager's directly-on-point statutory holding makes it exceedingly difficult for the Court to reach the result it desires today. To do so neatly and cleanly, it must either argue that our decision in *Braden* overruled *Eisentrager*, or admit that it is overruling *Eisentrager*. The former course would not pass the laugh test, inasmuch as *Braden* dealt with a detainee held within the territorial jurisdiction of a district court, and never mentioned *Eisentrager*. And the latter course would require the Court to explain why our almost categorical rule of *stare decisis* in statutory cases should be set aside in order to complicate the present war, and, having set it aside, to explain why the *habeas* statute does not mean what it plainly says. So instead the Court tries an oblique course: "*Braden*," it claims, "overruled the statutory predicate to *Eisentrager*'s holding."

Justice Kennedy, concurring, recognizes that *Eisentrager* controls, but misconstrues that opinion. He thinks it makes jurisdiction under the *habeas* statute turn on the circumstances of the detainees' confinement—including, apparently, the availability of legal proceedings and the length of detention. Among the consequences of making jurisdiction turn upon circumstances of confinement are (1) that courts would always have authority to inquire into circumstances of confinement, and (2) that the Executive would be unable to know with certainty that any given prisoner-of-war camp is immune from writs of *habeas corpus*. And among the questions this approach raises: When does definite detention become indefinite? How much process will suffice to stave off jurisdiction? If there is a terrorist attack at Guantanamo Bay, will the area suddenly fall outside the *habeas* statute because it is no longer "far removed from any hostilities"? Justice Kennedy's approach provides enticing law-school-exam imponderables in an area where certainty is called for.

The reality is this: Today's opinion, and today's opinion alone, overrules *Eisentrager*; today's opinion, and today's opinion alone, extends the *habeas* statute, for the first time, to aliens held beyond the sovereign territory of the United States and beyond the territorial jurisdiction of its courts. No reasons are given for this result; no acknowledgment of its consequences made. By spurious reliance on *Braden* the Court evades explaining why *stare decisis* can be disregarded, and why *Eisentrager* was wrong. Normally, we consider the interests of those who have relied on our decisions. Today, the Court springs a trap on the Executive, subjecting Guantanamo Bay to the oversight of the federal courts even though it has never before been thought to be within their jurisdiction—and thus making it a foolish place to have housed alien wartime detainees.

Today's carefree Court disregards, without a word of acknowledgment, the dire warning of a more circumspect Court in *Eisentrager*:

> To grant the writ to these prisoners might mean that our army must transport them across the seas for hearing. This would require allocation for shipping space, guarding personnel, billeting and rations. It might also require transportation for whatever witnesses the prisoners desired to call as well as transportation for those necessary to defend legality of the sentence. The writ, since it is held to be a matter of right, would be equally available to enemies during active hostilities as in the present twilight between war and peace. Such trials would hamper the war effort and bring aid and comfort to the enemy. They would diminish the prestige of our commanders, not only with enemies but with wavering neutrals. It would be difficult to devise more effective fettering of a field commander than to allow the very enemies he is ordered to reduce to submission to call him to account in his own civil courts and divert his efforts and attention from the military offensive abroad to the legal defensive at home. Nor is it unlikely that the result of such enemy litigiousness would be conflict between judicial and military opinion highly comforting to enemies of the United States.

These results should not be brought about lightly, and certainly not without a textual basis in the statute and on the strength of nothing more than a decision [*Braden*] dealing with an Alabama prisoner's ability to seek *habeas* in Kentucky.

The Court gives only two reasons why the presumption against extraterritorial effect does not apply to Guantanamo Bay. First, the Court says (without any further elaboration) that "the United States exercises 'complete jurisdiction and control' over the Guantanamo Bay Naval Base [under the terms of a 1903 lease agreement], and may continue to exercise such control permanently if it so chooses [under the terms of a 1934 Treaty]." But that lease agreement explicitly recognized "the continuance of the ultimate sovereignty of the Republic of Cuba over the [leased areas]," and the Executive Branch—whose head is "exclusively responsible" for the "conduct of diplomatic and foreign affairs"—affirms that the lease and treaty do not render Guantanamo Bay the sovereign territory of the United States.

The Court does not explain how "complete jurisdiction and control" without sovereignty causes an enclave to be part of the United States for purposes of its domestic laws. Since "jurisdiction and control" obtained through a lease is no different in effect from "jurisdiction and control" acquired by lawful force of arms, parts of Afghanistan and Iraq should logically be regarded as subject to our domestic laws. Indeed, if "jurisdiction and control" rather than sovereignty were the test, so should the Landsberg Prison in Germany, where the United States held the *Eisentrager* detainees.

The second and last reason the Court gives for the proposition that domestic law applies to Guantanamo Bay is the Solicitor General's concession that there would be *habeas* jurisdiction over a United States citizen in Guantanamo Bay. "Considering that the statute draws no distinction between Americans and aliens held in federal custody, there is little reason to think that Congress intended the geographical coverage of the statute to vary depending on the detainee's citizenship." But the reason the Solicitor General conceded there would be jurisdiction over a detainee who was a United States citizen had nothing to do with the special status of Guantanamo Bay: "Our answer to that question, Justice Souter, is that citizens of the United States, because of their constitutional circumstances, may have greater rights with respect to the scope and reach of the *Habeas* Statute as the Court has or would interpret it." Tr. of Oral Arg. 40. And that position—the position that United States citizens throughout the world may be entitled to *habeas corpus* rights—is precisely the position that this Court adopted in *Eisentrager*, even while holding that aliens abroad did not have *habeas corpus* rights. Quite obviously, the Court's second reason has no force whatsoever.

In sum, the Court's treatment of Guantanamo Bay, like its treatment of § 2241, is a wrenching departure from precedent. Departure from our rule of *stare decisis* in statutory cases is always extraordinary; it ought to be unthinkable when the departure has a potentially harmful effect upon the Nation's conduct of a war. The Commander in Chief and his subordinates had every reason to expect that the internment of combatants at Guantanamo Bay would not have the consequence of bringing the cumbersome machinery of our domestic courts into military affairs. Congress is in session. If it wished to change federal judges' *habeas* jurisdiction from what this Court had previously held that to be, it could have done so. And it could have done so by intelligent revision of the statute, instead of by today's clumsy, countertextual reinterpretation. For this Court to create such a monstrous scheme in time of war, and in frustration of our military commanders' reliance upon clearly stated prior law, is judicial adventurism of the worst sort. I dissent.

Yaser Esam Hamdi and Esam Fouad Hamdi, as next friend of
Yaser Esam Hamdi,
Petitioners,
v.
Donald H. Rumsfeld, Secretary of Defense, et al.

No. 03-6696.
Argued April 28, 2004
Decided June 28, 2004
542 U.S. ___, 124 S.Ct. 2633, 159 L.Ed.2d 578 (2004)

Justice O'Connor announced the judgment of the Court and delivered an opinion, in which the Chief Justice, Justice Kennedy, and Justice Breyer join.

At this difficult time in our Nation's history, we are called upon to consider the legality of the Government's detention of a United States citizen on United States soil as an "enemy combatant" and to address the process that is constitutionally owed to one who seeks to challenge his classification as such. We hold that although Congress authorized the detention of combatants in the narrow circumstances alleged here, due process demands that a citizen held in the United States as an enemy combatant be given a meaningful opportunity to contest the factual basis for that detention before a neutral decision maker.

On September 11, 2001, the al Qaeda terrorist network used hijacked commercial airliners to attack prominent targets in the United States. Approximately 3,000 people were killed in those attacks. One week later, in response to these "acts of treacherous violence," Congress passed a resolution authorizing the President to "use all necessary and appropriate force against those nations, organizations, or persons he determines planned, authorized, committed, or aided the terrorist attacks" or "harbored such organizations or persons, in order to prevent any future acts of international terrorism against the United States by such nations, organizations or persons." Authorization for Use of Military Force ("AUMF"). Soon thereafter, the President ordered United States Armed Forces to Afghanistan, with a mission to subdue al Qaeda and quell the Taliban regime that was known to support it.

This case arises out of the detention of a man whom the Government alleges took up arms with the Taliban during this conflict. His name is Yaser Esam Hamdi. Born an American citizen in Louisiana in 1980, Hamdi moved with his family to Saudi Arabia as a child. By 2001, the parties agree, he resided in Afghanistan. At some point that year, he was seized by members of the Northern Alliance, a coalition of military groups opposed to the Taliban government, and eventually was turned over to the United States military. The Government asserts that it initially detained and interrogated Hamdi in

Afghanistan before transferring him to the United States Naval Base in Guantanamo Bay in January 2002. In April 2002, upon learning that Hamdi is an American citizen, authorities transferred him to a naval brig in Norfolk, Virginia, where he remained until a recent transfer to a brig in Charleston, South Carolina. The Government contends that Hamdi is an "enemy combatant," and that this status justifies holding him in the United States indefinitely—without formal charges or proceedings—unless and until it makes the determination that access to counsel or further process is warranted.

In June 2002, Hamdi's father, Esam Fouad Hamdi, filed the present petition for a writ of *habeas corpus* under 28 U.S.C. § 2241 in the Eastern District of Virginia, naming as petitioners his son and himself as next friend. The *habeas* petition asks that the court, among other things, (1) appoint counsel for Hamdi; (2) order respondents to cease interrogating him; (3) declare that he is being held in violation of the Fifth and Fourteenth Amendments; (4) "[t]o the extent Respondents contest any material factual allegations in this Petition, schedule an evidentiary hearing, at which Petitioners may adduce proof in support of their allegations"; and (5) order that Hamdi be released from his "unlawful custody." Although his *habeas* petition provides no details with regard to the factual circumstances surrounding his son's capture and detention, Hamdi's father has asserted in documents found elsewhere in the record that his son went to Afghanistan to do "relief work," and that he had been in that country less than two months before September 11, 2001, and could not have received military training. The 20-year-old was traveling on his own for the first time, his father says, and "[b]ecause of his lack of experience, he was trapped in Afghanistan once that military campaign began."

The Government filed a response and a motion to dismiss the petition. It attached to its response a declaration from one Michael Mobbs ("Mobbs Declaration"), who identified himself as Special Advisor to the Under Secretary of Defense for Policy. Mobbs indicated that in this position, he has been "substantially involved with matters related to the detention of enemy combatants in the current war against the al Qaeda terrorists and those who support and harbor them (including the Taliban)." He expressed his "familiar[ity]" with Department of Defense and United States military policies and procedures applicable to the detention, control, and transfer of al Qaeda and Taliban personnel, and declared that "[b]ased upon my review of relevant records and reports, I am also familiar with the facts and circumstances related to the capture of . . . Hamdi and his detention by U.S. military forces."

Mobbs then set forth what remains the sole evidentiary support that the Government has provided to the courts for Hamdi's detention. The declaration states that Hamdi "traveled to Afghanistan" in July or August 2001, and that he thereafter "affiliated with a Taliban military unit and received weapons training." It asserts that Hamdi "remained with his Taliban unit following the attacks of September 11" and that, during the time when Northern Alliance forces were "engaged in battle with the Taliban," "Hamdi's Taliban unit surrendered" to those forces, after which he "surrender[ed] his Kalishnikov assault rifle" to them. The Mobbs Declaration also states that, because al Qaeda and the Taliban "were and are hostile forces engaged in armed conflict with the armed forces of the United States," "individuals associated with" those groups "were and continue to be enemy combatants." Mobbs states that Hamdi was labeled an enemy combatant "[b]ased upon his interviews and in light of his association with the Taliban." According to the declaration, a series of "U.S. military screening team[s]" determined that Hamdi met "the criteria for enemy combatants," and "a subsequent interview of Hamdi has confirmed that he surrendered and gave his firearm to Northern Alliance forces, which supports his classification as an enemy combatant."

The threshold question before us is whether the Executive has the authority to detain citizens who qualify as "enemy combatants." There is some debate as to the proper scope of this term, and the Government has never provided any court with the full criteria that it uses in classifying individuals as such. It has made clear, however, that, for purposes of this case, the "enemy combatant" that it is seeking to detain is an individual who, it alleges, was "'part of or supporting forces hostile to the United States or coalition partners'" in Afghanistan and who "'engaged in an armed conflict against the United States'" there. We therefore answer only the narrow question before us: whether the detention of citizens falling within that definition is authorized.

The Government maintains that no explicit congressional authorization is required, because the Executive possesses plenary authority to detain pursuant to Article II of the Constitution. We do not reach the question whether Article II provides such authority, however, because we agree with the Government's alternative position, that Congress has in fact authorized Hamdi's detention, through the AUMF.

Hamdi posits that his detention is forbidden by 18 U.S.C. § 4001(a). Section 4001(a) states that "[n]o citizen shall be imprisoned or otherwise detained by the United States except pursuant to an Act of Congress." Congress passed § 4001(a) in 1971 as part of a bill to repeal the Emergency Detention Act of 1950, which provided procedures for executive detention, during times of emergency, of individuals deemed likely to engage in espionage or sabotage. Congress was particularly concerned about the possibility that the Act could be used to reprise the Japanese internment camps of World War II. We conclude that the AUMF is explicit congressional authorization for the detention of individuals in the narrow category we describe (assuming, without deciding, that such authorization is required), and that the AUMF satisfied § 4001(a)'s requirement that a detention be "pursuant to an Act of Congress" (assuming, without deciding, that § 4001(a) applies to military detentions).

The AUMF authorizes the President to use "all necessary and appropriate force" against "nations, organizations, or persons" associated with the September 11, 2001, terrorist attacks. There can be no doubt that individuals who fought against the United States in Afghanistan as part of the Taliban, an organization known to have supported the al Qaeda terrorist network responsible for those attacks, are individuals Congress sought to target in passing the AUMF. We conclude that detention of individuals falling into the limited category we are considering, for the duration of the particular conflict in which they were captured, is so fundamental and accepted an incident to war as to be an exercise of the "necessary and appropriate force" Congress has authorized the President to use.

The capture and detention of lawful combatants and the capture, detention, and trial of unlawful combatants, by "universal agreement and practice," are "important incident[s] of war." *Ex parte Quirin* (1942). The purpose of detention is to prevent captured individuals from returning to the field of battle and taking up arms once again.

There is no bar to this Nation's holding one of its own citizens as an enemy combatant. In *Quirin*, one of the detainees, Haupt, alleged that he was a naturalized United States citizen. We held that "[c]itizens who associate themselves with the military arm of the enemy government, and with its aid, guidance and direction enter this country bent on hostile acts, are enemy belligerents within the meaning of . . . the law of war." While Haupt was tried for violations of the law of war, nothing in *Quirin* suggests that his citizenship would have precluded his mere detention for the duration of the relevant hostilities. Nor can we see any reason for drawing such a line here. A citizen, no less than an alien, can be "part of or supporting forces hostile to the United States or coalition partners" and "engaged in an armed conflict against the United States;" such a citizen, if released, would pose the same threat of returning to the front during the ongoing conflict.

In light of these principles, it is of no moment that the AUMF does not use specific language of detention. Because detention to prevent a combatant's return to the battlefield is a fundamental incident of waging war, in permitting the use of "necessary and appropriate force," Congress has clearly and unmistakably authorized detention in the narrow circumstances considered here.

Hamdi objects, nevertheless, that Congress has not authorized the indefinite detention to which he is now subject. The Government responds that "the detention of enemy combatants during World War II was just as 'indefinite' while that war was being fought." We take Hamdi's objection to be not to the lack of certainty regarding the date on which the conflict will end, but to the substantial prospect of perpetual detention. We recognize that the national security underpinnings of the "war on terror," although crucially important, are broad and malleable. As the Government concedes, "given its unconventional nature, the current conflict is unlikely to end with a formal cease-fire agreement." The prospect Hamdi raises is therefore not far-fetched. If the Government does not consider this unconventional war won for two generations, and if it maintains during that time that Hamdi might, if released, rejoin forces fighting against the United States, then the position it has taken throughout the litigation of this case suggests that Hamdi's detention could last for the rest of his life.

It is a clearly established principle of the law of war that detention may last no longer than active hostilities. Hamdi contends that the AUMF does not authorize indefinite or perpetual detention. Certainly, we agree that indefinite detention for the purpose of interrogation is not authorized. Further, we understand Congress' grant of authority for the use of "necessary and appropriate force" to include the authority to detain for the duration of the relevant conflict, and our understanding is based on longstanding law-of-war principles. If the practical circumstances of a given conflict are entirely unlike those of the conflicts that informed the development of the law of war, that understanding may unravel. But that is not the situation we face as of this date. Active combat operations against Taliban fighters apparently are ongoing in Afghanistan. The United States may detain, for the duration of these hostilities, individuals legitimately determined to be Taliban combatants who "engaged in an armed conflict against the United States." If the record establishes that United States troops are still involved in active combat in Afghanistan, those detentions are part of the exercise of "necessary and appropriate force," and therefore are authorized by the AUMF.

Ex parte Milligan (1866), does not undermine our holding about the Government's authority to seize enemy combatants, as we define that term today. In that case, the Court made repeated reference to the fact that its inquiry into whether the military tribunal had jurisdiction to try and punish Milligan turned in large part on the fact that Milligan was not a prisoner of war, but a resident of Indiana arrested while at home there. That fact was central to its conclusion. Had Milligan been captured while he was assisting Confederate soldiers by carrying a rifle against Union troops on a Confederate battlefield, the holding of the Court might well have been different. The Court's repeated explanations that Milligan was not a prisoner of war suggest that had these different circumstances been present he could have been detained under military authority for the duration of the conflict, whether or not he was a citizen.

Moreover, the Court in *Ex parte Quirin* (1942), dismissed the language of *Milligan* that the petitioners had suggested prevented them from being subject to military process. *Quirin* was a unanimous opinion. It both postdates and clarifies *Milligan*, providing us with the most apposite precedent that we have on the question of whether citizens may be detained in such circumstances. Brushing aside such precedent—particularly when doing so gives rise to a host of new questions never dealt with by this Court—is unjustified and unwise. To be clear, our opinion only finds legislative authority to detain under the AUMF once it is sufficiently clear that the individual is, in fact, an enemy combatant; whether that is established by concession or by some other process that verifies this fact with sufficient certainty seems beside the point.

Even in cases in which the detention of enemy combatants is legally authorized, there remains the question of what process is constitutionally due to a citizen who disputes his enemy-combatant status. Our resolution of this dispute requires a careful examination both of the writ of *habeas corpus*, which Hamdi now seeks to employ as a mechanism of judicial review, and of the Due Process Clause, which informs the procedural contours of that mechanism in this instance.

Though they reach radically different conclusions on the process that ought to attend the present proceeding, the parties begin on common ground. All agree that, absent suspension, the writ of *habeas corpus* remains available to every individual detained within the United States. U.S. Const., Art. I, § 9, cl. 2 ("The Privilege of the Writ of *Habeas Corpus* shall not be suspended, unless when in Cases of Rebellion or Invasion the public Safety may require it"). Only in the rarest of circumstances has Congress seen fit to suspend the writ. At all other times, it has remained a critical check on the Executive, ensuring that it does not detain individuals except in accordance with law. All agree suspension of the writ has not occurred here. Thus, it is undisputed that Hamdi was properly before an Article III court to challenge his detention under 28 U.S.C. § 2241. Further, all agree that § 2241 and its companion provisions provide at least a skeletal outline of the procedures to be afforded a petitioner in federal *habeas* review. Most notably, § 2243 provides that "the person detained may, under oath, deny any of the facts set forth in the return or allege any other material facts," and § 2246 allows the taking of evidence in *habeas* proceedings by deposition, affidavit, or interrogatories.

First, the Government urges that because it is "undisputed" that Hamdi's seizure took place in a combat zone, the *habeas* determination can be made purely as a matter of law, with no further hearing or fact-finding necessary. This argument is easily rejected. The circumstances surrounding Hamdi's seizure cannot in any way be characterized as "undisputed," as "those circumstances are neither conceded in fact, nor susceptible to concession in law, because Hamdi has not been permitted to speak for himself or even through counsel as to those circumstances." Further, the "facts" that constitute the alleged concession are insufficient to support Hamdi's detention. Under the definition of enemy combatant that we accept today as falling within the scope of Congress' authorization, Hamdi would need to be "part of or supporting forces hostile to the United States or coalition partners" and "engaged in an armed conflict against the United States" to justify his detention in the United States for the duration of the relevant conflict. Accordingly, we reject any argument that Hamdi has made concessions that eliminate any right to further process.

The Government's second argument requires closer consideration. This is the argument that further factual exploration is unwarranted and inappropriate in light of the extraordinary constitutional interests at stake. Under the Government's most extreme rendition of this argument, "[r]espect for separation of powers and the limited institutional capabilities of courts in matters of military decision-making in connection with an ongoing conflict" ought to eliminate entirely any individual process, restricting the courts to investigating only whether legal authorization exists for the broader detention scheme. At most, the Government argues, courts should review its determination that a citizen is an enemy combatant under a very deferential "some evidence" standard. Under this review, a court would assume the accuracy of the Government's articulated basis for Hamdi's detention, as set forth in the Mobbs Declaration, and assess only whether that articulated basis was a legitimate one.

In response, Hamdi emphasizes that this Court consistently has recognized that an individual challenging his detention may not be held at the will of the Executive without recourse to some proceeding before a neutral tribunal to determine whether the Executive's asserted justifications for that detention have basis in fact and warrant in law. He argues that the lower court inappropriately "ceded power to the Executive during wartime to define the conduct for which a citizen may be detained, judge whether that citizen has engaged in the proscribed conduct, and imprison that citizen indefinitely," and that due process demands that he receive a hearing in which he may challenge the Mobbs Declaration and adduce his own counter evidence.

Both of these positions highlight legitimate concerns. And both emphasize the tension that often exists between the autonomy that the Government asserts is necessary in order to pursue effectively a particular goal and the process that a citizen contends he is due before he is deprived of a constitutional right. The ordinary mechanism that we use for balancing such serious competing interests, and for determining the procedures that are necessary to ensure that a citizen is not "deprived of life, liberty, or property, without due process of law," U.S. Const., Amdt. 5, is the test that we articulated in *Mathews v. Eldridge* (1976). *Mathews* dictates that the process due in any given instance is determined by weighing "the private interest that will be affected by the official action" against the Government's asserted interest, "including the function involved" and the burdens the Government would face in providing greater process. The *Mathews* calculus then contemplates a judicious balancing of these concerns, through an analysis of "the risk of an erroneous deprivation" of the private interest if the process were reduced and the "probable value, if any, of additional or substitute safeguards.

It is beyond question that substantial interests lie on both sides of the scale in this case. Hamdi's "private interest . . . affected by the official action" is the most elemental of liberty interests—the interest in being free from physical detention by one's own government. "In our society liberty is the norm," and detention without trial "is the carefully limited exception." "We have always been careful not to 'minimize the importance and fundamental nature' of the individual's right to liberty," and we will not do so today.

Nor is the weight on this side of the *Mathews* scale offset by the circumstances of war or the accusation of treasonous behavior, for "[i]t is clear that commitment for any purpose constitutes a significant deprivation of liberty that requires due process protection," and at this stage in the *Mathews* calculus, we consider the interest of the erroneously detained individual. Indeed, as *amicus* briefs from media and relief organizations emphasize, the risk of erroneous deprivation of a citizen's liberty in the absence of sufficient process here is very real. Moreover, as critical as the Government's interest may be in detaining those who actually pose an immediate threat to the national security of the United States during ongoing international conflict, history and common sense teach us that an unchecked system of detention carries the potential to become a means for oppression and abuse of others who do not present that sort of threat.

On the other side of the scale are the weighty and sensitive governmental interests in ensuring that those who have in fact fought with the enemy during a war do not return to battle against the United States. As discussed above, the law of war and the realities of combat may render such detentions both necessary and appropriate, and our due process analysis need not blink at those realities. Without doubt, our Constitution recognizes that core strategic matters of warmaking belong in the hands of those who are best positioned and most politically accountable for making them.

The Government also argues at some length that its interests in reducing the process available to alleged enemy combatants are heightened by the practical difficulties that would accompany a system of trial-like process. In its view, military officers who are engaged in the serious work of waging battle would be unnecessarily and dangerously distracted by litigation half a world away, and discovery into military operations would both intrude on the sensitive secrets of national defense and result in a futile search for evidence buried under the rubble of war. To the extent that these burdens are triggered by heightened procedures, they are properly taken into account in our due process analysis.

Striking the proper constitutional balance here is of great importance to the Nation during this period of ongoing combat. But it is equally vital that our calculus not give short shrift to the values that this country holds dear or to the privilege that is American citizenship. It is during our most challenging and uncertain moments that our Nation's commitment to due process is most severely tested; and it is in those times that we must preserve our commitment at home to the principles for which we fight abroad.

We therefore hold that a citizen-detainee seeking to challenge his classification as an enemy combatant must receive notice of the factual basis for his classification, and a fair opportunity to rebut the Government's factual assertions before a neutral decisionmaker. "For more than a century the central meaning of procedural due process has been clear: 'Parties whose rights are to be affected are entitled to be heard; and in order that they may enjoy that right they must first be notified.' It is equally fundamental that the right to notice and an opportunity to be heard 'must be granted at a meaningful time and in a meaningful manner.'" These essential constitutional promises may not be eroded.

At the same time, the exigencies of the circumstances may demand that, aside from these core elements, enemy combatant proceedings may be tailored to alleviate their uncommon potential to burden the Executive at a time of ongoing military conflict. Hearsay, for example, may need to be accepted as the most reliable available evidence from the Government in such a proceeding. Likewise, the Constitution would not be offended by a presumption in favor of the Government's evidence, so long as that presumption remained a rebuttable one and fair opportunity for rebuttal were provided. Thus, once the Government puts forth credible evidence that the *habeas* petitioner meets the enemy-combatant criteria, the onus could shift to the petitioner to rebut that evidence with more persuasive evidence that he falls outside the criteria. A burden-shifting scheme of this sort would meet the goal of ensuring that the errant tourist, embedded journalist, or local aid worker has a chance to prove military error while giving due regard to the Executive once it has put forth meaningful support for its conclusion that the detainee is in fact an enemy combatant. Process of this sort would sufficiently address the "risk of erroneous deprivation" of a detainee's liberty interest while eliminating certain procedures that have questionable additional value in light of the burden on the Government.

We think it unlikely that this basic process will have the dire impact on the central functions of warmaking that the Government forecasts. The parties agree that initial captures on the battlefield need not receive the process we have discussed here; that process is due only when the determination is made to continue to hold those who have been seized. The Government has made clear in its briefing that documentation regarding battlefield detainees already is kept in the ordinary course of military affairs. Any fact-finding imposition created by requiring a knowledgeable affiant to summarize these records to an independent tribunal is a minimal one. Likewise, arguments that military officers ought not have to wage war under the threat of litigation lose much of their steam when factual disputes at enemy-combatant hearings are limited to the alleged combatant's acts. This focus meddles little, if at all, in the strategy or conduct of war, inquiring only into the appropriateness of continuing to detain an individual claimed to have taken up arms against the United States. While we accord the greatest respect and consideration to the judgments of military authorities in matters relating to the actual prosecution of a war, and recognize that the scope of that discretion necessarily is wide, it does not infringe on the core role of the military for the courts to exercise their own time-honored and constitutionally mandated roles of reviewing and resolving claims like those presented here.

In sum, while the full protections that accompany challenges to detentions in other settings may prove unworkable and inappropriate in the enemy-combatant setting, the threats to military operations posed by a basic system of independent review are not so weighty as to trump a citizen's core rights to challenge meaningfully the Government's case and to be heard by an impartial adjudicator.

In so holding, we necessarily reject the Government's assertion that separation of powers principles mandate a heavily circumscribed role for the courts in such circumstances. Indeed, the position that the courts must forgo any examination of the individual case and focus exclusively on the legality of the broader detention scheme cannot be mandated by any reasonable view of separation of powers, as this approach serves only to condense power into a single branch of government. We have long since made clear that a state of war is not a blank check for the President when it comes to the rights of the Nation's citizens. Whatever power the United States Constitution envisions for the Executive in its exchanges with other nations or with enemy organizations in times of conflict, it most assuredly envisions a role for all three branches when individual liberties are at stake. Likewise, we have made clear that, unless Congress acts to suspend it, the Great Writ of *habeas corpus* allows the Judicial Branch to play a necessary role in maintaining this delicate balance of governance, serving as an important judicial check on the Executive's discretion in the realm of detentions. Thus, while we do not question that our due process assessment must pay keen attention to the particular burdens faced by the Executive in the context of military action, it would turn our system of checks and balances on its head to suggest that a citizen could not make his way to court with a challenge to the factual basis for his detention by his government, simply because the Executive opposes making available such a challenge. Absent suspension of the writ by Congress, a citizen detained as an enemy combatant is entitled to this process.

Because we conclude that due process demands some system for a citizen detainee to refute his classification, the Government's proposed "some evidence" standard is inadequate. Any process, in which the Executive's factual assertions go wholly unchallenged or are simply presumed correct without any opportunity for the alleged combatant to demonstrate otherwise, falls constitutionally short. This standard is ill suited to the situation in which a *habeas* petitioner has received no prior proceedings before any tribunal and had no prior opportunity to rebut the Executive's factual assertions before a neutral decisionmaker.

Today we are faced only with such a case. Aside from unspecified "screening" processes, and military interrogations in which the Government suggests Hamdi could have contested his classification, Hamdi has received no process. An interrogation by one's captor, however effective an intelligence-gathering tool, hardly constitutes a constitutionally adequate fact-finding before a neutral decisionmaker. That even purportedly fair adjudicators "are disqualified by their interest in the controversy to be decided is, of course, the general rule." Plainly, the "process" Hamdi has received is not that to which he is entitled under the Due Process Clause.

There remains the possibility that the standards we have articulated could be met by an appropriately authorized and properly constituted military tribunal. Indeed, it is notable that military regulations already provide for such process in related instances, dictating that tribunals be made available to determine the status of enemy detainees who assert prisoner-of-war status under the Geneva Convention. In the absence of such process, however, a court that receives a petition for a writ of *habeas corpus* from an alleged enemy combatant must itself ensure that the minimum requirements of due process are achieved. Both courts below recognized as much, focusing their energies on the question of whether Hamdi was due an opportunity to rebut the Government's case against him. The Government, too, proceeded on this assumption, presenting its affidavit and then seeking that it be evaluated under a deferential standard of review based on burdens that it alleged would accompany any greater process. As we have discussed, a *habeas* court in a case such as this may accept affidavit evidence like that contained in the Mobbs Declaration, so long as it also permits the alleged combatant to present his own factual case to rebut the Government's return. We anticipate that a District Court would proceed with the caution that we have indicated is necessary in this setting, engaging in a fact-finding process that is both prudent and incremental. We have no reason to doubt that courts faced with these sensitive matters will pay proper heed both to the matters of national security that might arise in an individual case and to the constitutional limitations safeguarding essential liberties that remain vibrant even in times of security concerns.

Hamdi asks us to hold that the court below also erred by denying him immediate access to counsel upon his detention and by disposing of the case without permitting him to meet with an attorney. Since our grant of *certiorari* in this case, Hamdi has been appointed counsel, with whom he has met for consultation purposes on several occasions, and with whom he is now being granted unmonitored meetings. He unquestionably has the right to access to counsel in connection with the proceedings on remand. No further consideration of this issue is necessary at this stage of the case.

Justice Souter, with whom Justice Ginsburg joins, concurring in part, dissenting in part, and concurring in the judgment.

In these proceedings on Hamdi's petition, he seeks to challenge the facts claimed by the Government as the basis for holding him as an enemy combatant. And in this Court he presses the distinct argument that the Government's claim, even if true, would not implicate any authority for holding him that would satisfy 18 U.S.C. § 4001(a) (Non-Detention Act), which bars imprisonment or detention of a citizen "except pursuant to an Act of Congress."

The Government responds that Hamdi's *incommunicado* imprisonment as an enemy combatant seized on the field of battle falls within the President's power as Commander in Chief under the laws and usages of war, and is in any event authorized by two statutes. Accordingly, the Government contends that Hamdi has no basis for any challenge by petition for *habeas* except to his own status as an enemy combatant; and even that challenge may go no further than to enquire whether "some evidence" supports Hamdi's designation; if there is "some evidence," Hamdi should remain locked up at the discretion of the Executive. At the argument of this case, in fact, the Government went further and suggested that as long as a prisoner could challenge his enemy combatant designation when responding to interrogation during *incommunicado* detention he was accorded sufficient process to support his designation as an enemy combatant.

The plurality rejects any such limit on the exercise of *habeas* jurisdiction and so far I agree with its opinion. The plurality does, however, accept the Government's position that if Hamdi's designation as an enemy combatant is correct, his detention (at least as to some period) is authorized by an Act of

Congress as required by § 4001(a), that is, by the Authorization for Use of Military Force ("AUMF"). Here, I disagree and respectfully dissent. The Government has failed to demonstrate that the AUMF authorizes the detention complained of here even on the facts the Government claims. If the Government raises nothing further than the record now shows, the Non-Detention Act entitles Hamdi to be released.

The threshold issue is how broadly or narrowly to read the Non-Detention Act, the tone of which is severe: "No citizen shall be imprisoned or otherwise detained by the United States except pursuant to an Act of Congress." Should the severity of the Act be relieved when the Government's stated factual justification for *incommunicado* detention is a war on terrorism, so that the Government may be said to act "pursuant" to congressional terms that fall short of explicit authority to imprison individuals? With one possible though important qualification, the answer has to be no. For a number of reasons, the prohibition within § 4001(a) has to be read broadly to accord the statute a long reach and to impose a burden of justification on the Government. Under this principle of reading § 4001(a) robustly to require a clear statement of authorization to detain, none of the Government's arguments suffices to justify Hamdi's detention.

The Government's claim, accepted by the Court, is that the terms of the AUFM is adequate to authorize detention of an enemy combatant under the circumstances described, a claim the Government fails to support sufficiently to satisfy § 4001(a) as read to require a clear statement of authority to detain. Since the AUMF was adopted one week after the attacks of September 11, 2001, it naturally speaks with some generality, but its focus is clear, and that is on the use of military power. It is fairly read to authorize the use of armies and weapons, whether against other armies or individual terrorists. But it never so much as uses the word detention, and there is no reason to think Congress might have perceived any need to augment Executive power to deal with dangerous citizens within the United States, given the well-stocked statutory arsenal of defined criminal offenses covering the gamut of actions that a citizen sympathetic to terrorists might commit.

Since the Government has given no reason either to deflect the application of § 4001(a) or to hold it to be satisfied, I need to go no further; the Government hints of a constitutional challenge to the statute, but it presents none here. I will, however, stray across the line between statutory and constitutional territory just far enough to note the weakness of the Government's mixed claim of inherent, extra-statutory authority under a combination of Article II of the Constitution and the usages of war. It is in fact in this connection that the Government developed its argument that the exercise of war powers justifies the detention, and what I have just said about its inadequacy applies here as well. Beyond that, it is instructive to recall Justice Jackson's observation that the President is not Commander in Chief of the country, only of the military. *Youngstown Sheet & Tube Co. v. Sawyer* (1952) (Jackson, J., concurring) (Presidential authority is "at its lowest ebb" where the President acts contrary to congressional will).

There may be room for one qualification to Justice Jackson's statement, however: in a moment of genuine emergency, when the Government must act with no time for deliberation, the Executive may be able to detain a citizen if there is reason to fear he is an imminent threat to the safety of the Nation and its people (though I doubt there is any want of statutory authority). This case, however, does not present that question, because an emergency power of necessity must at least be limited by the emergency; Hamdi has been locked up for over two years.

Because I find Hamdi's detention forbidden by § 4001(a) and unauthorized by the AUMF, I would not reach any questions of what process he may be due in litigating disputed issues in a proceeding under the *habeas* statute or prior to the *habeas* enquiry itself. For me, it suffices that the Government has failed to justify holding him in the absence of a further Act of Congress, criminal charges, a showing that the detention conforms to the laws of war, or a demonstration that § 4001(a) is unconstitutional.

Since this disposition does not command a majority of the Court, however, the need to give practical effect to the conclusions of eight members of the Court rejecting the Government's position calls for me to join with the plurality in ordering remand on terms closest to those I would impose. Although I think litigation of Hamdi's status as an enemy combatant is unnecessary, the terms of the plurality's remand will allow Hamdi to offer evidence that he is not an enemy combatant, and he should at the least have the benefit of that opportunity. I join with the plurality in a judgment of the Court vacating the lower court's judgment and remanding the case.

Justice Scalia, with whom Justice Stevens joins, dissenting.

This case brings into conflict the competing demands of national security and our citizens' constitutional right to personal liberty. Although I share the Court's evident unease as it seeks to reconcile the two, I do not agree with its resolution. Where the Government accuses a citizen of waging war against it, our constitutional tradition has been to prosecute him in federal court for treason or some other crime. Where the exigencies of war prevent that, the Constitution's Suspension Clause, Art. I, § 9, cl. 2, allows Congress to relax the usual protections temporarily. Absent suspension, however, the Executive's assertion of military exigency has not been thought sufficient to permit detention without charge. No one contends that the congressional Authorization for Use of Military Force ("AUMF"), on which the Government relies to justify its actions here, is an implementation of the Suspension Clause.

The very core of liberty secured by our Anglo-Saxon system of separated powers has been freedom from indefinite imprisonment at the will of the Executive. Two central ideas of the English common law—due process as the right secured, and *habeas corpus* as the instrument by which due process could be insisted upon by a citizen illegally imprisoned—found expression in the Constitution's Due Process and Suspension Clauses. *See* Amdt. 5; Art. I, § 9, cl. 2.

The gist of the Due Process Clause, as understood at the founding and since, was to force the Government to follow those common-law procedures traditionally deemed necessary before depriving a person of life, liberty, or property. When a citizen was deprived of liberty because of alleged criminal conduct, those procedures typically required committal by a magistrate followed by indictment and trial. To be sure, certain types of permissible noncriminal detention—that is, those not dependent upon the contention that the citizen had committed a criminal act—did not require the protections of criminal procedure. However, these fell into a limited number of well-recognized exceptions—civil commitment of the mentally ill, for example, and temporary detention in quarantine of the infectious. It is unthinkable that the Executive could render otherwise criminal grounds for detention noncriminal merely by disclaiming an intent to prosecute, or by asserting that it was incapacitating dangerous offenders rather than punishing wrongdoing. These due process rights have historically been vindicated by the writ of *habeas corpus*.

The allegations here, of course, are no ordinary accusations of criminal activity. Yaser Esam Hamdi has been imprisoned because the Government believes he participated in the waging of war against the United States. The relevant question, then, is whether there is a different, special procedure for imprisonment of a citizen accused of wrongdoing by aiding the enemy in wartime.

Justice O'Connor, writing for a plurality of this Court, asserts that captured enemy combatants (other than those suspected of war crimes) have traditionally been detained until the cessation of hostilities and then released. That is probably an accurate description of wartime practice with respect to enemy aliens. The tradition with respect to American citizens, however, has been quite different. Citizens aiding the enemy have been treated as traitors subject to the criminal process.

Subjects accused of levying war against the King were routinely prosecuted for treason. The Founders inherited the understanding that a citizen's levying war against the Government was to be punished criminally. The Constitution provides: "Treason against the United States, shall consist only in levying War against them, or in adhering to their Enemies, giving them Aid and Comfort"; and establishes a heightened proof requirement (two witnesses) in order to "convic[t]" of that offense. Art. III, § 3, cl. 1.

In more recent times, too, citizens have been charged and tried in Article III courts for acts of war against the United States, even when their noncitizen co-conspirators were not. For example, two American citizens alleged to have participated during World War I in a spying conspiracy on behalf of Germany were tried in federal court. A German member of the same conspiracy was subjected to military process. During World War II, the famous German saboteurs of *Ex parte Quirin* (1942), received military process, but the citizens who associated with them (with the exception of one citizen-saboteur) were punished under the criminal process.

The modern treason statute is 18 U.S.C. § 2381; it basically tracks the language of the constitutional provision. Other provisions of Title 18 criminalize various acts of warmaking and adherence to the enemy. The only citizen other than Hamdi known to be imprisoned in connection with military hostilities in Afghanistan against the United States was subjected to criminal process and convicted upon a guilty plea. *See United States v. Lindh* (E.D. Va. 2002) (denying motions for dismissal).

There are times when military exigency renders resort to the traditional criminal process impracticable. English law accommodated such exigencies by allowing legislative suspension of the writ of *habeas corpus* for brief periods. Our Federal Constitution contains a provision explicitly permitting suspension, but limiting the situations in which it may be invoked: "The privilege of the Writ of *Habeas Corpus* shall not be suspended, unless when in Cases of Rebellion or Invasion the public Safety may require it." Art. I, § 9, cl. 2. Although this provision does not state that suspension must be effected by, or authorized by, a legislative act, it has been so understood, consistent with English practice and the Clause's placement in Article I. The Suspension Clause was by design a safety valve, the Constitution's only "express provision for exercise of extraordinary authority because of a crisis." *Youngstown Sheet & Tube Co. v. Sawyer* (1952) (Jackson, J., concurring). Criminal process was viewed as the primary means—and the only means absent congressional action suspending the writ—not only to punish traitors, but to incapacitate them.

The Government argues that our more recent jurisprudence ratifies its indefinite imprisonment of a citizen within the territorial jurisdiction of federal courts. It places primary reliance upon *Ex parte Quirin* (1942), a World War II case upholding the trial by military commission of eight German saboteurs, one of whom, Hans Haupt, was a U.S. citizen. The case was not this Court's finest hour. The Court upheld the commission and denied relief in a brief *per curiam* issued the day after oral argument concluded; a week later the Government carried out the commission's death sentence upon six saboteurs, including Haupt. The Court eventually explained its reasoning in a written opinion issued several months later.

Only three paragraphs of the Court's lengthy opinion dealt with the particular circumstances of Haupt's case. The Government argued that Haupt, like the other petitioners, could be tried by military commission under the laws of war. In agreeing with that contention, *Quirin* purported to interpret the language of *Ex parte Milligan* (1866) quoted above (the law of war "can never be applied to citizens in states which have upheld the authority of the government, and where the courts are open and their process unobstructed"). But even if *Quirin* gave a correct description of *Milligan*, or made an irrevocable revision of it, *Quirin* would still not justify denial of the writ here. In *Quirin* it was uncontested that the petitioners were members of enemy forces. They were "admitted enemy invaders," and it was "undisputed" that they had landed in the United States in service of German forces. The specific holding of the Court was only that, "upon the conceded facts," the petitioners were "plainly within [the] boundaries" of military jurisdiction. But where those jurisdictional facts are not conceded—where the petitioner insists that he is not a belligerent—*Quirin* left the pre-existing law in place: Absent suspension of the writ, a citizen held where the courts are open is entitled either to criminal trial or to a judicial decree requiring his release.

It follows from what I have said that Hamdi is entitled to a *habeas* decree requiring his release unless (1) criminal proceedings are promptly brought, or (2) Congress has suspended the writ of *habeas corpus*. A suspension of the writ could, of course, lay down conditions for continued detention, similar to those that today's opinion prescribes under the Due Process Clause. But there is a world of difference between the people's representatives' determining the need for that suspension (and prescribing the conditions for it), and this Court's doing so.

The plurality finds justification for Hamdi's imprisonment in the Authorization for Use of Military Force ("AUMF") which provides:

> That the President is authorized to use all necessary and appropriate force against those nations, organizations, or persons he determines planned, authorized, committed, or aided the terrorist attacks that occurred on September 11, 2001, or harbored such organizations or persons, in order to prevent any future acts of international terrorism against the United States by such nations, organizations or persons.

This is not remotely a congressional suspension of the writ, and no one claims that it is. Contrary to the plurality's view, I do not think this statute even authorizes detention of a citizen with the clarity necessary to satisfy the interpretive canon that statutes should be construed so as to avoid grave constitutional concerns, with the clarity necessary to comport with our prior cases or with the clarity necessary to overcome the statutory prescription that "[n]o citizen shall be imprisoned or otherwise detained by the United States except pursuant to an Act of Congress." 18 U.S.C. § 4001(a). But even if it did, I would not permit it to overcome Hamdi's entitlement to *habeas corpus* relief.

It should not be thought, however, that the plurality's evisceration of the Suspension Clause augments, principally, the power of Congress. As usual, the major effect of its constitutional improvisation is to increase the power of the Court. Having found a congressional authorization for detention of citizens where none clearly exists; and having discarded the categorical procedural protection of the Suspension Clause; the plurality then proceeds, under the guise of the Due Process Clause, to prescribe what procedural protections it thinks appropriate.

Having distorted the Suspension Clause, the plurality finishes up by transmogrifying the Great Writ—disposing of the present *habeas* petition by remanding for the District Court to "engag[e] in a fact-finding process that is both prudent and incremental. . . . In the absence of [the Executive's prior provision of procedures that satisfy due process], . . . a court that receives a petition for a writ of *habeas corpus* from an alleged enemy combatant must itself ensure that the minimum requirements of due process are achieved." This judicial remediation of executive default is unheard of. The role of *habeas corpus* is to determine the legality of executive detention, not to supply the omitted process necessary to make it legal.

Several limitations give my views in this matter a relatively narrow compass. They apply only to citizens, accused of being enemy combatants, who are detained within the territorial jurisdiction of a federal court. This is not likely to be a numerous group; currently we know of only two, Hamdi and Jose Padilla. Where the citizen is captured outside and held outside the United States, the constitutional requirements may be different. Moreover, even within the United States, the accused citizen-enemy combatant may lawfully be detained once prosecution is in progress or in contemplation. The Government has been notably successful in securing conviction, and hence long-term custody or execution, of those who have waged war against the state.

I frankly do not know whether these tools are sufficient to meet the Government's security needs, including the need to obtain intelligence through interrogation. It is far beyond my competence, or the Court's competence, to determine that. But it is not beyond Congress's. If the situation demands it, the Executive can ask Congress to authorize suspension of the writ—which can be made subject to whatever conditions Congress deems appropriate, including even the procedural novelties invented by the plurality today. To be sure, suspension is limited by the Constitution to cases of rebellion or invasion. But whether the attacks of September 11, 2001, constitute an "invasion," and whether those attacks still justify suspension several years later, are questions for Congress rather than this Court. If civil rights are to be curtailed during wartime, it must be done openly and democratically, as the Constitution requires, rather than by silent erosion through an opinion of this Court.

Many think it not only inevitable but entirely proper that liberty give way to security in times of national crisis—that, at the extremes of military exigency, *inter arma silent leges*. Whatever the general merits of the view that war silences law or modulates its voice, that view has no place in the interpretation and application of a Constitution designed precisely to confront war and, in a manner that accords with democratic principles, to accommodate it. Because the Court has proceeded to meet the current emergency in a manner the Constitution does not envision, I respectfully dissent.

Justice Thomas, dissenting.

The Executive Branch, acting pursuant to the powers vested in the President by the Constitution and with explicit congressional approval, has determined that Yaser Hamdi is an enemy combatant and should be detained. This detention falls squarely within the Federal Government's war powers, and we lack the expertise and capacity to second-guess that decision. As such, petitioners' *habeas* challenge should fail, and there is no reason to remand the case. The plurality reaches a contrary conclusion by failing adequately to consider basic principles of the constitutional structure as it relates to national security and foreign affairs and by using the balancing scheme of *Mathews v. Eldridge* (1976). I do not think that the Federal Government's war powers can be balanced away by this Court. Arguably, Congress could provide for additional procedural protections, but until it does, we have no right to insist upon them. But even if I were to agree with the general approach the plurality takes, I could not accept the particulars. The plurality utterly fails to account for the Government's compelling interests and for our own institutional inability to weigh competing concerns correctly. I respectfully dissent.

"It is 'obvious and unarguable' that no governmental interest is more compelling than the security of the Nation." The national security, after all, is the primary responsibility and purpose of the Federal Government. But because the Founders understood that they could not foresee the myriad potential threats to national security that might later arise, they chose to create a Federal Government that necessarily possesses sufficient power to handle any threat to the security of the Nation. The power to protect the Nation "ought to exist without limitation . . . [b]ecause it is impossible to foresee or define the extent and variety of national exigencies, or the correspondent extent & variety of the means which may be necessary to satisfy them. The circumstances that endanger the safety of nations are infinite; and for this reason no constitutional shackles can wisely be imposed on the power to which the care of it is committed." *The Federalist No. 23; see also The Federalist Nos. 34 and 41.*

The Founders intended that the President have primary responsibility— along with the necessary power—to protect the national security and to conduct the Nation's foreign relations. Congress, to be sure, has a substantial and essential role in both foreign affairs and national security. But it is crucial to recognize that judicial interference in these domains destroys the purpose of vesting primary responsibility in a unitary Executive. I cannot improve on Justice Jackson's words, speaking for the Court:

> The President, both as Commander-in-Chief and as the Nation's organ for foreign affairs, has available intelligence services whose reports are not and ought not to be published to the world. It would be intolerable that courts, without the relevant information, should review and perhaps nullify actions of the Executive taken on information properly held secret. Nor can courts sit *in camera* in order to be taken into executive confidences. But even if courts could require full disclosure, the very nature of executive decisions as to foreign policy is political, not judicial. Such decisions are wholly confided by our Constitution to the political departments of the government, Executive and Legislative. They are delicate, complex, and involve large elements of prophecy. They are and should be undertaken only by those directly responsible to the people whose welfare they advance or imperil. They are decisions of a kind for which the Judiciary has neither aptitude, facilities nor responsibility and which has long been held to belong in the domain of political power not subject to judicial intrusion or inquiry.

I acknowledge that the question whether Hamdi's executive detention is lawful is a question properly resolved by the Judicial Branch, though the question comes to the Court with the strongest presumptions in favor of the Government. The plurality agrees that Hamdi's detention is lawful if he is an enemy combatant. But the question whether Hamdi is actually an enemy combatant is "of a kind for which the Judiciary has neither aptitude, facilities nor responsibility and which has long been held to belong in the domain of political power not subject to judicial intrusion or inquiry." That is, although it is appropriate for the Court to determine the judicial question whether the President has the asserted authority, we lack the information and expertise to question whether Hamdi is actually an enemy combatant, a question the resolution of which is committed to other branches.

I agree with the plurality that the Federal Government has power to detain those that the Executive Branch determines to be enemy combatants. But I do not think that the plurality has adequately explained the breadth of the President's authority to detain enemy combatants, an authority that includes making virtually conclusive factual findings. In my view, the structural considerations discussed above, as recognized in our precedent, demonstrate that we lack the capacity and responsibility to second-guess this determination.

This makes complete sense once the process that is due Hamdi is made clear. As an initial matter, it is possible that the Due Process Clause requires only "that our Government must proceed according to the 'law of the land' — that is, according to written constitutional and statutory provisions." I need not go this far today because the Court has already explained the nature of due process in this context. In this context, due process requires nothing more than a good-faith executive determination. To be clear: The Court has held that an executive, acting pursuant to statutory and constitutional authority may, consistent with the Due Process Clause, unilaterally decide to detain an individual if the executive deems this necessary for the public safety even if he is mistaken. This Court has emphasized that this power "is conferred upon him by the Constitution and laws of the United States, and must therefore be respected and enforced in its judicial tribunals." Finally, this Court has explained that if the President abused this power "it would be in the power of Congress to apply the proper remedy. But the courts must administer the law as they find it." This Court has explained that the Due Process Clause "lays down [no] categorical imperative."

The Government's asserted authority to detain an individual that the President has determined to be an enemy combatant, at least while hostilities continue, comports with the Due Process Clause. As these cases also show, the Executive's decision that a detention is necessary to protect the public need not and should not be subjected to judicial second-guessing. Indeed, at least in the context of enemy-combatant determinations, this would defeat the unity, secrecy, and dispatch that the Founders believed to be so important to the warmaking function. I therefore cannot agree with Justice Scalia's conclusion that the Government must choose between using standard criminal processes and suspending the writ.

Accordingly, I conclude that the Government's detention of Hamdi as an enemy combatant does not violate the Constitution. By detaining Hamdi, the President, in the prosecution of a war and authorized by Congress, has acted well within his authority. Hamdi thereby received all the process to which he was due under the circumstances. I therefore believe that this is no occasion to balance the competing interests, as the plurality unconvincingly attempts to do.

Ultimately, the plurality's dismissive treatment of the Government's asserted interests arises from its apparent belief that enemy-combatant determinations are not part of "the actual prosecution of a war," or one of the "central functions of war making." This seems wrong: Taking and holding enemy combatants is a quintessential aspect of the prosecution of war. Undeniably, Hamdi has been deprived of a serious interest, one actually protected by the Due Process Clause. Against this, however, is the Government's overriding interest in protecting the Nation. If a deprivation of liberty can be justified by the need to protect a town, the protection of the Nation, *a fortiori*, justifies it.

NOTES

1. 124 S.Ct. 2711 (2004).
2. 124 S.Ct. at 2730.
3. *Id.* at 2735.

Epilogue

John F. Stack, Jr., and Thomas E. Baker

As our work on this book is concluding, in the spring of 2005, important legal questions and profound political issues are being heard in the federal court system and in the national public forum that echo the historical, constitutional, legal, and political leitmotifs sounded by the authors of the previous chapters. This chapter is a contextual postscript to link these chapters to current legal developments and the ongoing political debate.

The landmark decisions of the Supreme Court of the United States in *Rasul v. Bush*[1] and *Hamdi v. Rumsfeld*[2] presented in chapter 9 have served as a catalyst for numerous other cases that have been filed in the lower federal courts. These cases will present the next set of constitutional issues to be resolved ultimately by the Supreme Court. They will start showing up on the High Court's docket during its next term, beginning in October 2005.[3]

Hamdan v. Rumsfeld is the case that is farthest along: the U.S. District Court has granted Salim Hamdan's petition for *habeas corpus* relief.[4] Hamdan was a noncitizen combatant taken prisoner by the U.S. military in Afghanistan in 2001 and then transferred to the U.S. Naval Base in Guantanamo Bay, Cuba, in 2002. He was determined to have been a member of al Qaeda who allegedly had engaged in terrorism against the United States. Pursuant to a military order issued on November 13, 2001, by President Bush,[5] Hamden was designated for trial by a military commission rather than by a Military Court Marshall under the provisions of the *Uniform Code of Military Justice*. But the U.S. District Judge ruled that the commission could not proceed until the constitutional bases of two issues were determined: whether Hamdan was entitled to prisoner of war status under Article 4 of the *Geneva Convention Relative to the Treatment of Prisoners of War,* and whether Hamdan's trial before the military commission was subject to procedural protections included in the Uniform Code of Military Justice and consistent with due process.[6] The appeal from the District Court is pending on expedited review in the U.S. Court of Appeals for the District of Columbia Circuit, and no matter how that court rules we can expect a petition for *certiorari* review to the Supreme Court.

That same Court of Appeals for the D.C. Circuit is scheduled to review five consolidated cases in which Guantanamo detainees who are foreign nationals—taking their procedural cues from *Rasul v. Bush*—have filed *habeas corpus* petitions challenging their continued imprisonment. The Court of Appeals will likely expedite these cases to decide them over the next several months.[7]

Still more cases presenting more issues are pending at the District Court level. In *Abdah v. Bush*,[8] for example, thirteen Guantanamo detainees from Yemen are challenging the ability of the U.S. military and the United States to send them to other countries for continued detention and interrogation—at least until they have had the opportunity to consult with their lawyers and to challenge such transfers in federal court.[9] Time is of the essence in these cases, of course, because their physical transfer to foreign countries would compromise their ability to litigate their U.S. court challenges, and also would expose them to the vagaries of interrogation techniques that might not be countenanced under U.S. authority.[10] Indeed, the Yemeni have expressed their fears of the likelihood of torture at the hands of those other countries, but the U.S. government has resisted their legal pleadings and insisted that there is no legal basis whatsoever for intervention by the judicial branch in the decision to transfer them, a decision that the government characterizes as a matter of foreign relations and national security within the exclusive purview of the executive branch.[11]

These pending cases illustrate the first dimension of this book: What does the Constitution have to say about the way the government treats noncitizens in its military initiatives and in the conduct of international and foreign relations in the War on Terrorism? The War on Terrorism is being waged as a world war. The scope and nature of the War on Terrorism is so broadly conceived and justified so as to span the globe from Afghanistan to Iraq to the entire Middle East and beyond—arguably everywhere and anywhere outside the territorial sovereignty of the United States that the U.S. military conducts its operations. This necessarily raises a number of issues concerning the nature of due process to be afforded those individuals designated as noncitizen enemy combatants by the U.S. government before civilian and military forums, following their capture on the battlefield. How the lower federal courts and the Supreme Court of the United States will define and defend these rights will be critical in the War on Terrorism abroad and at home. Jules Lobel (chapter 3) explores the legacies of the "permanent" national security crises fueled for so long by the Cold War and now by the seemingly permanent War on Terror. His assessments shed light on the meaningfulness of *Hamdi* and *Rasul* for the cases now moving through the lower federal courts and for other future cases like them. Beyond peradventure, the rest of the world is watching the United States and what the government is doing to prosecute this war and measuring our policies against our own ideals as well as international norms.

The second dimension of this book revolves around the constitutional implications of the War on Terrorism for all American citizens. The contributions by Michael Greenberger (chapter 5) and Louis Fisher (chapter 6) address the expansive design of the USA PATRIOT Act and the dramatic expansion of federal law enforcement activities in the wake of the horrific 9/11 attacks. Central to the expansion of federal law enforcement activities has been continued congressional support for presidential prerogatives notwithstanding the trenchant criticisms in the 9/11 Commission Report describing the breakdown of intelligence gathering and analysis and a lack of coordination of counterterrorism efforts[12]—a generalized pattern of congressional acquiescence that persisted before and after George W. Bush's successful bid for a second term. Many in Congress seem reluctant to revisit their handiwork, although there are signs that some members may be coming around to question the need for and the continuing legitimacy of some of the more extreme measures in the USA PATRIOT Act.

Peter Irons (chapter 4) and John Ashcroft (chapter 2) also offer important and different historical perspectives. Irons points to the fragility of civil rights and civil liberties during national emergencies—the great depression of the 1930s and the prosecution of World War II. Under these grave conditions, civil rights and civil liberties, notwithstanding the rhetoric of the New Deal, were often a casualty of executive branch indifference or disdain. Irons' assessment of the power of the Department of Justice during the Roosevelt administration and willingly wielded by a number of Attorneys General during the 1930s and 1940s is sobering. Equally sobering, however, are the remarks of former Attorney General John Ashcroft in chapter 2. For Ashcroft, the paramount responsibility is how best to protect the national security of the United States to prevent future attacks as devastating as those of 9/11. The issue Irons and Ashcroft are debating is how a vast complex of governmental bureaucracies should balance the need for greater national security without sacrificing fundamental values of guaranteed liberty. The key question behind that question is how to avoid the mistaken excesses of the past. Associate Justice Stephen Breyer's contribution (chapter 2), written before the Supreme Court decisions in *Hamdi* and *Rasul,* gives testimony to his profound constitutional faith in the rule of law and evinces his basic trust in judicial process as the way to protect and defend the country and the Constitution at the same time. This represents the separation of powers among the three branches,—in theory how the Constitution creates mechanisms for checks and balances and in practice how the incumbents exercise their power during a crisis.

The third dimension of this book is an attempt to step back from the particulars to generalize and theorize as academics are wont to do—trying to understand the past, looking for meaning in the present, and always speaking truth to power. The manner in which civil rights and civil liberties have been addressed historically and philosophically form the essence of the contributions by Mark Graber (Chapter 7) and Mark Tushnet (Chapter 8). Graber offers a remarkably counterintuitive story of the progressively expanding ambit of voting rights during times of war and national emergencies. This is important because it places the evolving context of civil rights and civil liberties in a much larger context than any particular pending emergency. For Tushnet, the manner in which civil liberties are protected or not protected during a wartime crisis is perhaps the single most important and fundamental question that must be asked of any self-governing democracy that is premised on the rule of law embodied in a constitution. He explores variations on this theme. The power of judicial review does not operate on some ethereal plane. Rather, courts must operate within a system of constitutional powers separated and assigned to the three branches. In that system, the political or elected branches are expected to exercise more power because they are more accountable to the people, but the independent judiciary is supposed to be more accountable to the Constitution.

The chapters in this book might be likened to frames in a movie reel or stanzas in a poem. They provide segments of meaning and pieces of thought, but they are parts of a greater whole—they are connected at once to a past to be understood and to a future yet to be determined. The title of this book, *At War with Civil Rights and Civil Liberties,* describes a paradox for people anywhere and any time. As previous generations of Americans have been tested in the crucible of war and crisis, our generation's test is the War on Terrorism. How will we be judged in the court of history? We would do well to heed the warning of Thomas Jefferson: "A society that will trade a little liberty for a little order will deserve neither and will lose both."[13]

NOTES

1. 124 S. Ct. 2686 (2004).
2. 124 S. Ct. 2.633 (2004).

3. *See generally* Lyle Denniston, "Primer on Guantanamo Cases," (posted March 13, 2005 on SCOTUSblog, www.scotusblog.com).

4. Hamdan v. Rumsfeld, 344 F. Supp. 2d 152 (D. D.C. 2004).

5. *Id.* at 156. (The District Court specifically referenced several particular orders by the President as implemented by the U.S. Department of Defense.)

6. *Id.* at 173.

7. *See* Denniston, *supra* note 3. The consolidated cases are: *In re Guantanamo Cases* (05–8003); *Al Odah v. United States* (05–5064); *Boumedienne v. Bush* (05–5062); and *Khalid v. Bush* (05–5063).

8. *Id.* (*Abdah v. Bush,* (04–1254)).

9. Denniston, *supra* note 3.

10. *Id.*

11. *Id.*

12. Final Report of the National Commission on Terrorist Attacks upon the United States, government, ed., 2005, www.gpoaccess.gov/911.

13. *See* Williams v. Garrett, 722 F. Supp. 254, 256 (W.D. Va. 1989).

Index

About the Contributors

John Ashcroft served as attorney general of the United States from 2000 through 2004. He graduated with honors from Yale University in 1964 and earned a J.D. degree from the University of Chicago in 1967. He served two terms as attorney general of Missouri and was elected the chairman of the National Association of Attorneys General. He served as governor of Missouri from 1985 to 1993 and U.S. senator from 1994 to 2000.

Thomas E. Baker is a professor of law at Florida International University. Among his nine books are *Constitutional Analysis in a Nutshell*, *The Most Wonderful Work: Our Constitution Interpreted*, and *Rationing Justice on Appeal: The Problems of the U.S. Courts of Appeals*. He has published more than a hundred articles in the leading journals, including the law reviews at Harvard, Michigan, UCLA, Iowa, and William & Mary. Before joining the founding faculty at FIU, he held the James Madison Chair that Congress endowed at Drake University Law School, the Alvin R. Allison Distinguished Professorship at Texas Tech University School of Law, and the Distinguished Fulbright Professorship of American Constitutional Law at the University of Athens. He served at the Supreme Court, first as a judicial fellow and then as acting administrative assistant to Chief Justice William H. Rehnquist. He was a member of the Committee on Rules of Practice and Procedure of the Judicial Conference of the United States, by appointment of the chief justice, from 1990–1995. He received a formal Commendation for Distinguished Service from the Judicial Conference of the United States, and was the recipient of the Bicentennial of the Constitution Award in Legal Education.

Stephen G. Breyer is an associate justice of the Supreme Court of the United States. He received an A.B. from Stanford University, a B.A. from Magdalen College, Oxford, and an LL.B. from Harvard Law School. He served as a law clerk to Justice Arthur Goldberg of the Supreme Court of the United States during the 1964 term, as a special assistant to the assistant U.S. attorney general for antitrust, 1965–1967, as an assistant special prosecutor of the Watergate Special Prosecution Force, 1973, as special counsel of the U.S. Senate Judiciary Committee, 1974–1975, and as chief counsel of the committee, 1979–1980. He was an assistant professor, professor of law, and lecturer at Harvard Law School, 1967–1994, a professor at the Harvard University Kennedy School of Government, 1977–1980, and a visiting professor at the College of Law, Sydney, Australia, and at the University of Rome. From 1980 to 1990, he served as a judge of the United States Court of Appeals for the First Circuit, and as its chief judge, 1990–1994. He also served as a member of the Judicial Conference of the United States, 1990–1994, and of the United States Sentencing Commission, 1985–1989. President Clinton nominated him as an associate justice of the Supreme Court, and he took his seat August 3, 1994.

Louis Fisher serves as a Senior Specialist in American national government at the Congressional Research Service. He is author of numerous prominent books on the Constitution, Congress, and the Supreme Court, including *Presidential War Power*, *American Constitutional Law*, *The Politics of Shared Power: Congress and the Executive*, *Constitutional Dialogues: Interpretation as Political Process*, and *Constitutional Conflicts between Congress and the President.*

Mark A. Graber is professor of political science and associate chair of the Department of Political Science, University of Maryland. He teaches courses in the areas of public law, constitutionalism, American political development and political thought, and political theory. His research interests include the political history, theory and practice of judicial review, the economic prerequisites of civil liberties, American legal thought, the constitutional status of the law in action, and the nature of constitutional thinking in divided societies. His books include: *Dred Scott and the Problem of Constitutional Evil* (forthcoming); *Rethinking Abortion,* and *Transforming Free Speech*, as well as numerous articles and law reviews.

Michael Greenberger is director of the Center for Health and Homeland Security at the University of Maryland and professor at the School of Law. He was a partner for over twenty years in the Washington, D.C., law firm of Shea

& Gardner, where he served as lead counsel and argued cases before the United States Supreme Court, eight federal circuit courts of appeals, four state supreme courts, and various other federal and state trial courts. In 1997, Professor Greenberger left private practice to become the director of the Division of Trading and Markets at the Commodity Futures Trading Commission. In that capacity, he was responsible for supervising exchange traded futures and derivatives. In 1999, he served as counselor to U.S. Attorney General Janet Reno and then became the Justice Department's principal deputy associate attorney general overseeing five of six litigating divisions. He teaches Intellectual Property, Contracts, and Constitutional Law.

Peter Irons, Ph.D. Boston University, 1973, J.D. Harvard Law School, 1978, is professor of political science and director of the Earl Warren Bill of Rights Project. Professor Irons is the author of six books on the Supreme Court and constitutional litigation, including *The New Deal Lawyers*, *Justice at War*, *The Courage of Their Convictions*, *Justice Delayed*, *May It Please the Court*, and *Brennan vs. Rehnquist: The Battle for the Constitution*. He has also contributed to numerous law reviews and other journals. He was chosen in 1988 as the first Raoul Wallenberg Distinguished Visiting Professor of Human Rights at Rutgers University. He has been invited to lecture on constitutional law and civil liberties at the law schools of Harvard, Yale, Berkeley, Stanford, and more than twenty other schools. In addition to his academic work, Professor Irons has been active in public affairs. He is a practicing civil rights and liberties attorney, and was lead council in the 1980s in the successful effort to reverse the World War Two criminal convictions of Japanese Americans who challenged the curfew and relocation orders. He was also elected to two terms on the national board of the American Civil Liberties Union.

Jules Lobel is professor of law at the University of Pittsburgh. His areas of specialization include international law, constitutional law, civil rights, and comparative law. Through the U.S. Center for Constitutional Rights, he has litigated important issues regarding the application of international law in the U.S. courts. In the late 1980s, he advised the Nicaraguan government on the development of its first democratic constitution, and has also advised the Burundi government on constitutional law issues. He is editor of a text on civil rights litigation and of a collection of essays on the U.S. Constitution, *A Less Than Perfect Union*. He is author of numerous articles on international law, foreign affairs, and the U.S. Constitution in publications including *Yale Law Journal*, *Harvard International Law Journal*, *Cornell Law Review*, and *Virginia Law Review*. He is a member of the American Society of International Law.

John F. Stack, Jr., is professor of political science and law and the director of the Jack D. Gordon Institute for Public Policy and Citizenship Studies at Florida International University. He is the author, editor, and coeditor of ten books, including *International Conflict in an International City: Boston's Irish, Italians, and Jews 1935–1944*; and editor of *Ethnic Identities in a Transnational World*, and *The Primordial Challenge: Ethnicity in the Modern World*. He co-edited *The International Politics of Quebec Secession: State-Breaking and State-Making in North America*, *The Ethnic Entanglement: Conflict and Intervention in World Politics*, *Congress Confronts the Court*, *Congress and the Politics of Emerging Rights*, and *Congress and United States Foreign Policy*. He is the author and coauthor of more than forty articles in journals and edited books.

Mark V. Tushnet, Carmack Waterhouse Professor of Constitutional Law at Georgetown University Law Center. B.A., Harvard; M.A., J.D., Yale. Expertise: constitutional law, U.S. legal history. After receiving his J.D. from Yale, Professor Tushnet served as a clerk to Supreme Court Justice Thurgood Marshall from 1972–1973. He then was a member of the law faculty of the University of Wisconsin at Madison until joining the Georgetown faculty in 1981. He is coauthor of three casebooks: *Federal Courts in the Twenty-First Century: Policy and Practice*, *Constitutional Law: Cases and Commentary*, and *Comparative Constitutional Law* (with Vicki Jackson). His other recent publications include the NAACP's *Legal Strategy against Segregated Education 1925–1950*, which received the Littleton Griswold Award of the American Historical Association; *Red, White and Blue: A Critical Analysis of Constitutional Law*; *Making Civil Rights Law: Thurgood Marshall and the Supreme Court, 1936–1961*; *Making Constitutional Law: Thurgood Marshall and the Supreme Court, 1961–1991*; *Taking the Constitution away from the Courts*; and *The New Constitutional Order*. He was the secretary of the Conference on Critical Legal Studies from 1976–1985, and was president of the Association of American Law Schools for 2004.